D. H. LAWRENCE: A CALENDAR OF HIS WORKS

KEITH SAGAR

D. H. Lawrence:
A calendar of his works

with a checklist of the manuscripts of D. H. Lawrence
by LINDETH VASEY

University of Texas Press, Austin

International Standard Book Number 0–292–71519–6
Library of Congress Catalog Card Number 78–65562

Text set in 10/12 pt VIP Sabon, printed by photolithography,
and bound in Great Britain at The Pitman Press, Bath

CONTENTS

ACKNOWLEDGEMENTS

I should like to acknowledge my gratitude to the University of Manchester for a year's study-leave, and to my colleagues there for covering my absence; the United States–United Kingdom Educational Commission for the Fulbright Scholarship, and the British Academy for the research grant, which enabled me to spend three months in the U.S.A.; to Lin Vasey and everyone else at the Humanities Research Centre of the University of Texas at Austin, where most of the work was done; to the following Lawrence scholars whose work has particularly aided mine: Gerald Lacy, Harry T. Moore, Warren Roberts, James Boulton, David Farmer, Carole Ferrier, Brian Finney, Keith Cushman and John Worthen; to Monica Moore for help with the index and the proofs; to the editorial staff of the Manchester University Press; and to Gerald Pollinger and the D. H. Lawrence Estate for permission to quote widely from Lawrence's writings.

INTRODUCTION

Lawrence never stood still; neither in his life nor his work. He was continually incorporating his latest experiences and testing his latest ideas in his work, continually pushing outwards the frontiers of his life and work, creating 'that piece of supreme art, a man's life' (Moore 327), and supreme works of art out of that life.

The critic invariably finds himself sooner or later discussing Lawrence's development, both the development of individual works through their various stages or metamorphoses, and the development of his whole oeuvre from one phase to another. Yet often this discussion takes place with an inadequate grounding in the chronological facts.

I am not innocent of this myself. In *The Art of D. H. Lawrence* (Cambridge University Press, 1966), I wrote of *The Lost Girl* as a novel substantially written in 1913 and completed in 1920. I now know it was entirely written in 1920. More recently I have said in lectures that Loerke in *Women in Love* was based on Mark Gertler, and that the name itself is a combination of 'Loki', 'lurk' and 'Gertler'. I now know that Loerke already existed, with the same name, in the original *Sisters* (the ur-*Women in Love*), before Lawrence had ever heard of Mark Gertler.

It was partly to save myself from such errors that I began the *Calendar*, errors which anyone concerned, as I am, with the genesis of Lawrence's works, with that difficult terrain between biography and criticism, must guard against. Having embarked on it, I found it yielding other, perhaps more important benefits. It became a kind of selective biography—moving in close to the sources and the shaping of great imaginative art.

My decision to include Lawrence's paintings in his 'works' may cause some surprise. The early paintings, most of them copies of dreadful late-nineteenth-century watercolours, are of little or no intrinsic value, but are, as Carl Baron has shown, an essential part of the culture which gave Lawrence so much more than it deprived him of. But the original paintings done from 1926 onwards are another matter. Some are crude, some obviously miss what Lawrence was after: but in most he accomplished what many a professional painter never achieves in a lifetime—he put life on to canvas or paper; not the superficial appearance of life, but its very substance and charge. In *Boccaccio Story,* for example, there is a glow of life in the thighs of the sleeping gardener, in the spurting silvery olives at the field's edge, in the flushed faces of the bobbing nuns. *Resurrection, Red Willow Trees, Dance Sketch, Contadini, Renascence of Men, Lizard, Leda, Throwing Back the Apple,* would all be fine paintings if Lawrence had never written a word. Surely Lawrence's own assessment of his paintings, in a letter to Alfred Stieglitz, 15 August 1928, is just: *Don't be alarmed about the pictures—they're quite good. Anyhow, they contain something—which is more than you can say of most moderns, which are all excellent rind of the fruit, but no fruit. And because a picture has subject-matter it is not therefore less a picture. Besides, what's a deformed guitar and a shred of newspaper but subject-matter? There's the greatest lot of bunk talked about modern painting ever. If a picture is to hit deep into the senses, which is its business, it must hit down to the soul and up into the mind—that is, it has to mean something to the coordinating soul and the coordinating spirit which are central in man's consciousness: and the meaning has to come through direct sense-impression. I know what I'm about. As for their space composition and their mass-reaction and their arabesques, if that isn't all literary and idea-concept, what is? Such a lot of canary cages, and never a bird in one of 'em!* [Moore 1076–7]

The primary source for the *Calendar* is, of course, Lawrence's letters, of which over five thousand are known to be extant. The editors of the Cambridge University Press edition of *The Letters of D. H. Lawrence* have gathered together photocopies of these letters, and these I have been able to read. About two thousand of them are unpublished, and many more only partially published. I have not been able to quote from unpublished letters: copyright permission is being universally withheld until the completion of the CUP project. But all relevant information from them has been incorporated into the *Calendar*. References for which no published source is given can be assumed to be to unpublished letters. These can be identified by consulting the Lacy–Vasey *Calendar of the Letters of D. H. Lawrence*, to which I am much indebted.

Lawrence frequently did not date his letters. Many of the published sources, including Huxley and Moore, frequently give conjectural dates, often with no indication that they are conjectural. The editors of the Lacy–Vasey *Calendar*, with the help of the editors of the *Letters*, have been able to establish much more accurate dates for most of the letters. An asterisk before a date indicates that this is a conjectural date taken from the Lacy–Vasey *Calendar*. On the handful of occasions when I cannot accept that dating, I have indicated with a dagger that the conjecture is my own. Passages printed in italics are in every case verbatim quotations from Lawrence's writings.

Other sources I have used are letters to Lawrence (he did not keep any, but some of his correspondents kept carbons, including, fortunately, Curtis Brown's office), Lawrence's manuscripts (he rarely dated them, but they sometimes yield clues), his diary for the period 1920–4 (published in Tedlock), memoirs and biographies and bibilographies, and the internal evidence of the works. The published letters are so scattered in books and periodicals, many out of print, many obscure, that to search through them for information relevant to a specific text is a daunting task. Yet often major new information emerges simply from the juxtaposition of interlocking pieces, which, separately, tell little or nothing. When information is added from all the other sources, it is usually possible to date a work very accurately, from its conception to the correcting of the proofs, often to the day, almost always at least to the month. As with a jigsaw, the more pieces are fitted into place, the easier it gets to fit the rest.

From the overall pattern certain features emerge—the seasonal nature of Lawrence's creativity, its relationship to his physical, and still more, spiritual health (how can he write if he cannot believe there is anyone worth writing for?), to his financial state, to his environment. There are the amazing bursts of work, three or four months of rapid daily writing (over half *Women in Love* written in May 1916); the periods, again sometimes of months on end, of inability or refusal to do any work at all. There is all the careful revision, not throwing whole novels away and starting from scratch but incorporation of older material, insertion of new, interlinear revision on the holograph, on the typescript, on the proof, on the published text from a periodical when a piece was to be collected in a book. Sadly, there is the gradual sapping of his creative energy in the last years, when he had to turn more and more to painting, or to little poems and newspaper articles. Lawrence never found the energy to tackle the second half of *Etruscan Places*. In the last eighteen months of his life he completed not a single work of fiction.

D. H. LAWRENCE: A CALENDAR OF HIS WORKS

1897   At Walker Street, Eastwood, Nottinghamshire.

SUMMER   The eleven-year-old Bert wrote for his 'sweetheart' Mabel Thurlby a little poem no doubt not unlike those Miss Matthews had read him at Beauvale Board School:

We sit in a lovely meadow
  My sweetheart and me
And we are oh so happy
  Mid the flowers, birds, and the bees [Nehls 2, 32].

Scholars will no doubt see here a preliminary sketch for both *Birds, Bees and Flowers* and *Lady Chatterley's Lover.*

1901–6   At Walker Street until 1902, then at Lynn Croft, Eastwood.

SUMMARY   From the time he left school in July 1901 until the time he began a two-year teaching course at Nottingham University College in September 1906, Lawrence spent far more of his time and energy painting than writing.

May Chambers: 'There is one more memory of that kitchen: the table littered with water-colours and autograph albums, and Bert in his shirt sleeves painting furiously, surrounded by an admiring group of half-a-dozen girls and one boy, who had presented each other with albums for Christmas. . . . Bert painted a child with a watering-can over the flower bed and an umbrella over her own head in a heavy shower on a page of my album from himself, and wrote:

His 'prentice han' he tried on man
And then he made the lasses O.

Each one of us wanted a painting done for every one in the group, and Bert ran his fingers through his hair excitedly. "I tell you what, you'll have to have them, and I'll do them one by one. You won't mind what I choose, will you?" He was assured his choice would satisfy everyone.' [Nehls III 597]

Lawrence preferred to copy nineteenth-century water colours. Among the artists he copied were: H. B. Brabazon, Frank Brangwyn, Arnesby Brown, Hugh Cameron, Birket Foster, Maurice Greiffenhagen, Colin Hunter, B. W. Leader, G. H. Mason, W. L. Picknell, J. M. Swan, J. Walter West, J. Lawton Wingate, and Peter de Wint. [See 'D. H. Lawrence's Early Paintings' by C. E. Baron, *Young Bert* 32–40.] Many of these paintings survive, and several are reproduced in *Young Bert*, in Lawrence-Ada, and in Levy. *I learnt to paint from copying other pictures—usually reproductions, sometimes even photographs. When I was a boy, how I concentrated over it! Copying some*

2

perfectly worthless reproduction in some magazine. . . . Even if you only copy a purely banal reproduction of an old bridge, some sort of keen, delighted awareness of the old bridge or of its atmosphere, or the image it has kindled inside you, can go over onto the paper and give a certain touch of life to a banal conception [Making Pictures].

5 NOV. 1904   Lawrence presented two paintings to his sister Emily on the occasion of her wedding, one of a river and church, the other of an old bridge.

1904–5   Jessie Chambers: 'Lawrence was always tirelessly occupied and spent much of his spare time painting flower studies in oils and in water colours. He would sit on the sofa under the window in the living-room, often singing to himself in an undertone as he worked, quite undisturbed by the work and talk going on around him. He painted a study of fruits for me, figs and dark green leaves, and sent it with a note saying it was a gift of a day of his life.' [ET 62]

30 APRIL 1905   'He particularly wanted to show me some roses he had been painting.' [ET 71]

SPRING 1905   *The first poems I ever wrote, if poems they were, was when I was nineteen . . . I remember perfectly the Sunday afternoon when I perpetrated those first two pieces: 'To Guelder Roses' and 'To Campions'; in spring-time, of course* [CP 27]. The poems are published in CP 854.

1905–6   Lawrence says he wrote 'The Wild Common' when he was nineteen, and brackets with it 'Virgin Youth' as among the *earliest* poems [CP 28, 850]. Other poems which may date from this period are: 'Flapper', 'Discord in Childhood' (originally a much longer poem), 'Dog-Tired', 'Cherry Robbers', 'Renascence', 'In a Boat' and 'From a College Window'. An accurate dating of the early poems is almost impossible because of the amount of revising which took place (as Lawrence himself found when he came to try to arrange them chronologically for his *Collected Poems* in 1928).

1906   At Lynn Croft, Eastwood, except for a fortnight's holiday in August at Mablethorpe, Lincolnshire.

SUMMARY   At Easter Lawrence began his first novel *The White Peacock* (then called *Laetitia*). In September he entered Nottingham University College, where he wrote and re-wrote poems, making fair copies into a college notebook [E317]. In the autumn he may have written an early version of his first play *A Collier's Friday Night*.

SPRING   In a letter of 4 May 1908 [Moore 8] Lawrence claims to have begun his novel 'two years last Easter'.

Jessie Chambers: 'Lawrence now began to talk definitely of writing. He said he thought he should try a novel, and wanted me to write one too, so that we could compare notes. "The usual plan is to take two couples and develop their relationships," he said. "Most of George Eliot's are on that plan. Anyhow, I don't want a plot, I should be bored with it. I shall try two couples for a start."

'It was in the Whitsuntide holiday that he brought the first pages to me. . . . These first pages described himself standing on the banks of the mill-pond, watching the fish glide in and out. . . .

'"My time's so broken up. In the morning when I should love to sit down to it I have to go to school. And when you've done a day's teaching all your brightness has gone. By the time I get back to the writing I'm another man. I don't see how there can be any continuity about it. It will have to be a mosaic, a mosaic of moods"' [ET 103–4].

26 AUG.   Lawrence painted an Italian canal scene [Levy 83].

OCTOBER   Jessie Chambers: 'It may be that he never quite got over the treatment meted out to this first essay. The subject, I think, was "Autumn", and Lawrence began with a reference to Augustine Birrell, saying he would take a flying leap into his subject. He was obviously trying to strike an arresting note. He brought the essay to me after it had passed through the hands of the English Mistress. She had apparently interpreted his attempt to attract attention as impertinence. The essay was heavily scored in red ink with corrections, emendations and exhortations in the best manner of an elderly school-mistress putting a forward youth in his place.' [ET 78]

*29 OCT.   *You see how splendidly Madame has crushed me. She has asked me now to write the essay she wanted—viz the Description of a Picture. I'm not quite sure whether I shall comply—if so I shall merely do it as a written exercise. She told me some of my phrases are fine, but others ludicrous; that I was not entirely incapable of writing, but*

4

mixed up some sense with a great amount of absurdity. Therefore I must restrain myself to writing just what other people think, and are therefore willing to accept [Boulton 2].

NOVEMBER Lawrence later wrote on the MS of *A Collier's Friday Night* [A69]: *Written when I was twenty-one, almost before I'd done anything, it is most horribly green.* The action takes place on a Friday night six weeks before Christmas in 1906 or 1907, and gives the impression of having been written very close to the events. However, Jessie Chambers (who appears as a major character in the play) says that Lawrence first showed it to her in November 1909, and that he 'certainly wrote it that autumn' [Delavenay 694]. The MS contains several references which could not have been written before 1909, for example to the deaths of Meredith and Swinburne, which took place in the spring of that year. Lawrence could, however, have rewritten in 1909 a play first sketched in 1906.

1907 At Lynn Croft, Eastwood, except for holidays in August at Robin Hood's Bay, Yorkshire.

SUMMARY Lawrence continued to paint, though the only published painting actually dated 1907 is *Italian Scene* [Levy 84], and to write poems, though the only poem about college is 'Study' (rejected by the college magazine); but most of his creative energy went into *The White Peacock*.

Jessie Chambers: 'All the time he was in College Lawrence was working continuously on *The White Peacock*. He completed it for the first time by the end of the first college year, and during the second year he entirely rewrote it, altering and developing the story a great deal . . . I had not a high opinion of the first version of *The White Peacock*, in which George married Letty. . . . The novel, apart from its setting, seemed to me story-bookish and unreal. The upright young farmer, hopelessly in love with the superior young lady who had been served shabbily by a still more socially superior young man, married her after a puritanical exposition of the circumstances by her mother, and a highly dubious conjugal life began in the melancholy farmhouse, with, one imagined, Letty always in the parlour and George in the kitchen. . . . I think Lawrence despised the story from the bottom of his heart, for he immediately started to rewrite it. He must have shown it to his mother because when we were on holiday at Robin Hood's Bay I asked her what she thought of it, and she replied, in a pained voice: "To think that *my* son should have written such a story," referring presumably to Letty's situation' [ET 81 116–17].

Lawrence also wrote his first short stories, and achieved his first appearance in print with one of them, *A Prelude* [C1 A85 *Phoenix 2*] in the *Nottinghamshire Guardian*, 7 Dec. 1907. The others were 'Legend', later 'A Fragment of Stained Glass' [C7 A6], and 'The White Stocking' [A6].

EARLY 1907 Jessie Chambers dates 'Cruelty and Love' (later 'Love on the Farm') from about this time [ET 116].

JUNE 1907 In a letter of 4 May 1908 Lawrence wrote, of *The White Peacock*: *I finished the first writing last June* [Moore 9].

SUMMER Jessie Chambers: 'On a day in the summer of 1907 Lawrence went to her home to tea, giving me to understand that he meant to find out whether his feeling towards X. [Louie Burrows] was what he thought it was. Some days later he handed me, with a significant glance, the poem "Snapdragon"' [ET 142].

20 OCT. To Louie Burrows: *Perhaps you know that the* Nottm. Guardian *asks for three Christmas stories, and offers a prize of £3 for each. I have written two just for fun, and . . . I may write a third. They ask for*

6

an Amusing Adventure, a Legend, and an Enjoyable Christmas. But one person may not send in more than one story. So will you send in the Amusing in your name? . . . It is the Amusing I want you to send, because it is the only one that is cast in its final form. I want you to write it out again in your style, because mine would be recognised [Boulton 6]. This story was 'The White Stocking'.

AUTUMN   Jessie Chambers: 'Lawrence wrote three stories, and suggested that I, a college friend, and he, should each submit one story. As luck would have it the story I sent was accepted and came out under my name. It was a sentimental little story called "A Prelude to a Happy Christmas", and was Lawrence's first appearance in print. A cheque for three guineas came, so I signed and my father cashed Lawrence's first cheque. . . . The story that Lawrence submitted himself and that was rejected, he re-wrote, and it subsequently appeared in the *English Review* under the title of "A Fragment of Stained Glass". The third story probably formed the basis for "The White Stocking". It was an idealized picture of his mother as a young girl going to a ball at the Castle and drawing out a long white stocking in mistake for a pocket handkerchief' [ET 113–14]. For a fuller description of this version of 'The White Stocking', see Finney 2, 323.

1908   At Lynn Croft, Eastwood (except for holiday in Flamboro, Yorkshire, 8–22 August) until 12 October, then to 12 Colworth Road, Croydon, where Lawrence was now schoolteaching, until the Christmas holiday, spent back in Eastwood.

SUMMARY   Lawrence completed the second version of *The White Peacock*, and began the third. He continued with his poems and paintings, wrote 'Art and the Individual' [B34 and *Phoenix 2*], probably an early version of 'The Shadow in the Rose Garden' [C31 A6], 'A Lesson on a Tortoise' and 'Lessford's Rabbits' [both *Phoenix 2*], and possibly an early version of 'Love Among the Haystacks' [A56].

EARLY 1908   'The Vicar's Garden', a mere sketch for 'The Shadow in the Rose Garden', was apparently not written in time to be considered for the *Nottinghamshire Guardian* Christmas competition, but is on identical paper to 'Legend' [Tedlock 32]. See Delavenay 2, 192.

4 MAY   On *The White Peacock: I finished the first writing last June—since then I have written the whole thing again. But I have been busy at Coll. this year—and have been irritated between duty to swot Latin and trigonometry and my impulse to write. So, much of Laetitia is poor stuff, I fear, and I shall have it all to do over again* [Moore 9].

Jessie Chambers: 'In the second writing the story was radically altered and the characters became more like flesh and blood, except Cyril, who remained as he began, old-maidish. Lawrence concentrated upon George, and the figure of Annable emerged, at first only cynically brutal, but later developing into symbolic stature. I was horrifed at Annable's first appearance and remonstrated with Lawrence, but he shook his head decisively, and said: "He *has* to be there. Don't you see why? He makes a sort of balance. Otherwise it's too much one thing, too much *me*," and grinned' [ET 117].

13 MAY   To Blanch Jennings: *You may certainly read that paper on 'Art and the Individual'—better 'Art and Individual Development'—when I have written it out again* [Moore 12]. Blanche Jennings was a friend of Alice Dax at whose home Lawrence had met her. The piece as published opens: *These Thursday night meetings are for discussing social problems . . .*

Jessie Chambers: '"Art and the Individual" Lawrence read to a little gathering of the Eastwood "intelligentsia" on an evening in, I think, Whitsuntide holiday of 1909. I am sure of the *year*, but not quite certain whether it was Whitsuntide or Easter. The reading took place at the house of W. E. Hopkin; Mr and Mrs Dax were there, my

8

brother and I, . . . and Mr and Mrs Hopkin of course. Lawrence lay full length on the hearth rug to read to us, because he was shy no doubt' [Delavenay 682].

It seems likely that Jessie Chambers was, in fact, wrong about the date. The meeting must have been in the spring of 1908. Presumably Alice Dax had told Blanche Jennings of Lawrence's talk, and Blanche Jennings had asked Lawrence if she might see the text. Lawrence's desire to write it out again before sending it is understandable. The piece reads like an undistinguished undergraduate essay with nothing in it of the distinctive Lawrence either in style or content. Lawrence probably did not get round to the rewriting until August, since on 15 June he wrote: *I regret I have not been able to remit you that vapouring of mine on 'Art'; I have very little time to write it out—do you mind waiting a little longer?* [Moore 14] and he did not actually send it until 1 September. The MS now in the collection of John E. Baker probably is the one sent to Blanche Jennings. The opening reference to the Thursday night meetings has gone, as have the laboured attempts at the beginning and end to relate the subject to socialism. The essay is much longer and more fluent, and contains some characteristic Lawrentian insights, such as his statement that those who complain that a work of art is too vague, not sufficiently realistic, by which they mean photographic or programmatic, *should know that they are purposely led to the edge of the great darkness, where no word-lights twinkle.* Opposite a rather pedantic passage, Lawrence has written: *Pardon me if I am a schoolteacher,* which suggests that the MS was sent to someone. And the praise of Maurice Greiffenhagen's *Idyll* (which is not in the published text) probably inspired Blanche Jennings to send Lawrence a reproduction of this painting as a Christmas present. Ada Clarke probably did not know of this revised version when she printed the earlier one in *Young Lorenzo*, and the text in *Phoenix 2* was taken from there.

27 JULY An incident which may have inspired an early version of 'Love Among the Haystacks' took place on this date [Boulton 11, Moore 24].

6 OCT. *I spent all Sunday painting those nasturtiums; they look rather pretty* [Boulton 18]. This painting is reproduced in Levy. The original is in the possession of Mrs Margaret Needham.

4 NOV. *At present I am painting for dear life, and enjoying myself immensely. I have just finished my third landscape—I began the first ten days ago* [Moore 34].

11 NOV.   *I have nearly read* Laetitia. *It bores me mightily in parts. You can none of you find one essence of its failure: it is that I have dragged in conversations to explain matters that two lines of ordinary prose would have accomplished far better; I must cut out many pages of talk, and replace them with a few paragraphs of plain description or narrative; secondly, one is cloyed with metaphoric fancy; thirdly, folk talk about themes too much;—slight incidents—such as the sugar in* Eugenie—*should display character, not fine speeches; fourthly, I don't believe Lettie ever did break her enagement with Leslie—she married him.* . . . *The characters are often weak—the men—George and Leslie especially. Lettie herself is not bad. The rest are undeveloped. What the whole thing needs is that the essential should be differentiated from the non-essential. I will have another go at it this winter* [Moore 36].

Jessie Chambers: 'The phase of acute homesickness soon wore off. He settled down to the third writing of *The White Peacock*, and began to explore London, and to write about the lights that flowered when darkness came.' [ET 151] She seems to be referring to the poems 'Hyde Park at Night' and 'Piccadilly Circus at Night', but the position of these poems in E317 suggests the autumn of 1909 as a more likely date.

NOV.   In 'Lesson on a Tortoise' we are told that *November was darkening the early afternoon.* The similar piece 'Lessford's Rabbits' resembles a letter of 2 December [Moore 38–9].

1909 At 12 Colworth Road, Croydon during term time, and at Lynn Croft, Eastwood, during vacations, except for family holiday at Shanklin, Isle of White, 31 July–14 August.

SUMMARY   Lawrence wrote the third version of *The White Peacock*: *At Croydon I worked at it fairly steadily, in the evenings after school* ['Autobiographical Sketch']. He also wrote 'Goose Fair', published in the *English Review*, February 1910 [C3 A6], 'Odour of Chrysanthemums' *English Review* June 1911 [C6 A6] and 'A Modern Lover', not published until 1933 [C211 A71]; and probably some twenty-five or thirty of the poems in E317. (The painting *Evening* [Levy 84] was also done in 1909.)

20 JAN.   To Blanche Jennings: *Since coming back I have set down to write in earnest—now verses—now* Laetitia. . . . . *The baby poem I'll send you is a bit of Friday's work* [Moore 46–7]. Lawrence is referring to 'Baby Songs, Ten Months Old' [E317], since on the previous Friday (15th) Hilda Mary Jones, his landlord's daughter, had been exactly ten months old. Lawrence included four poems with this letter: the other three were: 'A Winter's Tale', which may have been recent, 'Cherry Robbers' and 'Renaissance', both certainly older.

28 FEB.   *I continue that old work of mine.* [The White Peacock] *Sometime, I hope, it will be finished. I have to do it over and over again, to make it decent* [Boulton 30]. Only two fragments, totalling fifty-eight pages, have survived from this version. Much of the material has nothing corresponding to it in the published text, but Tedlock quotes one long passage [5] which has its corresponding passage, much more restrained and direct, in the book. These Berkeley fragments reveal that in this version Lettie married George after bearing a child to Leslie [E430a].

MARCH   On 6 February Lawrence had visited the Royal Academy winter exhibition. One of the artists he admired there was Fritz Thaulow, whose snow scenes he recalls in the poem 'A Snowy Day at School':
How different, in the middle of snows, the great school rises red
Like a picture by Thaulow [CP 864].
In the same letter of 6 March in which Lawrence describes the exhibition to Blanche Jennings, he complains of the snow. The position of the poem in E317 confirms this dating rather than that of Helen Corke, who places it a year later [Corke 175–6].
The adjacent poems in E317, 'Letter from Town: The Almond Tree' and 'Letter from Town: The City' (later 'On a Grey morning in March') both probably also date from this month.

11

JUNE   Lawrence gave Jessie Chambers permission to send some of his poems, of her own choosing, to the *English Review*. 'I looked through the poems Lawrence had sent in letters to me since he left home, picked out what I thought were the best, and copied them out one beautiful June morning' [ET 157]. The poems she sent were 'Discipline' 'Dreams Old and Nascent' and 'Baby Movements'. These were published in the *English Review* November 1909 [C2 A9] and constituted Lawrence's first appearance in a serious literary periodical.

30 JUNE   To Louie Burrows: *I am glad you are writing stories. I can't do 'em myself. Send me them, please, and I'll see if I can put a bit of surface on them and publish them for you. We'll collaborate, shall we?* [Boulton 38]. The first story Louie sent was 'Goose Fair'. Lawrence rewrote it, then sent it to the London and Provincial Press Agency, who subsequently denied having received the 5s registration fee. Lawrence refused to send another 5s and demanded the story back.

27 JULY   Lawrence rewrote another of Louie's stories called 'Cupid and the Puppy': *Here is your tale—you will not like it* [Boulton 39].

19 AUG.   *Let me have the 'Puppy' and I'll go through it and revise it and send it* [Boulton 42]—to a new magaine called *The Tramp*.

11 SEPT.   *The editor of the* English Review *has accepted some of my verses, and wants to put them into the* English Review, *the November issue. But you see they are all in the rough, and want revising, so this week and so on I am very hard at work, slogging verse into form. I shall be glad when I have finished: then I may get on with the prose work* [Boulton 43].

It may well have been at this point that Lawrence started using the second of the two college notebooks [Ferrier MS5] which constitute the main repositories of his early poems, since revised versions of the *English Review* poems, which also appear two-thirds of the way through E317, are the first entries in the second book, in revised form.

1 NOV.   *I have just sent up to Mr Heuffer my novel, which I have rewritten, and which is much altered. I have added a third part, have married Lettie and Leslie and George and Meg, and Emily to a stranger and myself to nobody. Oh Lord—what a farce* [Moore 57].

Jessie Chambers: 'Lawrence entirely rewrote the novel and gave it its final shape during his first year in Croydon, and the story developed into a subtle study in self-portraiture. Cyril and Lettie are each aspects of Lawrence, with Emily as a foil to both. George developed from the simple, God-fearing yeoman into the man whose inner growth has been arrested, with the consequent proliferation into decay. . . . . The rounding off of the story Lawrence wrote during our brief moment of harmony. He said in a letter: "Do you mind if, *in the novel*, I make Emily marry Tom?" I didn't mind in the least. I thought the final turn to Emily's fortunes one of the happiest human touches in the book. Lawrence often said, "To write, I *must* be happy. I can't get on with things when I'm unhappy," and I know it was abundantly true' [ET 118–19].

NOV.   Jessie Chambers: 'When night came on he took me to Waterloo Bridge and made me look at the human wreckage preparing to spend the night on the Embankment. . . . . Finally we went to a theatre' [ET 165].

'After the Theatre' and 'Brotherhood' (later 'Embankment at Night') probably date from this time.

11 DEC.   *I sent the story* ['Goose Fair'] *with another I have written, up to Ford Madox Heuffer on Thursday* [Boulton 47]. The other story was almost certainly 'Odour of Chrysanthemums'. Jessie Chambers says she saw this story in 1909, and also 'A Modern Lover' in December 1909 [Delavenay 694]. In a letter of March 1912 Lawrence says he wrote 'A Modern Lover' *three years back* [Moore 102]. The text of this early version of 'Odour of Chrysanthemums' is published in Boulton 3.

1910 At 12 Colworth Road, Croydon, with school holidays in Eastwood. In mid-August Lawrence spent a week with George Neville in Blackpool and Barrow. He returned to his aunt Krenkow's in Leicester to find his mother ill. As she quickly deteriorated he took more and more time off school. On 3 December he became engaged to Louie Burrows. A week later his mother died. On 24 December Lawrence, his sister Ada and Frances Cooper went to Hove for a week's holiday. From there Lawrence went direct to the Burrows home in Quorn, Leicestershire.

SUMMARY Lawrence wrote the first version of *The Trespasser* [A2] as *The Saga of Siegmund* based on Helen Corke's *Freshwater Diary*. He produced two plays, *The Widowing of Mrs Holroyd* [A5] *The Merry-Go-Round* [C227], 'The Fly in the Ointment' [C22 B34 and *Phoenix* 2], 'Rachel Annand Taylor' [B34 and *Phoenix* 2], and many poems and paintings. In the autumn he began *Paul Morel*, later to become *Sons and Lovers* [A4].

23 JAN. *I have rewritten 'The White Stocking'. . . . My novel is practically accepted. I went up to Wm Heinnemann on Friday: he read me his readers crits: mostly good. I am to alter a bit in parts, then the thing will come out, and I shall have royalties* [Boulton 49].

*28 JAN. *I have been writing like the devil lately* [Moore 59]. Probably already revising *The White Peacock*.

FEB. Helen Corke: 'During many evenings, he and I sat in my mother's little green sitting-room, discussing points of revision' [Corke 2, 9].

9 MARCH *I have nearly finished the novel ready for the publisher. . . . Austin Harrison has just sent me the proofs of some verses which he is putting in next month* [Boulton 50]. 'Night Songs' [C4].

22 MARCH Lawrence wrote 'Throstles in the Cherry Tree', an intermediate version of 'Cherry Robbers'. Published *DHLR* 9, 2, 281–2.

APRIL Jessie Chambers: 'Towards the end of the [Easter] holiday he was planning his next novel. He told me he would write a "bright" story, and take one of my brothers as hero. Almost immediately on returning to Croydon he wrote, apparently very much disturbed, saying that he found he had to write the story of Siegmund. . . . It was in front of him and he had got to do it' [ET 181].

But perhaps the other novel was begun. There exists a MS from the Croydon period [Tedlock 37–9] of the first two chapters (forty-eight pages) of a novel beginning: *There is a small cottage off the Addiscome Road* . . . Tedlock gives a lengthy summary of the story, but no character emerges resembling a Chambers boy.

Helen Corke had shown Lawrence her diary of her experiences at

14

Freshwater, Isle of Wight, the previous summer. She had gone there with her lover, an older married man, who had killed himself shortly after his return, leaving her derelict. 'He returns to the subject later—comes with the request that he take the diary and expand its theme—use the poems as basis for a more comprehensive rendering of the story. ... One evening this spring D.H.L. brings me the first chapters of *The Saga of Siegmund*' [*Croydon* 7–8]. Helen Corke has given several slightly different accounts of her relationship with Lawrence and of the genesis of *The Trespasser*. [See bibliography. See also Sharpe.]

11 APRIL   Lawrence sent his final draft on *The White Peacock* to Pawling, saying that he had rewritten the whole of the third part, and removed all the words and phrases which might have offended the jeunes filles.

27 APRIL   To Sydney Pawling of Heinemann: *I think the novel* [The White Peacock] *is complete and final in its form as I have sent it you ... I have written about half of another novel* [Moore 61–2].

*12 MAY   *I write* Siegmund—*I keep writing, almost mechanically: very slowly, and mechanically* [Corke 182].

JUNE   Helen Corke: 'He brings me a short story just written, in which he quotes one of Jessie Chambers' letters to him. The story begins: "Muriel has sent me some mauve primroses"' [*Croydon* 10]. The story is 'The Fly in the Ointment'—but it has a winter setting. It was revised in July 1913.

14 JUNE   Heinemann did not like the title *Nethermere*. Lawrence suggested as possible alternatives: *Lapwings, Pee-wits, The Cry of the Peacock, The White Peacock, The Talent in the Napkin, The Talent, the Beggar, and the Box.*

24 JUNE   Lawrence rejects *The White Peacock* as too reminiscent of Ibsen or Wilkie Collins, and suggests further titles: *Tendrils, Tendril Outreach, Outreaching Tendrils, Outreach of Tendrils.*

9 JULY   *I have just hanged my latest hero* [Fraser 147]. The hanging of Siegmund takes place at the end of chapter XXVII. There are four chapters to follow.

15 JULY   Lawrence says he expects to finish the last half-dozen pages that evening. He suggests another title for *Nethermere—Crab-apples.*

24 JULY   *They have sent me back a rather nice story from the* English—*asking me to cut it 5 pages: a devilish business* [Boulton 52]. Probably 'Odour of Chrysanthemums', the first proofs of which are dated 10 March 1910. See March–April 1911.

4 AUG.   *I have just finished my second novel* [Fraser 147]. When Lawrence

15

sent the MS to Pawling in October, he said it was *the rapid work of three months* [Moore 66]. He was exaggerating a little. It had taken about four.

*2 SEPT.   *I sent mother some of the first batch of proofs of the novel* [The White Peacock] [Boulton 53].

9 SEPT.   *Here are some more proofs. . . . I go through the other set twice* [Boulton 54].

18 SEPT.   *Here are the last of the proofs: I am devoutly thankful to be done with them* [Boulton 54]. There is a set of partly corrected galleys at CLU [E430e], and the corrections are incorporated into the American edition, but they are not the galleys from which either edition was set up. [See Tedlock 6–7.].

30 SEPT.   To Rachel Annand Taylor: *Our 'English Association'—vague, middle-class Croydonians, mostly ladies, lingering remnants of the Pre-Raphaelites—asked me to give a paper on 'A Living Poet'. 'I will give you,' I said, 'Rachel Annand Taylor'* [Moore 64].

1 OCT.   According to Helen Corke [Croydon 16] 'Coldness in Love' was written about their experiences of that night in Seaford, Sussex.

18 OCT.   To Sydney Pawling: *I will give you my third novel,* Paul Morel, *which is plotted out very interestingly (to me), and about one-eighth of which is written.* Paul Morel *will be a novel—not a florid prose poem, or a decorated idyll running to seed in realism: but a restrained, somewhat impersonal novel. It interests me very much. I wish I were not so agitated just now, and could do more* [Moore 66–7].

LATE OCT.   According to Helen Corke [Corke 196–7] 'Excursion Train' is about their return journey to London from Nottingham at the 'end of half-term break'.

9 NOV.   Lawrence had promised to lend Grace Crawford the MS of *The Trespasser*, but, being unable to recover it, he writes: *Perhaps I can bring you another bit of MS if you like* [Fraser 150]. A week later he sent her *The Widowing of Mrs Holroyd*, with a request to pass it on to Violet Hunt. In an unpublished letter of 13 Dec. to Violet Hunt, Lawrence discusses the play in detail.

10 NOV.   The still-life of two apples reproduced in Lawrence-Ada and Levy bears this date.

*15 NOV.   To Rachel Annand Taylor: *To the Croydon folk I shall say of you nothing but good* [Moore 68].

18 NOV.   *The paper on Mrs Taylor went very well* [Moore 68].

DEC.   'Mrs King told V. de Sola Pinto that, during the many days that Lawrence spent by his mother's bedside when she was dying, he had this notebook with him and constantly wrote in it' [*CP* 1030]. The editors of *CP* suggest that this is E317, but though there are five poems written shortly after the death of Mrs Lawrence in that MS, there are none about her dying: those poems are in the other college notebook [Ferrier MS5], but *after* poems about bereavement, so Lawrence cannot have been writing direct into either notebook. He used both books for later drafts or fair copies of existing poems. It was also during this period that Lawrence, to relieve the intolerable weight of pain, wrote a romantic comedy, *The Merry-Go-Round*.

6 DEC. *I have been translating some of those Fellah songs which are done into German* [here Lawrence writes out two poems, 'Self-Contempt' and 'Near the Mark']. *They are ingenuous and touching, I think. But I am a bad translator. I am also copying a picture of Frank Brangwyn's for Ada: it is called* The Orange Market—*an impressionist, decorative thing, rather fine* [Boulton 58]. The songs were Egyptian folk-songs translated from Arabic into German by Fritz Krenkow, Lawrence's uncle. 'Self-Contempt' Lawrence later developed into 'Gipsy'. *The Orange Market* is reproduced in Lawrence-Ada.

9 DEC. On the night his mother died Lawrence began to copy Maurice Greiffenhagen's *Idyll*, a picture which had obsessed him since Blanche Jennings had given him a reproduction of it for Christmas 1908 [Moore 44]. He was to copy it many more times. Copies are reproduced in Lawrence-Ada, Levy, *Young Bert* and Spender.

13 DEC. Lawrence showed 'The End', 'The Bride' and 'The Virgin Mother' to Jessie Chambers [ET 184].

14 DEC. *I'm not going to write or read till January—not much, at any rate—just paint, which is soothing. The boys this morning began for exam. a ginger-jar with the straw handles, and 3 reddish oranges: it looks so pretty* [Boulton 60]. The following day Lawrence painted the ginger-jar himself. It is reproduced in *Young Bert* 50.

15 DEC. Lawrence sent Louie Burrows three more translations, one of which later became 'The Wind, the Rascal' [Boulton 62].

*17 DEC. *As for those translations—when I have written a letter I hastily seize the book and rattle them off. They never take me ten minutes: so don't talk about my working at them. At present I am merely painting* [Boulton 64].

1911 At 12 Colworth Road, Croydon in school terms until the end of September, when the Joneses moved to 16 Colworth Road. On 29 July Lawrence, Ada and Louie Burrows went to Prestatyn in North Wales for a fortnight. Lawrence spent frequent weekends at the Burrows home in Quorn.

SUMMARY ... *and, in the sick year after* [the death of his mother], *the collapse for me of Miriam* [Jessie Chambers], *of Helen* [Corke], *and of the other woman, the woman of 'Kisses in the Train' and 'Hands of the Betrothed'* [Louie Burrows]. *Then, in that year, for me, everything collapsed, save the mystery of death, and the haunting of death in life. I was twenty-five, and from the death of my mother, the world began to dissolve around me, beautiful, iridescent, but passing away substanceless. Till I almost dissolved away myself, and was very ill* [CP 851].

Lawrence continued to work on *Paul Morel*. He wrote the first versions of the stories ultimately known as 'The Witch a la Mode' [C215 A71], 'The Old Adam' [A71], 'Daughters of the Vicar' [A6], 'Second Best' [C9 A6], 'The Shades of Spring' [C18 A6] and rewrote most of his earlier stories. He completed the body of poems from which all the poems in *Amores* [A9], all but 'Bei Hennef' in *Love Poems* [A3], most of those in *New Poems* [A11], and several of those in *Bay* [A12] were to be drawn. He also did his first book-reviewing for the *English Review*. His writing was temporarily and his career as a schoolteacher permanently brought to an end by his severe attack of pneumonia in November.

EARLY 1911　There is no record of Lawrence doing any writing in the first three months after his mother's death, but he may have been continuing with the first draft of *Paul Morel*.

17 FEB.　Lawrence says he has been painting pictures for Nellie Allam.

1 MARCH　By this date he had done five, three for Nellie Allam and two for his aunt Ada Krenkow.

3 MARCH　*Tonight, for four hours, I have been drawing the* Idyll... *It is to be a big picture—as big as ever my board will hold. . . . It will take me to finish 12 or 14 hours in all. Then I will give it to you, and voila, a day of my life* [Boulton 82].

13 MARCH　*I have begun* Paul Morel *again. I am afraid it will be a terrible novel. But, if I can keep it to my idea and feeling, it will be a great one* [Boulton 83].

27 MARCH　To Ada Clarke: *I've painted you a little* Idyll, *about 14 by 7. Do you remember? I began to draw it the night mother died, and I said I should never finish it. Now I've done a big one for Louie, and a*

18

little one for you [Moore 75].

29 MARCH   *I began a new sketch, but have spoiled it through not being in the painting humour. Strange, when I can write I can't paint, and vice versa. I'm just amusing myself with a short story. Austin Harrison—English Review—wants to see some stories. I've got a dozen in rough but none done up. So I'll do one or two. Tomorrow I'm going to call in the evening to see him about the story he's got, which I think he wants altering a bit* [Boulton 87].

The next letter to Louie reveals that Lawrence was amusing himself turning 'Legend' into 'A Hole in the Window' (the title was changed again to 'A Fragment of Stained Glass' for publication in the *English Review* in September), and that the story Harrison wanted altering was 'Odour of Chrysanthemums'. This letter also contained an early draft of the poem 'Tease'.

1 APRIL   *I've done the transcript of the Legend tale. It's jolly good. If Austin Harrison wants it, you can have the proofs.—And soon, in a day or two, I'll send you the Chrysanthemums to copy* [Boulton 89].

2 APRIL   *Here are the MSS—it's a really good story. The desideratum is to shorten sufficiently the first part. Of course that part has to reveal the situation. I hope you can manage to make out all the alterations. . . . It has taken me such a long time to write those last two pages of the story. You have no idea how much delving it requires to get that deep into cause and effect* [Boulton 90–1].

The first proofs (heavily revised by Lawrence) are in the Burrows papers at the University of Nottingham, dated 10 March 1910. Louie's fair copy is at the University of Texas [E284]. Lawrence made minor revisions on it before sending it to Harrison. It appeared in the *English Review* in June.

6 APRIL   *Mind you leave out all I have crossed away. All the playing part—most of the kiddies share—goes out, I think. I intend it to. The story must work quicker to a climax. The other story wont want copying, I think* [Boulton 93]. This 26-page MS of 'A Fragment of Stained Glass' is in the Burrows papers at the University of Nottingham. The Texas MS of 'Legend' is only 8 pp. [E196].

12 APRIL   *I've finished the fourth story—it's the 'White Stocking' written up. . . . I have just done one folio, a dozen MSS pages, of* Paul Morel. *That great, terrible but unwritten novel, I am afraid it will die a mere conception* [Boulton 98].

The third story was probably 'Intimacy' ('Witch a la Mode'). 'Intimacy' was certainly written about this time [Corke 210]. The story describes a musical evening at the home of the pianist Laura Macartney at Purley. Lawrence attended several such evenings in the spring and summer of 1911, including 6 April. In the story, however, it is 'an evening of March'.

28 APRIL   *A week has gone by like a mist evaporating. Do you know I simply cannot work. I have done only about five pages of MSS,* Paul Morel, *and that only from sheer pressure of duty* [Boulton 100].

29 APRIL   *I'm going to do a bit of* Paul. *I send you this mass. . . . This is a quarter of the book.* [Boulton 101].

1 MAY   *At your behest I wrote yesterday fourteen pages of* Paul Morel, *and I sit with the paper before me to continue when this is done* [Boulton 102].

4 MAY   *I have written 90 pages of* Paul Morel. *I think about 7 of these pages may be called amusing, and 20 perhaps pleasant. The rest are 'navrant'. I wonder how* Paul *will work out* [Boulton 103].

7 MAY   *I have managed my ten pages of* Paul: *I'm now on with the 112th. I wonder what it will be like; at present it seems to me very rummy* [Boulton 103].

26 MAY   *At Whit. I will show you the first two hundred pages of* Paul, *that book of books* [Boulton 109].

*30 MAY   *J'ai été tellement occupé ce soir, ayant commencé un autre tableau pour ma tante: la femme d'un pêcheur, tenant son enfant, et regardant loin sur la mer* [Boulton 110].

1 JUNE   *I've painted till nightfall . . . I shall finish it tomorrow. It doesn't look bad, so far. I get quite a dab hand at manipulating water color. If I had time, I would do original stuff—but it is impossible* [Boulton 111].

14 JUNE   *I've worked quite hard: begun a picture, long promised, for Mac., and written a short story, 32 pages long, in two nights. Smart work, eh? . . . By the way, I've got a 'Swan' number of the* Studio. *Rather a nice tiger* [Boulton 112–13].

Lawrence saw Louie Burrows at Whitsuntide and apparently showed her his story 'The Old Adam' (*Why mustn't I write Old Adams?*). But the only surviving holograph MS of the 'The Old Adam' [E286] is only 27 pp. Possibly the 32-pp. MS was the first draft of 'Two Marriages' [E86]. See 15–16 July.

Lawrence made several copies of a tiger's head by John Macallan Swan. It is reproduced in Lawrence-Ada.

4 JULY   *I've done a fair amount of* Paul [Boulton 117]. This seems to represent the last work done on this version of *Paul Morel.* A fortnight

later Lawrence writes: *No, I've not done any* Paul *lately* [Boulton 122], and in October he writes: *I haven't done a stroke of* Paul *for months—don't want to touch it* [Boulton 140].

The Texas MS [E373] breaks off at p. 265. In October Lawrence showed this MS to Jessie Chambers, who gives a very accurate description of it: 'He had written about two-thirds of the story, and seemed to have come to a standstill. The whole thing was somehow tied up. The characters were locked together in a frustrating bondage, and there seemed no way out. The writing oppressed me with a sense of strain. It was extremely tired writing. I was sure that Lawrence had had to force himself to do it. The spontaneity that I had come to regard as the distinguishing feature of his writing was quite lacking. He was telling the story of his mother's married life, but the telling seemed to be at second hand, and lacked the living touch. I could not help feeling that his treatment of the theme was far behind the reality in vividness and dramatic strength. Now and again he seemed to strike a curious, half-apologetic note, bordering on the sentimental. . . . A nonconformist minister whose sermons the mother helped to compose was the foil to the brutal husband. . . . It was story-bookish. The elder brother Ernest, whose short career had always seemed to me most moving and dramatic, was not there at all. The character Lawrence called Miriam was in the story, but placed in a bourgeois setting, in the same family from which he later took the Alvina of *The Lost Girl*. He had placed Miriam in this household as a sort of foundling, and it was there that Paul Morel made her acquaintance. The theme developed into the mother's opposition to Paul's love for Miriam. . . . But the tissue was left quite unresolved. Lawrence had carried the situation to the point of deadlock and stopped there' [ET 190–1].

7 JULY   *I began a nice big Corot, half did it, spoiled it, and tore it in thirty pieces. Shame! Now I've begun a Little Idyll for Agnes Holt. She marries in early August, and has asked me for this picture. I must race and get her a couple done* [Boulton 117]. The second was *Wind on the Wold* [Levy] copied from a painting by G. H. Mason. Both are at the University of Nottingham.

*15 JULY   *Oh, I've been writing all day long, 38 pages of a long short story* [Boulton 121].

*16 JULY   *Well, I've finished the short story—called 'Two Marriages'* [Boulton 121]. This early version of 'Daughters of the Vicar' was published in *Time and Tide*, 24 March 1934 [C214].

21 JULY   Lawrence has corrected and returned the proofs of 'A Fragment

of Stained Glass'.

29 AUG. *I am just going to do another story for Austin Harrison. I did one last night—I will send him a couple. Then some for Edward Garnett* [Boulton 130].

1 SEPT. *I did not mean I had written a new story on Monday, but I've done one up. I sent two, yesterday evening, to Austin Harrison. . . . Tonight and tomorrow I am going to spend doing up a couple for* [Edward Garnett] [Boulton 131].

Apparently Harrison did not give Lawrence his decision about these two stories until 10 January, when he told Lawrence that 'Second Best' would be in the February number of the *English Review*, and returned the other story, which Lawrence promptly forwarded to Garnett, describing it as 'wicked' but 'clever'. The story was probably 'The Old Adam'.

10 SEPT. Two stories sent to Garnett [Moore 80]. One of them was 'Intimacy', the other 'Two Marriages'.

11 SEPT. *I am going to write another short story tonight, or part of one* [Boulton 134]. But a sentence in a letter of 15th suggests that he may not have done so: *This week I haven't written a scrap.*

21 SEPT. *Harrison is very friendly. He suggests that I do a bit of reviewing for the* English. *He bids me select from the forthcoming books one I should like to review. What shall it be?* [Boulton 136].

2 OCT. *Thanks for the return of 'Two Marriages' with such good hopes. I am doing it up, will split it in three, and will keep it between 12 and 15 thousand words* [Moore 81].

11 OCT. *It's eleven now, at night. I've been working since 7.0 at verse, getting it ready to take to Edward Garnett on Friday* [Moore 81]. Garnett was an editor for Duckworth.

23 OCT. Lawrence sent Garnett a second batch of poems which he described as more recent and more *anti-Daily News* than those Garnett had already read. On 7 November Lawrence wrote to Garnett: *You got the second bundle of verses a fortnight ago, didn't you—the one with 'Nils Likke' and 'Transformations' and 'Another Ophelia'* [Moore 84].

The batch was probably that described by Ferrier as MS19b, which did not contain 'Transformations', but did contain the other two. If this is so, at least one poem from *'Look! We Have Come Through!'*, the first, 'Moonrise', must have been written by this time, since it is in MS 19b. At least one other poem from *'Look!'* was written before Lawrence left Croydon, 'Martyr a la Mode'; and 'Elegy', which

Lawrence places before 'Martyr a la Mode', is signed Eastwood.

23 OCT. *I've had to withdraw the offer of the verse from Duckworth, and give Heinemann the promise of the things. I shall send in the MS in a week or so, and they'll be out in Jan. or February. . . . You can see I'm going to be kept most damnably up to the neck . . . I must get these damned verses shipshape* [Boulton 144]. It was, in fact, Duckworth who published *Love Poems* in February 1913.

3 NOV. *I think I have finished the verses. I must send them off at once. . . . Tonight I am going to begin* Paul Morel *again, for the third and last time* [Boulton 146]. Lawrence may have just received Jessie's suggestions: 'In my reply I told him I was very surprised he had kept so far from reality in his story; that I thought what had really happened was much more poignant and interesting than the situations he had invented. In particular I was surprised that he had omitted the story of Ernest, which seemed to me vital enough to be worth telling as it actually happened. Finally I suggested that he should write the whole story again, and keep it true to life . . . He fell in absolutely with my suggestion and asked me to write what I could remember of our early days, because, as he truthfully said, my recollection of those days was so much clearer than his. I agreed to do so, and began almost at once, but had not got very far when word came that Lawrence was dangerously ill with pneumonia' [ET 192–3]. Some ten pages of Jessie's notes have survived, and are at the University of Texas. They are incorporated almost word for word into the published text of *Sons and Lovers.*

7 NOV. *I've got another rather ripping long short story—shall I show it you? . . . I'm sending the last, best verses, the latest, and most substantial, to the Cearne tomorrow* [Moore 85]. The story is probably 'Love Among the Haystacks'. In a letter of 7 January 1912 Lawrence mentions it as a story Garnett has seen [Huxley 19].

8 NOV. *There is a review by me in the* English *of this month* [Moore 85]. This was a review of *Contemporary German Poetry*, ed. Jethro Bithell. Reprinted in *Encounter*, August 1969.

10 NOV. *I am really very tired of school—I can*not *get on with* Paul. *I am afraid I shall have to leave* [Boulton 148]. Lawrence spent the weekend of 18–19 Nov. at the Cearne, Edward Garnett's house in Kent. Waiting for trains on the way home he caught a chill which radpidly developed into pneumonia. He was confined to bed for over a month and never retured to school.

6 DEC. *I am allowed to read. I have got to review a book of German*

23

poetry and a book of Minnesinger translations. I like the German poetry, but not the translations [Moore 87].

13 DEC. *I have done the reviews and sent them off* [Boulton 154]. Lawrence's unsigned reviews of *The Oxford Book of German Verse*, ed. Fiedler, and *The Minnesingers*, ed. Bithell, appeared in *The English Review* in January 1912. They are reprinted in *Phoenix 2*.

*22 DEC. Lawrence sketched yet another *Idyll*, for McLeod.

30 DEC. *I think I'll send you this story. My sense of beauty and of interest comes back very strong. I wrote this story last week, in bed—before I could sit up much. You'll find it, perhaps, thin—maladif* [Moore 90]. A letter of 29 May 1913 identifies this as 'The Soiled Rose' (rewritten in 1914 as 'The Shades of Spring'): *I wrote it while I was still in Croydon—still in bed after the last illness. Don't you think it a bit affected? It is a bit stiff, like sick man's work.—So that the philosophy which is in 'The Soiled Rose' didn't hold good for me long after the writing of the story* [Moore 206].

When Lawrence left England for the first time in May 1912, with Frieda Weekley, he committed himself to being a professional writer. Not only did his output increase dramatically, but the material available for dating his work also increases, and his peregrinations begin. Therefore, from 1912 onwards, we shall follow him month by month.

JANUARY 1912 At 16 Colworth Road, Croydon until 6, then at Compton House, St Peter's road, Bournemouth.

SUMMARY *I do very little work—just the revising of the novel—no creative work* [Moore 95]. Lawrence completely revised *The Trespasser* [A2]. While convalescing in Bournemouth he also wrote 'The Sea' [C51 A10].

3 JAN. *I have begun the* Saga *again—done the first chapter—heaps, heaps better* [Moore 91].
19 JAN. *I have done the first 135 pages of* The Trespasser—*re-written them.* . . . *At the bottom of my heart I don't like the work* . . . *I hate it for its fluid, luscious quality* [Moore 93].
21 JAN. *I send you herewith the 180 or 190 pages of* The Trespasser *which I have done.* . . . *I hope the thing is knitted firm—I hate those pieces where the stitch is slack and loose.* . . . *I give myself away so much, and write what is my most palpitant, sensitive self, that I loathe the book, because it will betray me to a parcel of fools* [Moore 94].
29 JAN. The Trespasser *goes quite fast. I am past the 300th page now. It really isn't bad, is it?—but too florid, too chargé. But it can't be anything else—it is itself. I must let it stand* [Moore 97]. The MS, now at Berkeley, has 485 pages (487 in Lawrence's inaccurate numbering). Lawrence stayed closer to the earlier draft than was to be usual with him, which of course made for speed. Nevertheless the work must have continued into February. [See Tedlock 7–11.]

FEBRUARY 1912 At Bournemouth until 3, then to the Cearne, Edenbridge, Kent until 9, then to 13 Queen's Square, Eastwood.

SUMMARY On 4 Lawrence broke off his engagement to Louie Burrows, and on 28 resigned his post at Davidson Road, School, Croydon. He wrote 'The Miner at Home' [C10 and *Phoenix*], finished *The Trespasser*, and resumed work on *Paul Morel*.

3 FEB. Lawrence had his last meeting with Helen Corke, who claims that the poem 'Passing Visit to Helen' followed from it [Corke 215].
*14 FEB. *I send you these sketches. I think they're not bad. Would the* Saturday *or the* Nation *look at them?* . . . *The colliery one, apropos the strike, might go down* [More 100]. 'The colliery one' was 'The Miner at Home'. The other may have been 'The Fly in the Ointment', which Lawrence described as a 'sketch' in several letters at the time of

its publication in *The New Statesman* in 1913 [Moore 215, 217].

24 FEB.   *The only thing to do is to get on with this third novel. It goes pretty well. I think I shall finish it by May* [Moore 101].

MARCH 1912   At 13 Queen's Square, Eastwood, except for 2–8 with Harry and Alice Dax at Shirebrook, and 25–30 with George Neville at Mount Pleasant, Bradnop, Leek, Staffordshire.

SUMMARY   Lawrence worked hard at *Paul Morel*. He wrote 'A Sick Collier' [C25 A6], 'Her Turn' [C24 A71] and 'Strike Pay' [C26 A71]. In mid-March Lawrence met Frieda Weekley.

4 MARCH   Lawrence wrote to Walter de la Mare, who had succeeded Atkinson as reader for Heinemann, and had offered to help Lawrence with his poems, that he had no time to devote to verse, since he was trying to finish his novel before going to Germany in the spring.

6 MARCH   *I am very busy indeed at the collier novel. . . . I have done two thirds or more* [Moore 102].

8 MARCH   *It is good news from the* Forum! *I have altered the story much to my satisfaction. . . . I enclose a story I wrote three years back, and had forgotten. It is on the same theme* [Moore 102]. The *Forum* had accepted 'The Soiled Rose', which they published the following March. The other story was 'A Modern Lover'. (See December, 1909.)

14 MARCH   Lawrence received the proofs of 'The Miner at Home', and sent Garnett 'A Sick Collier'.

16 MARCH   Lawrence sent Garnett a second sketch.

17 MARCH   Lawrence sent Garnett a third sketch. These were 'Her Turn' and 'Strike Pay', published in the *Saturday Westminster Gazette*, 6 and 13 September, as 'Strike-Pay I, Her Turn' and 'Strike-Pay II, Ephraim's Half Sovereign'. Lawrence was now becoming aware of the need to support himself by his writing.

APRIL 1912   At 13 Queen's Square, Eastwood, except for a visit to Leicester on 23, to London (Oak Lodge, St George's Road, St Margaret's-on-Thames), 25–6, and to The Cearne, Edenbridge, 27–8 (with Frieda). Back in Leicester 28 and Eastwood 29.

SUMMARY   Lawrence finished the third draft of *Paul Morel*, and corrected the proofs of *The Trespasser*. He also wrote *The Married Man* [C226 and CPlays].

1 APRIL *The* Daily News *sent me back the article 'The Collier's Wife Scores'* [Moore 105]. Since there is nowhere any other mention of a piece by that name, I assume this is an early title for 'Her Turn'.

3 APRIL *I shall finish my colliery novel this week—the first draft. It'll want a bit of revising. It's by far the best thing I've done* [Moore 106].

5 APRIL *The first batch of proofs of* The Trespasser *arrived last night. I will wage war on my adjectives* [Moore 107]. Tedlock [11] gives an example: *That night she met his love with love as blazing as his own. They were not themselves, but transfigued in pure, fiery passion which they themselves merely held located, like the burning bush. They far transcended their own beings. It was a wonderful night to achieve.* In the published text this has become: *That night she met his passion with love. It was not his passion she wanted, actually. But she desired that he should want her madly, and that he should have all—everything. It was a wonderful night to him.*

11 APRIL Lawrence received the proofs of 'The Schoolmaster', but gave them only fleeting attention since he was still preoccupied with the proofs of *The Trespasser*. (De la Mare had arranged for seven of Lawrence's schoolteaching poems to appear in four consecutive numbers of the *Saturday Westminster Gazette*, from 11 May, under the general title of 'The Schoolmaster'.)

23 APRIL *I have written a comedy—middling good* [Moore 109]. *The Married Man* was not published until 1940, and has never, to my knowledge, been performed. The play was inspired by the recent marital adventures of Lawrence's old friend George Henry Neville [Moore 103].

28 APRIL 'At the Cearne' and the peoms sent with it to Edward Garnett, 'The Chief Mystery', 'Pear Blossom', 'Assuming the Burden', 'She Was a Good Little Wife', and 'Other women have reared in me . . .', were probably written during this weekend or shortly after.

MAY 1912   At Eastwood until 3. At Metz 4–7, 8–10 at Trier, 10 at Hennef on the way to Waldbröl, Rheinprovinz (c/o Frau Karl Krenkow). There until 24, then to Beuerberg for the rest of the month.

SUMMARY Lawrence was too busy 'making history', as Garnett put it, to give much thought to writing until he got to Trier, where he had time on his hands waiting for Frieda to join him. There he wrote 'Ballad of a Wilful Woman' [A10] and the first of his 'German Impressions'—'French Sons of

Germany' [C16 and *Phoenix*]. The second—'Hail in the Rhineland' [C17 and *Phoenix*] soon followed. He wrote 'Bei Hennef' [A10]; then returned to *Paul Morel.* At Beuerberg he wrote 'First Morning' [A10], and 'She Looks Back' [A10].

9 MAY *I have written a newspaper article that nobody on earth will print, because it's too plain and straight. . . . And I smoked a pensive cigarette, and philosophized about love and life and battle, and you and me. And I thought of a theme for my next novel* [Moore 115–16].

The article was 'French Sons of Germany'. The 'next novel' is, of course, hypothetical. Lawrence may never have begun it. The next novel he did begin was probably the one which was not written in its final form until 1920 and published as *The Lost Girl.* It is based on the life of Flossie Cullen. The Cullen family appears as the Houghtons both in *The Lost Girl* and in its unfinished 1913 predecessor, *The Insurrection of Miss Houghton.* They had figured prominently in the early *Paul Morel* as the Staynes family; Lawrence was clearly fascinated by them. The only surviving letter from Lawrence to Flossie Cullen is dated 11 May 1912. Lawrence says that he has heard from Ada that Flossie is cross with him, and begs her forgiveness. Nothing more. But perhaps it was this reminder of Flossie which gave Lawrence the idea of returning to the abandoned Cullen material, but this time with Flossie, not Jessie Chambers, as the heroine. It is certain that some time in 1912 he began such a novel. It begins 'My mother made a failure of her life . . .' [Tedlock 44–6], but breaks off after twenty pages. The narrator's name (the Flossie Cullen figure) is Elsa Culverwell.

†10 MAY *I am sitting like a sad swain beside a nice, twittering little river, waiting for the twilight to drop, and my last train to come* [Moore 117]. While waiting, Lawrence wrote 'Bei Hennef'.

14 MAY Lawrence corrected the proofs of 'Snap-Dragon', which was to appear in the *English Review* the following week [Moore 118–20].

*16 MAY Lawrence told de la Mare that he was revising his novel patiently, and expected to finish it in a fortnight. He enclosed 'Hail in the Rhineland', which describes a hail-storm of the previous day [Moore 122].

*19 MAY To Jessie Chambers: *I am going through* Paul Morel. *I'm sorry it has turned out as it has. You'll have to go on forgiving me* [Moore 127].

21 MAY *I am eating my heart out, and revising my immortal Heinemann*

28

novel, Paul Morel, *in this tiny village stuck up in the Rhineland* [Moore 124–5].

*23 MAY   Paul Morel *is finished all but ten pages* [Moore 126].

JUNE 1912   At the house of Alfred Weber at Icking, near Munich.

SUMMARY   Lawrence completed his revision of *Paul Morel*, wrote three short stories, probably 'The Christening' [A6] 'Delilah and Mr Bircumshaw' [C225 and *Phoenix 2*] and 'Once' [A56 and *Phoenix 2*], and several of the poems in '*Look! We Have Come Through!*' [A10].

6 JUNE   Corpus Christi, mentioned in the poem 'Frohnleichnam'.

9 JUNE   On this date Lawrence sent *Paul Morel* to Heinemann. He did not, however, regard it as finished, since 8 July he wrote to Garnett: *I will make what alterations you think advisable. It would be rather nice if you made me a few notes again. I will squash the first part together—it is too long* [Moore 131]. Lawrence resumed work on the novel in August.

29 JUNE   *While here I've written three* [short stories]. *But, under the influence of Frieda, I am afraid their moral tone would not agree with my countrymen* [Moore 133].

'The Christening' may have been written or at least begun earlier, since at the top of the first page is the address, crossed out, 13 Queen's Square, Eastwood, Notts., where Lawrence lived from February until his departure from England; perhaps in March when Lawrence heard that his friend George Neville had fathered a second illegitimate child [Moore 103].

JULY 1912   The Lawrences remained at Icking throughout July.

SUMMARY   Lawrence wrote more German sketches and at least part of a comedy. None of this material seems to have survived. Some seventeen poems in '*Look!*' seem to have been written at Icking, or nearby Wolfratshausen.

3 JULY   Lawrence received the proofs of 'French Sons of Germany', which appeared in the *Saturday Westminster Gazette*, 3 August.

*4 JULY   Lawrence received the MS of *Paul Morel* from de la Mare, and sent it off immediately to Garnett.

18 JULY   Lawrence told Garnett he was amusing himself writing a comedy.

1912

*22 JULY   To Edward Garnett: *I got* Paul Morel *this morning, and the list of notes from Duckworth. The latter are awfully nice and detailed. What a Trojan of energy and conscientiousness you are! I'm going to slave like a Turk at the novel—see if I won't do you credit. I begin in earnest tomorrow—having spent the day in thought (?)* [Moore 135]. It seems that the combined force of the criticisms Lawrence received from de la Mare, Garnett, and, most of all, Frieda, convinced Lawrence at this stage that the novel would have to be written again.

AUGUST 1912   Lawrence and Frieda left Icking 5 to walk to Mayrhofen, where they arrived 9, leaving 27 to walk to Sterzing am Brenner.

SUMMARY   Lawrence probably wrote 'A Chapel Among the Mountains' [A56 and *Phoenix* 2], 'A Hay Hut Among the Mountains' [A56 and *Phoenix* 2] and 'The Young Soldier with Bloody Spurs' [CP 732], 'Song of a Man Who is Not Loved' [A10] and 'Sinners' [A10].

4 AUG.   Lawrence sent Austin Harrison three more stories, presumably the three written in June. None was accepted. He says that he has written five German sketches in all, and that three have been accepted by the *Westminster Gazette*. In fact only two appeared there. Of the three unpublished ones there is no trace. *I am going to write six short stories. I must try and make running money. I am going to write* Paul Morel *over again—it'll take me 3 months. . . . I've thought of a new novel—purely of the common people—fearfully interesting* [Moore 137].

Lawrence wrote no short stories at all until the following spring. He did rewrite *Paul Morel*, and it took him just over three months. He could not, therefore, begin a new novel until December, q.v.

8 AUG.   If Lawrence is to be taken literally in describing, in 'A Chapel Among the Mountains', the events of the story as happening 'yesterday', then the story was written 8 at Glasshutte. The poem 'Song of a Man Who is Not Loved' is also signed Glasshutte, and 'Sinners' Mayrhofen.

13 AUG.   Lawrence sent Garnett 'The Young Soldier with Bloody Spurs'.

22 AUG.   Lawrence tells Garnett that two of his articles have been rejected by the *Westminster Gazette* as too anti-German.

30

SEPTEMBER 1912   Lawrence and Frieda arrived at Sterzing 2. From there they went to Riva by train, arriving 4 or 5. On 18 they moved to Villa Igea, Villa, Gargnano, Lago di Garda, which was to be their home until the end of March 1913.

SUMMARY   Lawrence wrote 'Christs in the Tirol' [C20, A56b, and *Phoenix*] and worked hard on the revision of *Paul Morel*. He also wrote 'Misery' [A10] and, probably, 'Meeting Among the Mountains' [A10].

2 SEPT.   *I must soon begin to write again, for I've done absolutely nothing lately. I want to get a few articles done for the W.G.* [Moore 142].

5 SEPT.   Lawrence sends de la Mare three articles for the *Westminster Gazette*. He must have written 'Christs in the Tirol' (published there 22 March 1913) to add to the 'Chapel' and the 'Hay Hut'.

7 SEPT.   *I am glad to be settling down, to get at that novel. I am rather keen on it. I shall recast the first part altogether* [Moore 143].

11 SEPT.   *I am working like hell at my novel* [Moore 145].

*16 SEPT.   *I shall correct the proofs* [Love Poems] *in Gargnano* [Moore 146].

*17 SEPT.   Paul Morel *is better than* The White Peacock *or* The Trespasser. *I'm inwardly very proud of it, though I haven't yet licked it into form—am still at that labour of love* [Moore 147].

OCTOBER 1912   At Villa Igea, Gargnano, Lago di Garda, Italy.

SUMMARY   Lawrence wrote *The Fight for Barbara* [C213, CPlays], continued to revise *Paul Morel*, and corrected the proofs of *Love Poems* [A3].

3 OCT.   *I do my novel well, I'm sure. It's half done* [Moore 149].

*4 OCT.   Lawrence read *Anna of the Five Towns* by Arnold Bennett, to which *The Insurrection of Miss Houghton* was shortly to be his answer.

5 OCT.   The first proofs of *Love Poems* arrived [Moore 150].

*15 OCT.   *You'll see I returned the corrected proofs of the poems to Duckworth before I got your letter. . . . And I only made corrections of the most unrespectable lines—I was a bit hurried. . . . I have done ⅗ of* Paul Morel. *Can I call it* Sons and Lovers [Moore 153–4].

30 OCT.   *I've written the comedy I send you by this post in the last three days, as a sort of interlude to* Paul Morel. *I've done all but the last hundred or so pages of that great work, and those I funk. But it'll be*

done easily in a fortnight, then I start Scargill Street. . . . *I've written 400 pages of* Paul Morel. . . . *I've made the book heaps better—a million times* [Moore 152–3].

On 2 Nov. Lawrence names the comedy: *I'm dying to know what you think of the* Fight for Barbara [Moore 155].

Lawrence says *Scargill Street* as though the name should mean something to Garnett. Unless there is a missing letter, Lawrence had never mentioned it to him (or anyone else in the surviving correspondence). He had, however, told Garnett three months earlier, that he had thought of a new novel, 'purely of the common people'. Perhaps Lawrence had now got used to thinking of the new novel waiting for *Sons and Lovers* to be finished, by this title. *Scargill Street* is in Eastwood: *Down the steep between the squares, Scargill Street, the Wesleyans' chapel was put up, and I was born in the little corner shop just above* ['Nottingham and the Mining Countryside', *Phoenix* 134].

NOVEMBER 1912   At the Villa Igea, Gargnano.

SUMMARY   Lawrence wrote 'Giorno dei Morti', 'All Souls' and probably other *'Look!'* poems, and finished *Sons and Lovers* [A4], which was published by Duckworth in May 1913.

2 NOV.   All Souls' Day. Presumably 'Giorno dei Morti' and 'All Souls' were written on this day or shortly afterwards.

19 NOV.   *I hasten to tell you I sent the MS of the* Paul Morel *novel to Duckworth registered, yesterday. And I want to defend it, quick. I wrote it again, pruning it and shaping it and filling it in. I tell you it has got form—form: haven't I made it patiently, out of sweat as well as blood* [Moore 160].

Lawrence goes on to give Garnett his famous synopsis of the novel. Garnett was not as impressed as Lawrence clearly expected him to be, and suggested extensive pruning. Lawrence asked him to take out what he thought necessary. He removed about a tenth, very skilfully, improving the novel a good deal. When Lawrence saw the proofs he wrote to Garnett (18 February 1913): *You did the pruning jolly well, and I am grateful. I hope you'll live a very long time, to barber up my novels for me before they're published. I wish I were not so profuse—or prolix* [Moore 186].

The 19 November letter also asks Garnett to return his plays so that he can do some recasting of them *before I really set to work on my next novel—which I have conceived.* There is no evidence that Lawrence received the plays. The 'next novel' is presumably still the one to be called *Scargill Street*.

DECEMBER 1912   At Villa Igea, Gargnano.

SUMMARY *I'm going to begin again my work. One works in two bursts—Sept. to the beginning of Dec.—and Jan. till March or April. The rest are more or less trivial and barren months. I feel I am resisting too hard to write poetry—resisting the strain of Weekley, and the tragedy there is in keeping Frieda. To write poetry one has to let oneself fuse in the current—but I daren't* [Moore 168].

Lawrence did two paintings, began and abandoned his Burns novel, wrote a few poems including, presumably, 'December Night' [A10] and 'New Year's Eve' [A10], and began *The Insurrection of Miss Houghton*.

2 DEC.   To A. W. McLeod: *Oh, I've actually painted two pictures. I'm doing several—when they're finished I shall send them and let you have your pick. This is the interlude between novels* [Moore 164].

On 24 December Lawrence was to write to Collings: *I sketch in water-colour myself, as a hopeless amateur. But it is such healing work, I find, to paint a bit, even if it is only to copy, after one has frayed out one's soul with damned emotional drawing. To copy a nice Peter de Wint is the most soothing thing I can do, and to copy a Frank Brangwyn is a joy, so refreshing* [Moore 171]. Lawrence's copy of Peter de Wint's *A Harvest Scene* is reproduced in *Young Bert*, 48. It may have been done at this time.

17 DEC.   *I am thinking so hard of my new novel, and since I am feeling hard pushed again, am in the right tune for it. It is to be a life of Robert Burns—but I shall make him live near home, as a Derbyshire man and shall fictionalise the circumstances. I think I can do him almost like an autobiography. . ... I haven't done any stories or anything lately* [Moore 167–8].

To Edward Garnett: *I've thought of a new novel I'm keen on. It's a sort of life of Robert Burns. But I'm not Scotch. So I shall just transplant him to home—or on the hills of Derbyshire—and do as I like with him as far as circumstances go, but I shall stick to the man* [Moore 169].

All that survives of the Burns novel is some twelve pages of MS which were left with Else Jaffe. They are published in Nehls 1,

184–95. Since Lawrence began *The Insurrection of Miss Houghton* very shortly after this, and wrote to MacLeod on 17 January. *As for my book, my novel on the subject* [Burns], *I wonder if I shall ever get it done* [Moore 178] it is quite possible that no more than this was ever written. It is not clear from the letters whether this is or is not *Scargill Street*, or the novel of the common people Lawrence had been waiting to write since August. This could be one and the same novel or three different ones; or the first two could have been the same, but the Burns new. Lawrence had apparently asked Agnes Mason to send him Lockhart's *Life of Burns*, and had received it in time to have read it by 17 December [Moore 168]. He may have sent for the book because he was already planning the novel, or been inspired to attempt the novel by reading the book. The setting of the fragment we have is not Eastwood, but the area just to the north. The hero, Jack Haseldine, is from Haggs Farm; his girl, Mary Renshaw, from Jacksdale a few miles to the north. It is back in the days of gin-pits, probably before there was a Scargill Street, in the time of Robert Burns.

29 DEC.   *I've stewed my next novel inside me for a week or so, and have begun dishing it up. It's going to have a bit of a plot, and I don't think it'll be unwieldy, because it will be further off from me and won't come down on my head so often* [Moore 174]. It seems that the Burns project is now abandoned, and Lawrence is beginning *The Insurrection of Miss Houghton*.

JANUARY 1913 At Villa Igea, Gargnano.

SUMMARY *I couldn't have done any more at that novel* [Sons and Lovers]—*at least for six months. I must go on producing, producing, and the stuff must come more and more to shape each year. But trim and garnish my stuff I cannot—it must go. The plays I can rewrite and re-create: I shall love it* [Moore 176].

Lawrence wrote 'New Year's Night' [A10], *The Daughter-in-Law* [CPlays] and the Foreword to *Sons and Lovers* [Huxley 95–102], and about the first hundred pages of *The Insurrection of Miss Houghton*; also possibly, 'The Theatre' [C23 A8].

12 JAN. *I am going to send you a new play I have written. It is neither a comedy nor a tragedy—just ordinary. It is quite objective, as far as that term goes, and though no doubt, like most of my stuff, it wants weeding out a bit, yet I think the whole thing is there, laid out properly, planned and progressive. . . . I do think this play might have a chance on the stage. It'll bear cutting, but I don't think it lacks the stuff for the theatre. . . . I'm simmering a new work that I shall not tell you about, because it may not come off. But the thought fills me with a curious pleasure—venomous, almost* [Moore 175–6]. This play can only be *The Daughter-in-Law*.

16 JAN. The sketches in *Twilight in Italy* grouped together as 'On the Lago di Garda', can be dated only on internal evidence. 'The Theatre' may well have been the earliest, since the performance of *Hamlet* it describes was on 16 January.

17 JAN. *I have written 80 pages of a new novel: a most curious work, which gives me great joy to write, but which, I am afraid, will give most folk extreme annoyance to read, if it doesn't bore them* [Moore 178]. In succeeding letters Lawrence describes closely the progress of this novel, but does not name it until 2 May, by which time it has been set aside.

*20 JAN. *I was fearfully anxious to write a foreword to* Sons and Lovers, *and this is what I did. I am a fool—but it will amuse you* [Huxley 95]. In this next letter to Garnett, Lawrence made clear that the Foreword was not intended for publication: *I should die of shame if that Foreword were printed* [Moore 182].

26 JAN. To Katherine Mansfield, editor of *Rhythm*: *Let me have something interesting to review for March—German if you like* [Moore 181 misdated]. The March number of *Rhythm* contained Lawrence's review 'The Georgian Renaissance'. This was the last number of

Rhythm. But Katherine Mansfield and John Middleton Murry immediately started the *Blue Review*, the third and last number of which (July) carried Lawrence's essay on Thomas Mann [C21]. See May.

FEBRUARY 1913   At Villa Igea, Gargnano.

SUMMARY   Lawrence continued writing *The Insurrection of Miss Houghton*, but most of his time was taken up with the proofs of *Sons and Lovers.* He also wrote one or two '*Look!*' poems, including 'Valentine's Night', his review of *Georgian Poetry* [C19 and *Phoenix*], and, possibly, 'The Spinner and the Monks' [C23 A8]. In 'The Spinner and the Monks' the season is very early spring. There are primroses, crocuses and periwinkles, but also the last of the Christmas roses, and evening begins at four.

1 FEB.   *I have done 100 pages of a novel. I think you will hate it, but I think, when it is rewritten, it might find a good public amongst the Meredithy public. It is quite different in manner from my other stuff—far less visualised. . . . 106 pages are written* [Moore 183].

*5 FEB.   *I am doing proofs of* Sons and Lovers [Huxley 103].

*18 FEB.   *I corrected and returned the first batch of* Sons and Lovers. . . . *The new novel is going quite fast. It is awfully exciting, thrilling, to my mind—a bit outspoken, perhaps. I shall write it as long as I like to start with, then write it smaller. I must always write my books twice* [Moore 186].

24 FEB.   *I am correcting proofs of my novel* [Moore 190].

*25 FEB.   *The last proofs of* Sons and Lovers *came today* [Huxley 110]. Lawrence returned them before the end of the month [Moore 190].

MARCH 1913   At Villa Igea, Gargnano.

SUMMARY   Lawrence reached page 200 of *The Insurrection of Miss Houghton*, then set it aside to begin *The Sisters.*

5 MARCH   *My new novel is a weird thing. I rather love it. It's half written* [Moore 193].

11 MARCH   *I've written rather more than half of a most fascinating (to me) novel. But nobody will ever dare to publish it. I feel I could knock my head against the wall. Yet I love and adore this new book. It's all crude as yet, like one of Tony's clumsy prehistorical beasts—most cumber-*

some and floundering—but I think it's great—so new, so really a stratum deeper than I think anybody has ever gone, in a novel. But there, you see, it's my latest. It is all analytical—quite unlike Sons and Lovers, not a bit visualised. But nobody will publish it. I wish I had never been born. But I am going to stick at it, get it done, and then write another, shorter, absolute impeccable—as far as morals go—novel. . . . The novel is not about Frieda and me, nor about a Baroness neither [Moore 194].

This letter is often quoted as though it referred to *The Sisters*, the very novel he here announces, at the end, his intention to write, or even *The Rainbow*, which is still months away. The novel Lawrence thought so highly of was *The Insurrection of Miss Houghton*. The appropriateness of Lawrence's claims for it cannot be tested, since it does not survive; we cannot know how drastically Lawrence changed it when he rewrote it in 1920 as *The Lost Girl*. Even Frieda thought the *Insurrection* was 'improper!' [Moore 208]; but between it and *The Lost Girl* came the *Rainbow* prosecution.

22 MARCH   *I have also been trying to draw collieries. It is beastly difficult. One needs the technique of a proper illustrator. I have also written the brief notice for the wrapper. I began a new lighter novel and have done 46 pages. It will be quite decent (D.V.). The other one has my love. It will be none the worse for waiting a while* [Heilbrun 153]. Edward Garnett had asked Lawrence to provide an illustration of colliery headstocks and a synopsis for the dust-wrapper of *Sons and Lovers*. Lawrence had so little success with his attempts at the drawing, that he asked Ernest Collings to do it. Collings submitted a sketch which Lawrence liked, but, in the event, the wrapper bore no illustration. The 'brief notice' reads: *Mr D. H. Lawrence's new novel covers a wide field: life in a colliery, on a farm, in a manufacturing centre. It is concerned with the contrasting outlook on life of two generations. The title, Sons and Lovers, indicates the conflicting claims of a young man's mother and sweetheart for predominance.* The 'new lighter novel' is, as we shall see, *The Sisters*.

APRIL 1913   At San Gaudenzio, Gargnano, until 11, then to Verona until 14, then to Munich. By 17 at Villa Jaffe, Irschenhausen.

SUMMARY   Lawrence continued to write *The Sisters*. He also wrote four or five of the sections of *Twilight in Italy*, and two or three poems for

'*Look!*', including 'Spring Morning', which is signed 'San Gaudenzio'. He corrected the revised proofs of *Sons and Lovers*.

5 APRIL   *I sit and write in a deserted lemon-garden. . . . I did 200 pages of a novel—a novel I love—then I put it aside to do a pot-boiler—it was too improper. The pot-boiler is at page 110, and has developed into an earnest and painful work—God help it and me. I'm so sick of the last lot of proofs of* Sons and Lovers, *that I have scarcely patience to correct them* [Moore 196–7].

> Though Lawrence places 'The Lemon Gardens' before 'The Theatre' in *Twilight in Italy*, it seems more likely to have been written at San Gaudenzio than at the Villa Igea. The four sections beginning with 'San Gaudenzio' itself were almost certainly written there. All these sketches were to be much revised and extended for book publication in 1915. The 'pot-boiler' is *The Sisters*.

*23 APRIL   *I am doing a novel which I have never grasped. Damn its eyes, there I am at page 145, and I've no notion what it's about. I hate it. F. says it is good. But it's like a novel in a foreign language I don't know very well—I can only just make out what it is about* [Moore 203].

MAY 1913   At Villa Jaffe, Irschenhausen.

SUMMARY   Lawrence continued with *The Sisters*. He also wrote his essay on *Thomas Mann* [C21 and *Phoenix*] and, possibly, 'The Shades of Spring' [A6] and 'The Prussian Officer' [C34 A6].

8 MAY   Lawrence sent Harriet Monroe a batch of poems including those published in *Poetry* in December 1914: 'Grief' [C30 B5 CP], 'Memories' [A9 as 'The End'], 'Weariness' [A9 as 'Sorrow'], 'Service of All the Dead' [C28 A10 as 'Giorno dei Morti'], 'Don Juan' [A10] and 'Song' [C32 A11 as 'Flapper'].

*9 MAY   *I am only doing* reviews *for the* Blue Monthly, *or whatever it is. Shall I send some poems, and a story, for the* Forum? *I have written 180 pages of my newest novel* The Sisters. *It is a queer novel, which seems to have come by itself. I will send it to you. You may dislike it—it hasn't got hard outlines—and of course it's only first draft—but it's pretty neat, for me, in composition. Then I've got 200 pages of a novel which I'm saving—which is very lumbering—which I'll call, provisionally,* The Insurrection of Miss Houghton. *That I shan't send you yet, but it is, to me, fearfully exciting. It lies next my heart, for the* *present. But I am finishing* The Sisters. *It will only have 300 pages. It was meant to be for the* 'jeunes filles', *but already it has fallen from grace. . . . In a month* The Sisters *will be finished (D.V.)* [Moore 200].

'German Books: Thomas Mann' appeared in *The Blue Review* the following month. *The Forum* published nothing else of Lawrence's until 1927. The story Lawrence proposes to send may be an old one, or even one not yet written. At last Lawrence here gives us titles by which we can identify, retrospectively, the two novels he has been describing in his letters for several months.

13 MAY   *I am going it strong enough with a new novel, that is two-thirds done* [Huxley 123].

17 or 19   *I hope in about a fortnight to have finished* The Sisters. . . . *We got Miss Chambers' novel* [Moore 205]. Lawrence's 7s and 9s are not always easily distinguishable. This one looks more like a 9, but could be 7, and there is an envelope to Garnett postmarked 17 which would otherwise be unaccounted for. Lawrence read the MS of Jessie Chambers' *The Rathe Primrose* (which she subsequently destroyed), and was made very miserable by it. This may have stimulated him to rewrite 'The Soiled Rose' as 'The Dead Rose' [Huxley 201]. The title was changed to 'The Shades of Spring' for *The Prussian Officer*. On 10 June Lawrence is to speak of having written an 'autobiographical' story.

†21 or 27   To Edward Garnett: *I was glad of your letter about* The Sisters. *Don't schimpf, I shall make it all right when I rewrite it. I shall put it in the third person. All along I knew what ailed the book. But it did me good to theorise myself out, and to depict Frieda's Good Almightiness in all its glory. That was the first crude fermenting of the book. I'll make it into art now. I've done 256 pages, but still can't see the end very clear. But it's coming. Frieda is so cross, since your letter came, with the book* [Moore 208].

Garnett had complained about the 'remarkable females' (Frieda calls them 'beastly, superior, arrogant females') one of whom, Ella Templeman, was at this stage the narrator, and was based closely on Frieda. It seems self-evident to me that this letter must follow the preceding one, as in Moore. The Lacy–Vasey *Calendar* has reversed them.

JUNE 1913   At Villa Jaffe, Irschenhausen, until 17. By 21 at The Cearne, Edenbridge, Kent.

1913

SUMMARY   Lawrence completed the first draft of *The Sisters*, and wrote 'The Thorn in the Flesh' [C33 A6].

*1 JUNE   Lawrence tells Garnett that he has reached page 283 of *The Sisters*. He must have completed it shortly afterwards, since on 10 he is asking Garnett if he has received the second half.

Mark Kinkead-Weekes has argued [414] that the first of the two Texas MS fragments E44lb is from this first draft of *The Sisters* on the grounds of the similarity of the paper to that of the Foreword to *Sons and Lovers* and of the page numbers 291–6. If correct, this disposes of the suggestion that the name Loerke is related to that of Gertler, whom Lawrence did not meet until the autumn of 1914. The first page has the last fourteen lines of an earlier section about Gerald's mother, which corresponds roughly with a paragraph in the 'Industrial Magnate' chapter of *Women in Love*. The following chapter in *Women in Love* is 'Rabbit', which may have derived from Gerald's recollection, later in the fragment, of a rabbit running to a groom for protection from a cat, as no creature ever came to him for protection or tenderness. The rest of the fragment is about Gerald going to Gudrun's house in Beldover to ask her to marry him (she is already pregnant by him), and finding Loerke there already on the same errand. There are threats of violence, but Loerke eventually leaves, his face broken in an agony of emotion. Gerald and Gudrun are then reconciled, and the fragment ends: *There was a good deal that hurt still, between them. But he was humble to her. Only, she must love him—she must love him or else everything was barren. This aloofness of hers—she came to him as the father of her child, not as to a lover, a husband. Well he had had a chance, and lost it. He had been a fool. Now he must make the best of it, and get her again. But it hurt that she did not seem to want him very much. It hurt keenly. Then while he was thinking, with his forehead hard with pain, she kissed him, drawing him to her, murmuring 'My love!'*

This is page 296. A month earlier Lawrence had estimated that the novel would be three hundred pages. So this may well be the ending, especially as Lawrence has squeezed the last line on to the page so as not to have to start another sheet.

*10 JUNE   *I have written the best short story I have ever done—about a German officer in the army and his orderly. Then there is another good autobiographical story. I think it is good: then there is another story in course of completion which interests me* [Moore 209]. The

40

first story was 'Honour and Arms', the second, I think, 'The Dead Rose' (see May); the third is identified as 'Vin Ordinaire', later 'The Thorn in the Flesh', by a letter of 21 June: *Now I have written three good short stories just before we came to England—two about German soldier-life* [Moore 211].

JULY 1913   At the Cearne until 9 then to 28 Percy Avenue, Kingsgate. Broadstairs, Kent, until 30, then to London.

SUMMARY   *I have been grubbing away among the short stories. God, I shall be glad when it is done. I shall begin my novel again in Germany. We bathe and I write among the babies of the foreshore: it is an innocent life and a dull one* [Moore 215].

Lawrence wrote 'History' [A10] and 'New Eve and Old Adam' [A71] at the Cearne, and 'The Primrose Path' [A23] at Kingsgate. He revised several of his earlier short stories before sending them to Douglas Clayton to be typed.

*8 JULY   Lawrence sent a batch of MSS to Clayton. Apparently it included 'The New Eve', since Lawrence wrote to Edward Garnett on 14: *Mrs Clayton said she thought the story I called 'The New Eve'—previously I think 'Renegade Eve'—that is the one where the telegram comes 'Meet me Marble Arch 7.30 Richard'—was unworthy of me, and so Douglas didn't type it. Perhaps she's right—it amuses me* [Moore 212].

*11 JULY   Lawrence wrote to David Garnett to ask if he had left 'Intimacy' at the Cearne. Two days later he wrote again to say he had found it, and changed the title. On the same day he sent another story to Mrs Clayton, probably 'Intimacy' revised, and with the title changed to 'The White Woman' [Powell 20].

*14 JULY   *I am drudging away revising the Stories. How glad I shall be when I have cleared that mess up!* [Moore 213].

*16 JULY   *Shall I send these Syndicate people some of my short things? You don't know how nice they look, and how convincing, now I have revised them and they are type-written. They haven't all come yet, and so I can't send them out for a day or two.—I thought I might let this Syndicate have 'A Sick Collier', and perhaps 'The Baker's Man'—the one when they christen the illegitimate child. I rewrote the end and made it good. . . . I am swotting away at the short stories—and shall be so glad to get them done* [Moore 213–14].

The Syndicate was the Northern Newspaper Syndicate, which rejected the stories on the ground that they were too long. 'The Baker's Man' was later retitled 'The Christening'. It was first published in *The Smart Set*, February 1914.

20 JULY Lawrence wrote to Edward Garnett that he had sent two stories to the Syndicate, three for the *North American Review* (none appeared there), was sending two to Garnett for Pinker or the *English Review*, and was keeping three short ones. The *English Review* published 'Vin Ordinaire' and 'Honour and Arms' in June and August 1914. The ten stories which Clayton had typed by this date were probably: 'The Sick Collier', 'The Baker's Man', 'Vin Ordinaire', 'Honour and Arms', 'The White Woman', 'The Fly in the Ointment', which Lawrence sent to *The New Statesman* on 28, 'Her Turn' and 'Ephraim's Half Sovereign', which appeared in *The Saturday Westminster Gazette*, 6 and 13 September, 'The Shadow in the Rose Garden', which appeared in *The Smart Set*, March 1914, and 'Once', which *The Smart Set* rejected [Moore 229]. Lawrence's rewriting was particularly heavy for 'The Shadow in the Rose Garden', for which 'The Vicar's Garden' had been a mere seven-page sketch [See Cushman, 2; Finney 2].

On the same date Lawrence sent Clayton 'Daughters of the Vicar' (much expanded from 'Two Marriages') to type, and 'Love Among the Haystacks' and two more little things to pitch in a drawer. One of these was probably 'The Shades of Spring'. [On 'Daughters of the Vicar' see Finney, *op. cit.*, 329.] If 'The White Stocking' was the story sent for typing on 21 August, and if we add the stories already published, this accounts for all the stories which were to form *The Prussian Officer*.

*28 JULY Lawrence sent Clayton 'The Primrose Path'. Before sending 'The Fly in the Ointment' to *The New Statesman* on this date, Lawrence revised it. The revised typescript is at Texas. This was published in *The New Statesman*, 13 August 1913, and is reprinted in *The Mortal Coil and Other Stories* (Penguin, 1971). The text in Lawrence-Ada and in *Phoenix 2* is that of the earlier, unrevised version.

AUGUST 1913 At the Cearne until 2, then to Eastwood until 6, then, after two nights in London, to Germany. By 9 at Villa Jaffe, Irschenhausen.

SUMMARY Lawrence wrote a sketch of Eastwood, revised *The Widowing of Mrs Holroyd*, corrected the proofs of three Italian sketches, and resumed work on *The Sisters*.

I I AUG   *I have written today my first sketch—on Eastwood. It interests me very much. I propose to do a bookful of sketches—publish them in the papers first. You, Willie Hopkin, must tell me all the things that happen, and sometimes send me a Rag. And remember I am going to do an article on the Artists of Eastwood. I do the Primitive Methodist chapel next* [Moore 218]. The Eastwood sketch is lost, as are the rest, if Lawrence did any more.

13 AUG   *I have been very busy reading the play to Frieda. It wants a lot of altering. I have made it heaps better. You must by no means let the MS go to the printer before I have it—neither here nor in America. What a jolly fine play it is, too, when I have pulled it together. I shall be glad if you'll send me the typed copy when you can, so I may alter it. Must I find another title? The Widowing of Mrs Holroyd describes it, but doesn't sound very well* [Moore 218]. *The Widowing of Mrs Holroyd*, originally written in 1910, was published by Mitchell Kennerley in New York and Duckworth in London in April 1914.

*21 AUG.   Lawrence sends Clayton another story to forward to Pinker. This may have been 'The White Stocking', which Pinker had accepted by *The Smart Set* on 12 March 1914.

24 AUG.   *I send the revised MS of the play to Duckworth. It is pretty much altered, and much improved. If Kennerley has printed, I must have the MS back to correct proofs by. . . . The Sisters is the devil—I've made two false starts already—but it'll go—* [Huxley 136–7].

Lawrence described in more detail the alterations he had made in a letter of 8 September to Kennerley: *Particularly I hated it in the last act, where the man and woman wrangled rather shallowly across the dead body of the husband. And it seemed nasty that they should make love where he lay drunk. I hope to heaven I have come in time to have it made decent* [Moore 223].

SEPTEMBER 1913   At Villa Jaffe, Irschenhausen until 18, then to Constance. To Schaffhausen 19, whence Lawrence walked via Zurich to Lucerne, arriving 22. To Milan 26, to meet Frieda. By 30 at Lerici.

SUMMARY   Lawrence worked exclusively on *The Sisters*.

4 SEPT.   To Edward Garnett: *I will do what you say, and leave short stories for a while. I shall not be able to settle down here to work, I know. . . . The Sisters has quite a new beginning—a new basis altogether. I hope I can get on with it. It is much more interesting in its new form—not so*

43

damned flippant. I can feel myself getting ready for my autumn burst of work [Moore 223].

*15 SEPT. The Sisters *is going well. I've done a hundred pages. . . . It is queer. It is rather fine, I think. I am in it now, deep. . . . I am walking a week in Switzerland . . . I shall take* The Sisters *in a rucksack. I shan't do anything but* The Sisters *now. I hope to have it done in a month. . . . It's a weird novel you'll get from me this time: but perfectly proper. The libraries will put it on their Sunday School prize list* [Moore 224].

Two years later *The Rainbow* was burned by the public hangman as obscene. In fact Lawrence did not take the MS in his rucksack, but left it in Munich to be forwarded.

OCTOBER 1913   At Lerici per Fiascherino, Golfo della Spezia, Italy. The Lawrences lived at Villino Ettore Gambrosier until June 1914.

SUMMARY   Lawrence continued to work on *The Sisters*. He wrote 'Italians in Exile' and 'The Return Jouney', the last two sections of *Twilight in Italy* [A8]. He corrected the proofs of *The Widowing of Mrs Holroyd*, and probably wrote 'The Mortal Coil' [C49 and *Phoenix 2*].

*4 OCT.   Lawrence tried to correct the proofs of *The Widowing of Mrs Holroyd*, which he had just received from Garnett, but found he could not do so adequately, lacking the revised MS which he had sent to Kennerley in New York. There was one speech, particularly, which he felt he could not recreate, which was the keystone of the play. The following day he heard from Kennerley that Edwin Bjorkman would correct the proofs in American from the revised MS to avoid the delay of having to return it to Lawrence. On 22 September Kennerley had written to Garnett that he would make all the changes Lawrence desired, and shortly send him a revised proof. In 1924 Lawrence wrote: *I always remember how, in a cottage by the sea, in Italy, I rewrote almost entirely that play,* The Widowing of Mrs. Holroyd, *right on the proofs which Mitchell Kennerley had sent me. And he nobly forbore with me* [*Phoenix* 233]. Since on 21 December Lawrence tells Garnett that he has no duplicate proofs, it is possible that Kennerley never sent revised proofs, and Lawrence had to do this revision over again on the proofs he already had.

6 OCT.   Austin Harrison had offered Lawrence £15 each for a series of four stories for *The English Review*. Lawrence asks Garnett to send 'Vin

Ordinaire', 'Honour and Arms' and 'Once', adding: *For a fourth, I think I would write one I have had in my mind for a long time* [Moore 229].

On 26 October Lawrence told McLeod that Harrison had got *three soldier stories* [Moore 235]. 'Once' could conceivably be described as a soldier story, but it is more likely that Lawrence had sent 'The Mortal Coil', based on an experience of Frieda's father, which Lawrence must have known about for a long time.

6 OCT. *I am working away at* The Sisters. *It is so different, so different from anything I have yet written, that I do nothing but wonder what it is like. When I get to page 200 I shall send you the MS for your opinion* [Moore 230].

23 OCT. Frieda Lawrence to Lady Cynthia Asquith: 'L. has just put your black *crêpe de Chine* blouse with the big opal in a story! It's jolly, to watch the stories coming' [Frieda 200]. I have not been able to find this blouse. Anita, in 'Once', wears crêpe de Chine, but it is blue, and there is no opal.

28 OCT. To Edward Marsh: *I've copied out quite a lot of poems. Tell me if you like them* [Moore 237]. Lawrence was almost incapable of copying out poems without revising them at the same time. The poems he sent to Marsh were: 'Song of a Man Who is Loved' [A10b], 'Afterwards' (later 'Grey Evening' and 'Firelight and Nightfall') [A9], 'Don Juan' [C35 A10], 'Storm in Rose-Time' (later 'Love Storm'] [A11], 'Purity' (later 'Paradise Re-Entered') [A10], 'Mystery' [A9], 'Illicit' (later 'On the Balcony') [C29 A10], 'A Kiss' [CP], 'The Wind, the Rascal' [C29 A70 CP], 'The Inheritance' [A9] (later 'Noise of Battle' [A11]), and 'Ballad of a Wayward Woman' (later 'Ballad of a Wilful Woman') [A10]. See Ferrier MS20b.

*31 OCT. Lawrence told Garnett that he had been doing the stories for the *English Review*, and was just finishing the last. This implies that the three existing stories were revised. Only 'Vin Ordinaire' and 'Honour and Arms' were printed in the *English Review*. Lawrence also says that he has made no progress with *The Sisters*.

NOVEMBER 1913   At Lerici.

SUMMARY   Lawrence worked exclusively on *The Sisters*.

*2 NOV. Lawrence wrote to Garnett that he had finished the last of the *English Review* stories, and had 'started' *The Sisters*.

*18 NOV.   To Edward Marsh: *Don't talk to me any more about poetry for months—unless it is other men's work. I really love verse, even rubbish. But I'm fearfully busy at a novel, and brush all the gossamer of verse off my face* [Moore 245].

*24 NOV.   *We seem to have been very busy. I writing away at my novel, then visits to pay and to receive. I have done 340 pages of my novel. It is very different from* Sons and Lovers. *The Laocoön writhing and shrieking have gone from my new work, and I think there is a bit of stillness, like the wide, still, unseeing eyes of a Venus of Melos* [Moore 241].

Shortly after this date Lawrence must have written the second E441b fragment, which is numbered 373–8. It deals with Birkin's visit to Ella to propose to her when her parents are away on holiday, but is completely different from the proposal scene in chapter 19 of *Women in Love*. It is quoted at length by Kinkead-Weekes [376–7]. At the end of the fragment, the girls go to Filey where they see Ella's former lover Ben Templeman.

DECEMBER 1913   At Lerici.

SUMMARY   *I am writing my novel slowly—it will be a beautiful novel— when it's done. But here, it is too beautiful, one can't work. I was out rowing on the sea all afternoon* [Moore 249].

17 DEC.   To Edward Marsh: *I send you a poem which you ought to like* [Moore 253]. The poem was a slightly different version of 'Grief', Ferrier MS21.

Lina Waterfield: 'He described his first impression when he walked in the roof-garden one evening and looked at the mountains. It seemed to him as though wild beasts were circling round a fire and he was filled with a feeling of apprehension' [Waterfield 140]. Lawrence uses this image in the penultimate chapter of *The Rainbow*.

21 DEC.   To Edward Garnett: *The novel goes slowly forward. . . . In a few day's time I shall send you the first half of the MS* [Moore 256].

30 DEC.   *In a few day's time I shall send you the first half of* The Sisters—*which I should rather call* The Wedding Ring—*to Duckworth's. It is* very different from Sons and Lovers: *written in another language almost. . . . I shan't write in the same manner as* Sons and Lovers *again, I think—in that hard, violent style full of sensation and presentation* [Moore 259].

JANUARY 1914   At Lerici.

SUMMARY   Lawrence nearly finished the second version of *The Sisters*, now called *The Wedding Ring*, then abandoned it.

6 JAN.   Lawrence sent Garnett the first half of *The Sisters*, saying that he expected to finish it in six or eight weeks.

24 JAN.   Lawrence reveals that the name of his cat is Mino. Mino gives his name to chapter 13 of *Women in Love*.

29 JAN.   To Edward Garnett: *I am not very much surprised, nor even very much hurt by your letter—and I agree with you. I agree with you about the Templeman episode. In the scheme of the novel, however, I must have Ella get some experience before she meets her Mr Birkin. I also felt that the character was inclined to fall into two halves—and graduations between them. It came of trying to graft on to the character of Louie, the character, more or less, of Frieda. That I ought not to have done. To your two main criticisms, that the Templeman episode is wrong, and that the character of Ella is incoherent, I agree. Then about the artistic side being in the background. It is that which troubles me most. I have no longer the joy in creating vivid scenes, that I had in* Sons and Lovers. *I don't care much more about accumulating objects in the powerful light of emotion, and making a scene of them. I have to write differently. I am most anxious about your criticism of this, the second half of the novel, a hundred and fifty pages of which I send you tomorrow. Tell me very frankly what you think of it: and if it pleases you, tell me whether you think Ella would be possible, as she now stands, unless she had some experience of love and men. I think, impossible. Then she must have a love episode, a significant one. But it must not be a Templeman episode.*

I shall go on now to the end of the book. It will not take me long. Then I will go over it all again, and I shall be very glad to hear all you have to say. But if this, the second half, also disappoints you, I will, when I come to the end, leave this book altogether. Then I should propose to write a story with a plot, and to abandon the exhaustive method entirely—write pure object and story.

I am going through a transition stage myself. I am a slow writer, really—I only have great outbursts of work. So that I do not much mind if I put all this novel in the fire, because it is the vaguer results of transition. I write with everything vague—plenty of fire underneath, but like bulbs in the ground, only shadowy flowers that must be beaten and sustained, for another spring. I feel that this second half of

The Sisters *is very beautiful, but it may not be sufficiently incorporated to please you. I do not try to incorporate it very much—I prefer the permeating beauty* [Moore 263–4].

Lawrence did not finish this version, nor did he send what he had already written of the second half to Garnett: *I didn't send those other pages, because I thought I'd do the whole thing again* [Tedlock 203]. Lawrence received a second letter of criticism from Garnett which upset him because it seemed to him to insult not so much his failings as his very intentions. It seems that Lawrence did not write to Garnett again for over two months. Then he sent Garnett as much as was typed of the third version, adding: *From this part that I have sent you, follows on the original* Sisters—*the School Inspector, and so on* [Moore 272]. He is obviously referring to something Garnett has read, and this is unlikely to be what he has recently read, which Lawrence a moment later carefully designates as *the first draft of* The Wedding Ring. *The original* Sisters must mean what it says, the very first version Garnett saw in May 1913.

It follows that *The Sisters* must originally have begun where *Women in Love* begins, with the meeting of Ella/Ursula and Rupert Birkin. The second version was 'widened' to take in an earlier part of Ella's life, including an affair with her cousin, Ben Templeman, which was later replaced by her relationship with her cousin Charles, later Anton, Skrebensky. Ursula is probably to have more of Frieda and less of Louie in her than Ella (Frieda blamed her own non-participation for the failure of the second draft, and promised to throw herself into the novel now), but Will Brangwen in *The Rainbow* is still closely modelled on Louie Burrows' father, so he was probably there in the second draft. In other words, it seems that Lawrence set out to write about *Frieda and me*, about marriage. The 'widening' he found the theme demanded was backwards in time. He could not do justice to Ella in her relationship with Birkin without giving her a past. So what had been the beginning of *the original* Sisters becomes the second half of the third writing, and is to be pushed out altogether at the fourth. *The Rainbow* ends at the point where Ursula is ready to meet her Mr Birkin. It is likely that the original *Sisters* contained not one word of *The Rainbow*, though some of it no doubt found its way eventually into *Women in Love*.

FEBRUARY 1914   At Lerici.

SUMMARY   Lawrence restarted *The Sisters* as *The Wedding Ring.*

9 FEB.   *I have begun my novel again—for about the seventh time. . . . I had nearly finished it. It was full of beautiful things, but it missed—I knew that it just missed being itself. So here I am, must sit down and write it out again. I know it is quite a lovely novel really—you know that the perfect statue is in the marble, the kernel of it. But the thing is the getting it out clean. I think I shall manage it pretty well. You must say a prayer for me sometimes* [Moore 264].

MARCH 1914   At Lerici.

SUMMARY   Another month of solid work on *The Wedding Ring. I wish to God I needn't write and needn't do anything. Oh it is such a beautiful spring: I wish I could just walk out of the house and into the hills, and on and on at my own sweet will* [Moore 268].

7 MARCH   *I began my novel for about the eleventh time. It is on its legs and is going strong, but I shall be glad when it is finished* [Moore 267].
14 MARCH   *My novel goes on slowly. It ought to be something when it is done, the amount of me I have given it* [Huxley 181].
22 MARCH   *I am getting on with a novel—I have been lazy this year* [Huxley 185].

The Wedding Ring was being typed by Sir Thomas Dacre Dunlop, the British consul at Spezia. Kinkead-Weekes has established that the sixty-three pages of typescript which Lawrence inserted into the Texas holograph of *The Rainbow* [E331a] are from this version. The complete typescript was to be about five hundred pages [Kinkead-Weekes 379], and Lawrence claimed to have done two-thirds on 3 April. Therefore these pages, numbered 219–275 and 279–284, must have been written in late March. They deal with Ursula's career as a teacher at Brinsley Street School, and correspond to most of chapters 13 and 14 of *The Rainbow.* When Lawrence incorporated these pages into *The Rainbow*, the numbering became 548–604 and 608–613. Thus Ursula reaches a stage half way through *The Wedding Ring* which she reaches only three chapters from the end of *The Rainbow.*

APRIL 1914   At Lerici.

SUMMARY   Lawrence worked hard on *The Wedding Ring*.

3 APRIL   *Oh, I tried so hard to work, this last year. I began a novel seven times. I have written quite a thousand pages that I shall burn. But now, thank God, Frieda and I are together, and the work is of me and her, and it is beautiful, I think. I have done two-thirds* [Moore 270].

22 APRIL   To Edward Garnett: *I send you by this post as much of* The Wedding Ring *as the consul has yet typed. I have only some 80 pages more to write. In a fortnight it should be done. . . . I am sure of this now, this novel. It is a big and beautiful work. Before, I could not get my soul into it. That was because of the struggle and the resistance between Frieda and me. Now you will find her and me in the novel, I think, and the work is of both of us. . . . In the work as it stands now, there will, if anything, be only small prolixities to cut down* [Moore 272].

MAY 1914   At Lerici.

SUMMARY   Lawrence finished *The Wedding Ring*.

8 MAY   *Four days, and I shall have finished my novel, pray God* [Moore 275].

9 MAY   *It's a* magnum opus *with a vengeance. I have got about three thousand more words to write—two more days, and then* basta. *Frieda wants the novel to be called* The Rainbow. *It doesn't look it at first sight, but I think it is a good title* [Moore 275–6].

The rainbow imagery, with its associated images of arches and colours, is so pervasive throughout *The Rainbow* and central to its structure, that, for the title to have been thought appropriate at this stage, we must assume a great deal of the novel as we know it to have been there in this version.

'*The Wedding Ring* may have included, then, the story of Ella's parents [excluding Lincoln Cathedral], her childhood and youth, the first girlish affair with Skrebensky, a return to schoolteaching, and the final finding of themselves of Ella and Birkin. Of the episodes that may have caused the banning of *The Rainbow*, we can say definitely that the last relationship between Anna and Will, and Ursula's relationship with Winifred Inger, were not in the novel; and that the handling of the affair with Skrebensky had not struck Lawrence as indiscreet, so

that he was dumbfounded at the reaction of his new publisher'
[Kinkead-Weekes 379–80].

*16 MAY   *The novel is finished, and I have gone through the sheets. . . . I
have not begun to work again yet, only to think of a new novel which
has been lying very small in my mind these three months. I ought to do
some Ligurian sketches—I have some lovely matter—but just yet I
don't want to* [Moore 276–7]. It seems that Lawrence neither began
the novel nor wrote any sketches.

**JUNE 1914   At Lerici until 9, then to Turin, Aosta (10), Grand St Bernard
(11), Martingny (12 or 13). By 18 in Heidelberg. By 24 in London, 9
Selwood Terrace, South Kensington.**

SUMMARY   Lawrence wrote nothing whatever during this month.

2 JUNE   *I want to write an essay about Futurism, when I have the
inspiration and wit thereunto* [Moore 281]. Lawrence's famous letter
of 5 June to Edward Garnett is the nearest he got to writing such an
essay. That he thought of it as notes towards an essay is evident from
its conclusion: *Please keep this letter, because I want to write on
futurism and it will help me* [Moore 283]. In the letter Lawrence
attempts to explain the more revolutionary aspects of his own style,
form, and, particularly, characterisation, in terms of the futurists, then
in terms of chemistry, and finally in terms of Chladni Figures [see
Notes and Queries, September 1973].

**JULY 1914   At 9 Selwood Terrace, South Kensington, London, with a visit
to Ripley 18–22.**

SUMMARY   On 30 June Lawrence had appointed J. B. Pinker as his
agent, given Pinker *The Rainbow* for Methuen, who had offered an advance
of £300, and given Duckworth instead the offer of a book of short stories.
The whole month was spent gathering together short stories for *The
Prussian Officer* [A6], as the volume was ultimately called, and rewriting
several of them. Lawrence and Frieda were married at Kensington Registry
Office on 13. 'Song of a Man Who Is Loved' [A10] and 'Song of a Man Who
Has Come Through' [A10] were probably written just before and just after
the wedding.

2 JULY   Lawrence wrote to Douglas Clayton asking if he had the MS of

'Love Among the Haystacks' (which Lawrence said he wanted to go over before it was typed), 'New Eve and Old Adam' and 'The White Stocking', and typed copies of 'Once' and 'A Sick Collier'. Of these, only 'The White Stocking' and 'A Sick Collier' were to go into *The Prussian Officer.*

7 JULY   To Sir Thomas Dacre Dunlop: *Your most vital necessity in this life is that you shall love your wife completely and implicitly and in entire nakedness of body and spirit. Then you will have peace and inner security, no matter how many things go wrong* [Moore 285]. This reads like a paraphrase of 'Song of a Man Who Is Loved'.

8 JULY   Lawrence wrote to Pinker that he had been invited by Bertram Christian of Nisbet's to do a little book of about fifteen-thousand words on Thomas Hardy. It seems Lawrence did not begin the book until September.

*9 JULY   Lawrence asked Clayton for the MS of 'The Shadow in the Rose Garden' so that he could revise it before it was typed. On this date Lawrence sent the first batch of stories to Duckworth [Huxley 202].

*14 JULY   To Edward Garnett: *I send you herewith another batch of the short stories. There remains only one to send—one story. It is the German soldier story that came in last month's* English Review. *I find it wants writing over again, to pull it together. I have gone over the stories very carefully. I wish you would go through the selection I have sent in, and see if there is any you would leave out, and any you would like putting in. I think all the stories have been already printed, except* 'Daughters of the Vicar'. *I would like them arranging so.*

		about
1.	*A Fragment of Stained Glass*	6,000 *words*
2.	*Goose Fair*	6,000
3.	*A Sick Collier*	2,500
4.	*The Christening*	3,300
5.	*Odour of Chrysanthemus*	8,000
6.	*Daughters of the Vicar*	18,980
7.	*Second Best*	5,000
8.	*The Shadow in the Rose Garden*	6,000
9.	*The Dead Rose*	7,000
10.	*The White Stocking*	8,000
11.	*Vin Ordinaire*	9,500
12.	*Honour and Arms*	9,600

. . . *I will send the last story—*'Vin Ordinaire'*— within a day or two* [Huxley 201–2].

These twelve stories were chosen, but were printed in a completely different order, and several of the titles were changed. 'The Dead Rose' became 'The Shades of Spring', 'Vin Ordinaire' became 'The Thorn in the Flesh', and 'Honour and Arms' became 'The Prussian Officer'. Lawrence's word estimates are far out, in seven cases by over one thousand and in three by over two thousand. The most spectacular divergence is in the case of 'A Fragment of Stained Glass', which is actually only 3,500 words. In all but two cases Lawrence has overestimated. The exceptions are 'The White Stocking' which is about one thousand words longer, and 'Daughters of the Vicar', which, despite his apparently precise count in that case (not 19,000 but 18,980) is two thousand longer than his estimate. This may argue either bad counting, or subsequent revision, or both.

The change of the title of 'Honour and Arms' was Garnett's, not Lawrence's, as was the decision to make this the title story. 'The Prussian Officer' is some fifteen hundred words longer in the book than in *The English Review*. This does not represent revision: the story had been cut by that extent by Norman Douglas for *The English Review*. For a detailed account of the textual history of these stories see Cushman 2. See also Sagar 3 on 'The Shades of Spring'; Littlewood on 'The Thorn in the Flesh', 'Odour of Chrysanthemums' and 'Daughters of the Vicar'; and Finney 2 on 'The White Stocking', 'Daughters of the Vicar' and 'The Shadow in the Rose Garden'. On the three endings of 'Odour of Chrysanthemums' see Kalnins.

*17 JULY   Lawrence sent 'Vin Ordinaire' to Garnett, suggesting that its title be changed to 'The Thorn in the Flesh', and that this should be the title of the whole volume. Garnett had apparently suggested placing the story first. He also tells Garnett that he is going to fill the next few weeks writing his book on Thomas Hardy.

*25 JULY   Lawrence sent 'Once' and 'The Primrose Path' to Clayton to be typed and forwarded to Pinker. Presumably he had revised them both. He also sent another story direct to Pinker, the only one he had by him.

*27 JULY   Lawrence sent 'A Chapel among the Mountains' to be typed.

*31 JULY   Lawrence sent 'A Hay Hut among the Mountains' to be typed and sent with the other to the editor of the *New Statesman*. Presumably he would have sent them together had he not been revising them.

AUGUST 1914   On 31 July Lawrence had set off with three friends on a walking tour in the Lake District. They came down 5 August into Barrow-in-Furness to find that war had been declared. Lawrence returned 8 to 9 Selwood Terrace. By 16 the Lawrences were living at The Triangle, Bellingdon Lane, Nr. Chesham, Bucks., where they remained until January 1915.

SUMMARY   Lawrence wrote 'With the Guns' [*Manchester Guardian*, 18 August 1914, reprinted in *Encounter*, August 1969].

SEPTEMBER 1914   At The Triangle, near Chesham.

SUMMARY   Lawrence began 'A Study of Thomas Hardy' [*Phoenix*].

5 SEPT.   *What a miserable world. What colossal idiocy, this war. Out of sheer rage I've begun my book about Thomas Hardy* [Moore 290].

OCTOBER 1914   At The Triangle, near Chesham.

SUMMARY   . . . *this God-forsaken little hole where I sit like a wise rabbit with my pen behind my ear, and listen to distant noises* [Huxley 208]. Lawrence continued with 'A Study of Thomas Hardy' and corrected the proofs of *The Prussian Officer*.

5 OCT.   To Koteliansky: *Will you really type-write me my book—which is supposed to be about Thomas Hardy, but which seems to be about anything else in the world but that. I have done about 50 pages—re-written them* [Zytaruk 5]. The Texas typescript, which corresponds almost exactly with the published version, is obviously the work of an untrained typist. Both this typescript and the one at Berkeley are titled *Le Gai Savaire*.

13 OCT.   *The proofs of the stories keep on coming. What good printers these Plymouth people are. They never make a mistake. And how good my stories are, after the first two. It really surprises me. Shall they be called The Fighting Line? After all, this is the real fighting line, not where soldiers pull triggers. . . . I have been writing my book more or less—very much less—about Thomas Hardy, I have done a third of it* [Moore 292–3].

There was further revision of some of the stories at proof stage, particularly 'The Christening', which had two paragraphs added at the end, 'The Shades of Spring' and 'The Shadow in the Rose Garden'. The corrected proofs are at Nottingham County Library.

29 OCT.   Lawrence wrote to Pinker that he did not feel in the humour for tackling the novel, but would go over the whole thing thoroughly in a month's time.

31 OCT.   Lawrence sent some more Thomas Hardy MS to Koteliansky.

NOVEMBER 1914   At The Triangle, near Chesham.

SUMMARY   Lawrence wrote a war poem, probably 'Eloi, Eloi Lama Sabachthani?' [C37 and *CP*], continued to write 'A Study of Thomas Hardy', and resumed work on *The Rainbow*.

17 NOV.   To Harriet Monroe: *In a real fury I had to write my war poem, because it breaks my heart, this war. . . . Take care now you regard my war poem—it is good* [Moore 294–5]. The rest of this letter is very similar in spirit to a poem 'Ecce Homo', which only survives in the form of passages copied out by Harriet Monroe [*DHLR* 9, 2, 269–71]. A different version was published under the title 'Eloi, Eloi Lama Sabachthani'. [See Ferrier MS24.]

LATE   There is no mention of the novel in the November letters, but since Lawrence had a hundred pages ready to send to Pinker on 5 December, he must have begun in November.

DECEMBER 1914   At The Triangle, Chesham. In London 5–10, Ripley 10–12.

SUMMARY   Lawrence finished 'A Study of Thomas Hardy' [*Phoenix*] and continued work on *The Rainbow*.

*3 DEC.   *I am working* frightfully *hard—rewriting my novel* [Moore 295].

5 DEC.   To Koteliansky: *I send you the last of the MS* [Zytaruk 17].

Zytaruk suggests that this does not necessarily mean the conclusion of the MS, but that Lawrence and Frieda took over the typing themselves at this point. (See 18 December.) This seems to me unlikely for four reasons:

1. Only two days earlier Lawrence had written to Koteliansky: *Do please get my typing done. If I can send it in, I may get a little money for it* [Moore 295]. This surely implies that Koteliansky has almost the whole thing.

2. On the same day Lawrence wrote to Pinker of the novel: *I began to type it. But it took me hours, and I am too busy writing. . . . But if it must be done, will you have it done for me?* [Moore 296]. Lawrence is surely unlikely, on the same day, to take other typing out of Koteliansky's hands into his own.

3. Both surviving typescripts of 'A Study of Thomas Hardy' are complete. I have no evidence that the Texas typescript is Koteliansky's but it is certainly the work of an untrained typist.

4. On 18 Lawrence speaks of writing the Study 'again'. He was to continue to speak of it as 'Le Gai Savaire' through several drafts on its way to becoming 'The Crown'. What we now know as 'A Study of Thomas Hardy' may well have been the first draft finished at this time.

To Pinker: *I send you the first hundred or so pages of my novel, which I am writing over. It needs the final running through. It is a beautiful piece of work, really. It will be, when I have finished it: the body of it is so new. . . . I shall finish the thing by the end of January—perhaps earlier* [Moore 296].

*17 DEC.   *I am so busy writing my novel* [Zytaruk 19].

18 DEC.   *My wife and I we type away at my book on Thomas Hardy, which has turned out as a sort of Story of My Heart, or a* Confessio Fidei: *which I must write again, still another time* [Moore 298].

Lawrence was to continue to rewrite his philosophy for several months, under several titles—first 'Le Gai Savaire', which is also his title for 'A Study of Thomas Hardy' on both typescripts, then 'The Signal', 'The Phoenix' and 'Morgenrot' before arriving at 'The Crown'.

JANUARY 1915 At The Triangle, near Chesham until 21, then to Hampstead for two days with the Eders. From 23 at Greatham, Pulborough, Sussex.

SUMMARY *My heart has been as cold as a lump of dead earth, all this time, because of the War. But now I don't feel so dead. I feel hopeful. I couldn't tell you how fragile and tender this hope is—the new shoot of life* [Moore 310].

Lawrence worked on *The Rainbow*, and possibly wrote 'New Heaven and Earth' [B6, as 'Terra Nuova', A10].

5 JAN. *. . . still revising* The Rainbow—*putting a good deal of work into it. I have done 300 pages. It'll be a new sort of me for you to get used to* [*Priest* 213].

7 JAN. To Pinker: *Here is another hundred pages of the novel. I am going to split the book into two volumes: it was so unwieldy* [Moore 306].

  The Rainbow as we have it cannot be very different from the first half of the composite novel, since it took Lawrence only seven weeks to finish it. Though Lawrence continued to speak of *Women in Love* as volume two, or a sequel to *The Rainbow*, and cherished the idea in 1920 of putting them together again, so much of *Women in Love* was rewritten in 1916 and later, and in a spirit very different from the tender hopefulness of the early months of 1915, and out of new experiences and relationships of the interim, as to make it an utterly distinct and new novel.

*31 JAN. The letter to Lady Cynthia Asquith of this date is very close in spirit to the poem 'New Heaven and Earth', which is signed 'Greatham' and refers to the woman *at whose side I have lain for over a thousand nights*.

FEBRUARY 1915 At Greatham, Pulborough.

SUMMARY Frieda Lawrence: 'L. is writing hard, we go for long walks, the estate is very beautiful, much the most beautiful country I have seen in England. Such a nice letter from Katherine [Mansfield]. I am glad the Lord made her. Lady Ottoline [Morrell] is nice, she is coming on Saturday with Bertrand Russell; our Rananim will come off in some form or other [*Frieda* 207].

Lawrence worked exclusively on *The Rainbow*.

1 FEB. *I wish I had done that novel. I seem so long. But it will certainly be*

*done by the end of this month, February, for I have done 450 pages
out of 600 or so. . . . Tell Methuen . . . that there shall be no very
flagrant love-passages in it (at least to my thinking)* [Huxley 219].

The MS is over seven hundred pages in Lawrence's numbering and
over eight hundred in fact. One of the most 'flagrant' love passages
was added to the typescript, probably in April.

*2 FEB. To Gordon Campbell: *Oh, one of my characters in my
novel—minor—is a subaltern in the Engineers—does one say Royal
Engineers?—he is 21 years old, son of a parson, not poor. What would
he be? What would he earn? What would he do? Where would he live?
Have patience, and tell me* [Moore 313]. Anton Skrebensky must have
been a very minor character at this stage if Lawrence had not yet
established such basic aspects of him.

*5 FEB. *I have got into the stride of my novel, and am working gallantly.
But I doubt I shall be too late for spring publication. However, I don't
care. What is the use of giving books to the swinish public in its
present state* [Moore 314].

*11 FEB. *My novel is getting along. I hope the publishers will not think it
impossible to print it as it stands* [Moore 316]. Lawrence's sudden
anxiety on this score suggests that he had been developing the sexual
relationship of Ursula and Skrebensky.

24 FEB. *I am very, very near the end of the novel. But Miss Meynell is
somewhat behind with the typing* [Moore 322].

To Bertrand Russell: *I wrote a book about these things—I used to
call it* Le Gai Savaire. *I want now to rewrite this stuff, and make it as
good as I can, and publish it in pamphlets, weekly or fortnightly, and
so start a campaign for this freer life* [Moore 324 misdated]. 'Le Gai
Savaire' was 'A Study of Thomas Hardy'. This scheme was to result in
the publication of a fortnightly periodical *The Signature* in October.
Each of the three numbers carried a section of Lawrence's 'The
Crown'.

**MARCH 1915   At Greatham, Pulborough, except for 6–7 at Cambridge,
and 20–21 in London.**

SUMMARY Lawrence finished *The Rainbow* and returned to his
'philosophy'.

2 MARCH To Viola Meynell: *I have finished my* Rainbow, *bended it and
set it firm. Now off and away to find the pots of gold at its feet. I don't*

hear from Pinker—but from Methuen asking for 70 words descriptive for his autumn announcements. . . . Will you keep the MS at your house, and send me the typed copy in batches, so I can run through it. . . . I am going to begin a book about Life—more rainbows, but in different skies—which I want to publish in pamphlet form week by week—my initiation of the great and happy revolution. . . . Tell me which parts you think the publisher will decidedly object to [Moore 328].

Lawrence's seventy words were probably also used as the dust-wrapper synopsis, which reads: *This story, by one of the most remarkable of the younger school of novelists, contains a history of the Brangwen character through its developing crises of love, religion, and social passion. It ends with Ursula, the leading-shoot of the restless, fearless family, waiting at the advance-post of our time to blaze a path into the future.*

To Bertrand Russell: *I have finished my novel so am very glad. I am also very excited about my novel. I feel like a bird in spring that is amazed at the colours of its own coat. Also I feel very profound about my book* The Signal—Le Gai Saver—*or whatever it is—which I am re-beginning. It is my revolutionary utterance. I take on a very important attitude of profundity to it, and so feel happy* [Moore 327].

4 MARCH To Lady Ottoline Morrell: *I am doing my philosophish book—called (pro tem)* The Signal—*or* The Phoenix *(which?). I want you to read this. I am also doing a Van Gogh—one of those sketches in a letter, with colour directions—of a dock and raising bridge* [Schorer 49–50].

While at Greatham Lawrence also painted, as a gift for Viola Meynell, a copy of Giotto's *Joachim and the Shepherds.*

6 MARCH Lawrence was taken by Russell to Cambridge for the weekend, to meet people he hoped would be his allies in *the great and happy revolution.* It was a 'momentous' occasion for him, but in the event completely destroyed the gladness which had carried him through to the end of *The Rainbow.*

*15 MARCH To Bertrand Russell: *I wanted to write to you when there was something to write about: also when I could send you some of the 'philosophy'. But the time goes by, and I haven't done enough of the writing, and there isn't any news. I shall send the philosophy when I have done these first crucial chapters* [Moore 329].

*19 MARCH To Russell: *I was too sad to write my 'philosophy' (forgive the word) any more. I can't write it when I am depressed or hopeless. But*

it comes back all right, the philosophy and the belief [Moore 330].
LATE   To Lady Ottoline Morrell: *I have been revising my novel—but I've only got the first 71 typed pages* [Schorer 50].

APRIL 1915   At Greatham, Pulborough.

SUMMARY   Lawrence revised *The Rainbow* and began his 'philosophy' again, possibly now in the version which was to become 'The Crown' [C39, 40, 41, A32, *Phoenix*].

*2 APRIL   To Lady Ottoline Morrell: *Viola Meynell is typing my novel, and does it slowly, so I am delayed sending it to you. But next week there will be a moderately good batch ready, which I shall send you. As for my 'Contrat Social', wait, wait, wait, for I can't do it yet* [Schorer 51].

*8 APRIL   To Lady Ottoline Morrell: *I send you so much of my novel as is typed. It is perhaps one-half or one-third of the whole—one-third I should say. . . . To-day I have begun again my philosophy—Morgenrot is my new name for it. I feel as if I can do it now. God preserve me from getting out of my depths* [Huxley 236–7].

   To Koteliansky: *I think I shall send you my philosophy to type again for me. I have begun it again. I will not tell them, for people, this time that they are angels in disguise. Curse them, I will tell them they are dogs and swine, bloodsuckers* [Moore 331].

*10 APRIL   To Koteliansky: *I send you the first Chapter of my philosophy* [Zytaruk 38].

*20 APRIL   To Koteliansky: *I have not sent you any more MS because I am very slow, and I thought you wanted to be* lentissimo *yourself. Herewith I forward a little more* [Moore 333].

   To Lady Ottoline Morrell: *Page 40 of my philosophy. It is very good and rather terrible, and nobody will ever publish it* [Schorer 52].

23 APRIL   To Pinker: *Miss Meynell told me you wanted the MS of the novel. Lady Ottoline Morrell is reading it just now: she will send it on to you as she reads it.*

   I hope you are willing to fight for this novel. It is nearly three years of hard work, and I am proud of it, and it must be stood up for. I'm afraid there are parts of it Methuen won't want to publish. He must. I will take out sentences and phrases, but I won't take out paragraphs or pages. So you must tell me in detail if there are real objections to printing any parts. You see a novel, after all this period of coming into being, has a definite organic form, just as a man has when he is grown.

And we don't ask a man to cut his nose off because the public don't like it: because he must have a nose, and his own nose, too.

Oh God, I hope I'm not going to have a miserable time over this book, now I've at last got it pretty much to its real being.

Very soon I shall have no money [Moore 334].

Lawrence's anxiety relates to the fact that he had added to the batch of MS sent that same day to Lady Ottoline Morrell the bulk of the chapter called 'The Child', with Will's adventure with the girl he picks up at the cinema, and the subsequent violent sensuality of his relationship with his wife.

I send you another batch of MS. . . . If you haven't sent off the last MS will you look at the last page of it and correct my numbering, in duplicate, on the new batch, for a few pages—or perhaps all through it if you would be so good. I forgot what page we had come to, so started these at 250 at random. Tell me next time you write, if you can, what is the last page of all the MS you have—the number please [Moore 335]. The number Lawrence should have started at was 263. In his next letter to Lady Ottoline Lawrence asks her if the number of the last page of 'this secondary numbering' is 356. In fact the second and longer of the passages Lawrence had inserted into the typescript in holograph ends at 355. This passage I have described above. The other is a mere five pages in the Cathedral chapter beginning: *She too was overcome with wonder and awe,* and describing how Anna seizes on the gargoyles to destroy Will's absolute.

MAY 1915   At Greatham, Pulborough. The Lawrences went to London 7 for four or five days, and returned by way of Brighton where they stayed two days with the Asquiths.

SUMMARY   Lawrence's mornings were entirely taken up teaching Mary Saleeby. He continued to struggle with his philosophy, and finished the revision of *The Rainbow*.

5 MAY   Lawrence sent Lady Ottoline another batch of MS of *The Rainbow*, and told her that he was getting stuck with his philosophy.

18 MAY   To Eleanor Farjeon: *I have decided to try to type my MS myself. When I break down, I shall come to you for help* [Moore 344]. Lawrence is referring to his philosophy.

*19 MAY   To Lady Ottoline Morrell: *I send you the next batch of the MS. There will only be one more lot* [Huxley 222]. The one-legged soldier described in this letter also appears in Chapter 5 of 'The Crown'.

29 MAY   To Pinker: *I will try to write a story for the* Strand. . . . *The MS is being finished by Miss Meynell this very day. I have only to revise it and let you have it* [Moore 345]. A few days later Lawrence was to begin 'England, My England', which did not appear in the *Strand*.

31 MAY   To Pinker: *I send you the final batch of MS of* The Rainbow. . . . *It did not seem to me very improper, as I went through it. But then I feel very incompetent to judge on that point. My beloved book, I am sorry to give it to you to be printed. I could weep tears in my heart when I read these pages. . . . I want on the fly-leaf, in German characters, the inscription ZU ELSE* [Moore 346–7]. That inscription cannot have helped Lawrence when his beloved book came before a magistrate whose son had just been killed at the front.

JUNE 1915   At Greatham, but for a visit to Garsington for four or five days 12, and a visit to the Asquiths at Littlehampton, Sussex 21.

SUMMARY   Lawrence wrote 'England, My England' [C38 A23] and worked on his philosophy.

2 JUNE   Lawrence tells Lady Ottoline that he is typing his philosophy, recomposing as he goes.

6 JUNE   Lawrence sends Pinker 'England, My England': *A story about the Lucases. . . . the story of most men and women who are married today—of most men at the War, and wives at home* [Moore 364] and promises to write some short stories when the book of philosophy is finished.

8 JUNE   To Bertrand Russell: *I send you the first quarter of my philosophy. You mustn't think it bosh. I depend on you to help me with it* [Russell 49].

†30 JUNE   *I have dropped writing my philosophy, but I go on working very hard in my soul. . . . I have been wrong, much too Christian, in my philosophy. These early Greeks have clarified my soul. I must drop all about God* [Moore 352].

When Russell visited the Lawrences for the weekend of 19–20, he had probably taken Lawrence a copy of Burnet's *Early Greek Philosophy*. Moore's guess, 7 July, for this letter seems to me possible, but the Lacy–Vasey 21 July quite wrong. It must come well before the letter of 19 July to Lady Ottoline Morrell.

JULY 1915   At Greatham, Pulborough until 30. Weekends of 10–11 and 17–18 in London.

SUMMARY   *I really think I shall give some lectures on Eternity. I shrink from it very much. . . . God help me, I would rather have done anything else. I would like to be remote, in Italy, writing my soul's words. To have to speak in the body is a violation to me—you don't know how much. However, anything for the new infinite relation that must come to pass* [Moore 353].

Lawrence resumed teaching Mary Saleeby. He corrected the proofs of *The Rainbow*, and began his philosophy again. He rewrote 'Christs in the Tirol' as 'The Crucifix Across the Mountains' [A8].

*7 JULY   Lawrence tells Forster he has left off his philosophy in the middle, to think again.

9 JULY   *I have broken down in the middle of my philosophy—I suppose I shall go on later when I am freer. I am correcting the proofs of the Rainbow* [Huxley 240].

*12 JULY   *As for my philosophy, I shall write it again* [Moore 353].

*19 JULY   *I shall write all my philosophy again. Last time I came out of the Christian Camp. This time I must come out of these early Greek philosophers. I am so sure of what I know, and what is true, now, that I am sure I am stronger, in the truth, in the knowledge I have, than all the world outside that knowledge* [Moore 351].

26 JULY   To Pinker: *I send you back the slips and pages. I have cut out, as I said I would, all the phrases objected to. The passages and paragraphs marked I cannot alter. There is nothing offensive in them beyond the very substance they contain. And that is no more offensive than that of all the rest of the novel . . . I can't cut them out, because they are living parts of an organic whole. . . . These slips and pages I return to you are not revised proofs. I am now at page 192 of the revised proofs, the final form, and I must go on from there* [Moore 356–7].

29 JULY   Lawrence told Pinker of his intention to prepare *Twilight in Italy* [A8] for Duckworth, saying he would send Pinker a copy of each essay as he got it ready, and enclosing the first, formerly 'Christs in the Tirol' [C20] but now more than twice as long and quite different.

AUGUST 1915   At Littlehampton, Sussex until 4, then at 1 Byron Villas, Vale of Health, Hampstead, London.

SUMMARY   *I don't know how to begin to lecture or write, publicly, these things of the real truth and the living spirit. . . . One must start direct with the open public, without associates. But how to begin, and when, I don't know yet* [Moore 363].

Lawrence rewrote several sections of *Twilight in Italy* [A8].

20 AUG.   Lawrence sent 'The Spinner and the Monks' to Clayton to be typed. The content was much the same as the version which had appeared in the *English Review* [C23], but Lawrence had completely rewritten it, with several new paragraphs at the beginning and end.

*24 AUG.   Lawrence sent Clayton 'The Lemon Gardens'. This time he had not only rewritten the existing material, but added some twenty pages of 'philosophy'. There had been no philosophy in any of the *English Review* versions, which were pure travel sketches. There had been rather more in the original version about the lemon gardens. Much philosophy was also to be added to 'The Theatre'.

SEPTEMBER 1915   At 1 Byron Villas, Vale of Health, Hampstead.

SUMMARY   *Only I feel, that even if we are all going to be rushed down to extinction, one must hold up the other, living truth, of Right and pure reality, the reality of the clear, eternal spirit. One must speak for life and growth, amid all this mass of destruction and disintegration* [Moore 369].

Lawrence rewrote 'The Theatre' and 'San Gaudenzio' and prepared 'The Crown' for publication [C39 40 41, A32, *Phoenix 2*].

1 SEPT.   Lawrence sent Clayton the beginning of 'The Theatre' to be going on with, promising the rest the following day.

5 SEPT.   Lawrence returned Clayton's typescript of 'The Lemon Gardens' asking him to take out pages 4–10 and to replace three paragraphs with new material. The new material begins: *It is time to leave off . . .* and concludes *I make nullity, nihil.* The paragraphs they replace read:

   It is time to turn round, the flesh, new issued from the Infinite, strong and dark from the creative Infinite, becomes now the supreme threshold of creative eternity. But it is time that we looked outwards from the threshold, that we passed out to the great, luminous, uncreated world. So long we have stopped to the doorway of the flesh, and gone in unto the flushed, sensual darkness, and beyond the sensual darkness, into the far spaces of scientific research, the everlasting night, the first cold, grey twilight of the dawn of creation, beyond the hot flush of life. It is the great and wonderful retrogression to the Orginal Creation, to the Original Eternity, to the Original God.

But there is also, at the threshold of the flesh, the beginning of the world that is to be, the Uncreated World, that shall become the future. Looking outward from the doorway of the senses, from the threshold of the original eternity, clarified and confident from our return to the creative Infinite, we look forth again, and see the great impediments to our going forth, great stumbling-blocks, immense falsities that we have gropingly reared against ourselves. But beyond these is the golden chaos of morning, which is waiting for us to order into being. Once beyond the obstructions, once these are removed, there is a new world for us to create, to bring into being. We know that it exists in Eternity, because we have been received back into the original Eternity, through the senses, and our late experience of death, universal death. We know that in Eternity exists a great world of truth, which here, in this falsity and confusion, is denied and obscured. And it is our business to set the whole living world into relation to the eternal truth.

When we have done that, we shall have re-created Paradise, there will be complete Heaven. We can at any rate begin the job. To finish it may be beyond us. But we must make a start, nevertheless. The success will be greater than the failure, however we fail, we shall be in closer relation to the Infinite Truth than we were, we shall have our place in the Eternity of Truth.

To Bertrand Russell: *We are going to start a little paper, myself and Murry and Katherine Mansfield—and you and Cannan if you care to join. . . . I think we shall call it* The Signature. *. . . I shall be the preacher* [Russell 57]. The split with Russell came a week later. For Lawrence's fuller, though not quite accurate, account of the *Signature* venture, see his introductory note to 'The Crown' in *Reflections on the Death of a Porcupine* [A32], reprinted in *Phoenix 2*.

6 SEPT.   Lawrence sends the rest of 'The Theatre' to Clayton.

*11 SEPT.   Lawrence sends Clayton 'San Gaudenzio'. At this point he seems to have broken off his work on the Italian sketches for some weeks to prepare his material for *The Signature*.

20 SEPT.   *Today I have sent in the MS of the first number. . . . My contribution is purely philosophic and metaphysical, and on these grounds sociological* [Huxley 257]. Lawrence's contribution was part 1 of 'The Crown'. Only three of the six parts of 'The Crown' appeared, because *The Signature* 'fizzled out' after only three num-

bers. The rest of 'The Crown' was not published until *Reflections* in 1925.

22 SEPT.   Lawrence sent Edward Marsh an altered version of the penultimate stanza of 'Meeting Among the Mountains'. Marsh was considering several Lawrence poems for inclusion in *Georgian Poetry 1913–1915* [B3]. Lawrence asked for the others to be returned to him so that he might make a little improvement.

25 SEPT.   Lawrence returns the altered poems, inviting Marsh to alter them back if he doesn't care for the alterations. Lawrence says he does not care for 'Cruelty and Love', which was not in the event used. The two Lawrence poems in the anthology were 'Service of All the Dead' (later 'Giorno dei Morti') and 'Meeting Among the Mountains', both to be collected in *'Look! We Have Come Through!'* [A10].

OCTOBER 1915   At 1 Byron Villas, Vale of Health, Hampstead.

SUMMARY   *I am English, and my Englishness is my very vision. But now I must go away, if my soul is sightless for ever. Let it then be blind, rather than commit the vast wickedness of acquiescence* [Moore 371].
   Lawrence completed 'The Crown' and his revision of the Italian sketches. He wrote 'The Thimble' [C44 and *Phoenix 2*] and 'Resurrection' [B12 C47 CP].

2 OCT.   *I have done my six papers* ['The Crown'] . . . *I think my papers are very beautiful and very good. I feel if only people, decent people, would read them, somehow a new era might set in* [Huxley 259].

8 OCT.   Lawrence wrote to Douglas Clayton that he was going on with the Italian sketches after an interval, and sent 'Il Duro'.

*12 OCT.   Lawrence sent Clayton 'Italians in Exile'.

19 OCT.   Lawrence sent 'On the Road', the last of the Italian sketches.

25 OCT.   Lawrence finished 'Resurrection', which he sent to Harriet Monroe the following day. He must have been working on it for some time, despite telling her that it was 'done in these last days', for there is another draft dated September 1915. [See Ferrier MS22 and 25.]

29 OCT.   To Lady Cynthia Asquith: *I have done a rather good word-sketch of you: in a story. I think it good. When the story is finished, and I've got it typed, I'll give you the MS to see what you think of your likeness* [Moore 372].

30 OCT.   *This is the story: I don't know what you'll think of it. The fact of resurrection, in this life, is all in all to me now. I don't know what the*

story is like, as a story. I don't want to read it over—not yet [Moore 372].

Lady Cynthia recorded in her diary what she thought of it: 'It is . . . extremely well written, I think, though the symbolism of the thimble is somewhat obscure. I *was* amused to see the "word-picture" of me. He has quite gratuitously put in the large feet. I think some of his character hints are damnably good. He has kept fairly close to the model in the circumstances.'

NOVEMBER 1915   At 1 Byron Villas, Vale of Health, Hampstead. 8–10 and 29–30 at Garsington.

SUMMARY   *The authorities have suppressed the sale of* The Rainbow, *and Methuen's are under orders of the magistrate to deliver up all existing copies. Isn't this monstrous! We must do something about it. We must get a body of people to have the thing altered. . . .*

I hope to be going away in about a fortnight's time: to America: there is a man who more or less offers us a cottage in Florida: but nothing is settled yet. We have got passports. It is the end of my writing for England. I will try to change my public [Moore 376].

Lawrence wrote 'The Turning Back', published as 'Erinnyes' [B4 *CP*].

1 NOV.   The MS of 'The Turning Back' bears this date. On the following day Lawrence sent it to Lady Cynthia Asquith [Moore 374]. [See Farmer, 121.]

DECEMBER 1915   At 1 Byron Villas until 21. On 22 at 2 Hurst Close, Garden Suburb, London NW; 23–29 at Ripley; 30 to Porthcothan, St Merryn, Padstow, Cornwall.

SUMMARY   *I haven't written a line these many weeks. It is winter with me, my heart is frost-bound. We'll thaw it out one day. If only I could go away. . . . I am laid up in bed with a violent cold, and wonder why one should ever trouble to get up, into this filthy world. The war stinks worse and worse* [Moore 399]. Lawrence postponed indefinitely his plan to go to Florida.

JANUARY 1916 At Porthcothan, St Merryn, Padstow, Cornwall.

SUMMARY *We still love it down here—but I am nearly always in bed. If I get up and go out I get worse again at once. But I can sit in bed and read or do my poems and look at the sea and see the sun set, so I am not unhappy* [Nehls 1, 356].

Lawrence suffered a mild paralysis which made writing difficult. He made a new start on his 'philosophy', began 'The Horse Dealer's Daughter' [C91 A23], prepared his poems for *Amores* [A9], and corrected the proofs of *Twilight in Italy*.

31 DEC. *Soon I shall begin to write a story—a midwinter story of oblivion* [Carswell 43].

5 JAN. *I am once more beginning to write a sort of philosophy: a maturer and more intelligible* Signature. *At last, this time, I have got it: the fifth time of writing* [Nehls 1, 345–6].

9 JAN. *I have written the first part of a short story, but I don't know how to go on. You see one must break into a new world and it is so difficult* [Moore 411].

On 13 Nov. Lawrence had written to Pinker: *Then I have another short story on hand, which I shall finish when I've sent off the novel* [Huxley 378]. On 12 January 1917 Lawrence sent Pinker 'The Miracle' (later 'The Horse Dealer's · Daughter'). The heroine seeks oblivion by walking into a pond in winter, and is miraculously brought back to life by a young doctor. In the same letter of 9 January quoted above Lawrence says: *One always believes in the miracle. We are going to write, all of us together, a comedy for the stage, about Heseltine and Puma and so on* [Moore 412]. 'All of us' meant, presumably, Lawrence, Frieda, Kouyoumdjian and Heseltine, who was staying with them. Puma was Heseltine's girl-friend, later his wife, Minnie Lucie Channing.

13 JAN. *I'm doing my philosophy. It's come at last. I am satisfied, and as sure as a lark in the sky* [Moore 414]. Lawrence did not mention his philosophy again in his letters until mid-February, and probably set it aside to work on his poems. Its eventual title was *Goats and Compasses*.

*15 JAN. Lawrence thanked Sir Thomas Dacre Dunlop for sending him from Italy his two red college notebooks (*They* are *my past, indeed*) and a black book of *new scribble*, from which he began at once to select the poems for *Amores*.

20 JAN. *At night we write a play, which is rather fun* [Priest 253]. The play

seems not to have survived, though some of it may have been transmuted into those scenes in *Women in Love* where Heseltine appears as Halliday, and Puma as Pussum/Minette.

24 JAN.   Lawrence was still working on the poems and also on the proofs of *Twilight in Italy*.

25 JAN.   Lawrence deleted the last five stanzas of 'Drunk'. The MS of the unpublished longer version is at Harvard [Ferrier 2, 351].

31 JAN.   Lawrence completed his work on *Amores*.

FEBRUARY 1916   At Porthcothan.

SUMMARY   *We shall stay in Cornwall till our money is gone—which will take three or four months—then I think we may as well all go and drown ourselves. For I see no prospect of the war's ever ending, and not a ghost of a hope that people will ever want sincere work from any artist* [Huxley 319].

Nevertheless Lawrence and Heseltine planned to found a publishing company, Rainbow Books and Music, to publish first *The Rainbow*, then *Goats and Compasses*, which Lawrence finished this month. For the prospectus and history of the project see Nehls 1, 349–51.

2 FEB.   Lawrence anticipates finishing the proofs of *Twilight in Italy* in two days.

10 FEB.   The printers have held Lawrence up and there are still the last six pages of proofs to come.

15 FEB.   *I have nearly done the first, the destructive, half of my philosophy. At last it can stand. It is the last word* [Moore 427].

25 FEB.   *I send you now the first, the destructive half of my philosophy. . . . There remains the new half to write* [Moore 437]. Cecil Gray described *Goats and Compasses* as 'a bombastic, pseudo-mystical, psycho-philosophical treatise dealing largely with homosexuality' [Nehls 1, 582]. According to Gray, Lawrence destroyed one copy and Heseltine the other. For a discussion of the possible nature of the work and its relation to *Women in Love* and 'The Reality of Peace' see *DHLR* 4, 3, 280–6; 6, 1, 33–46; 6, 3, 303–8.

MARCH 1916   At the Tinners' Arms, Zennor, Cornwall, until 16, then at Higher Tregerthen, Zennor.

SUMMARY *I'm afraid I can't come to London—no money. What is more, I can't write stories to make money, because I don't want to. Curse the idiotic editors and the more idiotic people who read: shall I pander to their maudlin taste?* [Moore 443].

What with cleaning the cottage and making and buying furniture, Lawrence had *hardly a place to sit down in* and wrote nothing. There were only about thirty replies to the six hundred circulars for Rainbow Books and Music, and the project collapsed.

15 MARCH *I am writing nothing just at present. I shall begin when we are settled in our cottage: but I am not quite sure what I shall do. If I can get a manuscript from Germany, I shall go on with that. It is a novel I began three years ago* [Ross, 200]. The *two-thirds finished* novel was *The Insurrection of Miss Houghton*, which Lawrence did not secure until Jan. 1920, when he rewrote it as *The Lost Girl*.

28 MARCH Lawrence first suggests the title *Amores* for his new book of poems.

APRIL 1916   At Higher Tregerthen, Zennor, Cornwall.

SUMMARY *I begin really to feel better, strong again. Soon I shall begin to work. I am waiting for a novel manuscript to come from Germany. But after this lapse, one is slow and reluctant* [Moore 447].

At the beginning of the month the Murrys arrived to occupy the adjacent cottage, and Lawrence was busy helping them to decorate and furnish it. Towards the end of the month he began *Women in Love* [A15].

26 APRIL *I am doing another novel—that really occupies me* [Huxley 347]. For the history of the composition of *Women in Love* see Ford, ch. 8; Kinkead-Weekes; Ross.

MAY 1916   At Higher Tregerthen.

SUMMARY *I have begun the second half of* The Rainbow. *But already it is beyond all hope of ever being published, because of the things it says. And more than that, it is beyond all possibility even to offer it to a world, a putrescent mankind like ours. I feel I cannot touch humanity, even in thought, it is abhorrent to me. But a work of art is an act of faith, as Michael Angelo says, and one goes on writing, to the unseen witnesses* [Moore 449].

*5 MAY   *I have begun a new novel: a thing that is a stranger to me even as I write it. I don't know what the end will be* [Moore 451].

16 MAY   *I have corrected proofs of my new volume of poems* Amores, *which Duckworth is bringing out* [Nehls 1, 383].

19 MAY   *I am half way through a novel, which is a sequel to* The Rainbow, *though quite unlike it* [Huxley 350].

24 MAY   *I have got a long way with my novel. It comes rapidly, and is very good. When one is shaken to the very depths, one finds reality in the unreal world. At present my real world is the world of my inner soul, which reflects on to the novel I write* [Moore 453].

30 MAY   *I have married Ursula—yesterday. Two-thirds of the novel are written. It goes on pretty fast, and very easy. I have not travailed over it. It is the book of my free soul* [Moore 454]. The marriage of Ursula Brangwen and Rupert Birkin takes place in chapter XXVII of *Women in Love*, about three-quarters of the way through the novel as we know it.

JUNE 1916   At Higher Tregerthen. Lawrence's second medical examination at Bodmin 28.

SUMMARY   Lawrence finished this draft of the novel he was still calling *The Sisters*.

12 JUNE   *Fennimore Cooper is lovely beyond words* Last of the Mohicans, Deerslayer. . . . *Then Herman Melville's* Moby Dick *is a real masterpiece, and* very good *is Dana's* Two Years Before the Mast. *These are books worth preserving in every language* [Zytaruk 80–1]. That Lawrence should be asking for, reading, and recommending such books, suggests that he may already be planning to write on them.

19 JUNE   *I have nearly done my new novel* [Moore 455].

30 JUNE   *I have finished* The Sisters, *in effect* [Moore 457], The 'in effect' is explained by a letter of 9 July to Pinker: *There is a last chapter to write, some time, when one's heart is not so contracted* [Moore 460].

Not only the medical examination had drained him of the faith he needed to finish the novel, but the war in general, poverty, his conviction that the novel could not be published, and the defection of the Murrys. We cannot assume that the unwritten chapter was 'Exeunt'. See 31 October.

JULY 1916 At Higher Tregerthen.

SUMMARY At the beginning of July Lawrence had only £6 in the world, and could not afford to pay for the typing of his novel. He tried to do it himself, estimating that it would take him three months, but had to give up within a fortnight: *It got on my nerves and knocked me up* [Moore 469]. Possibly he wrote 'Love' and 'Life' [C52 C53 and *Phoenix*].

13 JULY *Shall I call the novel* Women in Love? *I'm not good at titles—never know if they're good or bad* [Moore 463].

16 JULY Lawrence's letter to Catherine Carswell [Moore 465] is very similar to his essays 'Love' and 'Life'.

21 JULY *I am scribbling out the final draft in pencil . . . It is ⅘ done now. This is the fourth and the final draft* [Moore 469].

AUGUST 1916 At Higher Tregerthen.

SUMMARY Lawrence resumed the typing of *Women in Love*: *I recomposed all the first part on the typewriter* [Ross, 201].

23 AUG. After discussing Crèvecoeur, Melville and Dana, Lawrence says: *But your classic American literature, I find to my surprise, is* older *than our English* [Damon 371]. This is Lawrence's first use of the phrase which is to provide his ultimate title for *Studies in Classic American Literature*.

SEPTEMBER 1916 At Higher Tregerthen.

SUMMARY Lawrence continued to type and revise *Women in Love*.

*4 SEPT. To Kotcliansky: *Your 'Dostoevsky evening' gives me a queer contraction of the heart. It frightens me. When I think of London, the Cafe Royal—you actually there, and Katherine—terror overcomes me, and I take to my heels, and hide myself in a bush. It is a real feeling of horror* [Zytaruk 91].

Kotcliansky had described how Katherine Mansfield, hearing Heseltine on another table at the Cafe Royal reading aloud from *Amores* with malicious mockery, had snatched the book from his hands and stalked out with it. Lawrence incorporated this incident into chapter XXVIII of *Women in Love*, 'Gudrun at the Pompadour'.

9 SEPT. Lawrence told Pinker that the novel was only half done.

26 SEPT.   *I only want to finish this novel, which is like a malady or a madness while it lasts. It will take only a week or two* [Moore 475].

OCTOBER 1916   At Higher Tregerthen.

SUMMARY   Lawrence finished *Women in Love*, wrote a few poems, and rewrote 'The Mortal Coil' [C49 and *Phoenix 2*]. *As for my novel, I don't know if I hate it or not. I think everybody else will hate it. But this cannot be helped. I know it is true, the book. And it is another world, in which I can live apart from this foul world which I will not accept or acknowledge or even enter. The world of my novel is big and fearless—yes, I love it, and love it passionately. It only seems to me horrible to have to publish it* [Moore 477].

3 OCT.   *I shall call my novel I think* The Latter Days [Moore 477].

9 OCT.   Lawrence received from Gertler a photograph of his latest painting *The Merry-Go-Round*. Loerke's granite frieze in chapter XXIX of *Women in Love* is given some of the characteristics of this painting.

11 OCT.   To Catherine Carswell: *I've had a cold and been seedy since you went, so haven't done anything—novel at a standstill till this very day* [Huxley 370]. She had spent a few days with the Lawrences at the beginning of the month [Moore 477].

    Today I sent a few poems to Hilda Aldington for the new American anthology [Nehls 1, 403]. *Some Imagist Poets 1917* [B6] contained only one Lawrence poem 'Terra Nuova' (see January 1915). Several poems were written at Zennor, including 'Elysium' [A10], 'Manifesto' [A10], 'Autumn Rain' [C42 A10], 'Craving for Spring' [A10] and 'Reality of Peace 1916' [A11].

12 OCT.   *I am still typing away at my new novel: it takes a tremendous time: and the novel itself is one of the labours of Hercules* [Damon 385].

13 OCT.   Lawrence wrote to Clayton that he had typed out about two-thirds of the novel, but could do no more, and would have to write out the rest.

25 OCT.   To Pinker: *I send you nearly the whole of the untyped MS of the novel. I have very, very nearly finished—only the concluding chapter to do. I shall probably cut it down a little when I have the typescript—the whole novel* [Moore 480]. Pinker had offered to have the typing done in his office free. Lawrence sent him the final third of the novel in ten small exercise books.

31 OCT. To Pinker: *I send you the conclusion of the novel* Women in Love *(which Mrs Lawrence wants to be called* Dies Irae*)—all but the last chapter, which, being a sort of epilogue, I want to write later—when I get the typescript back from you.*

The last exercise book contains the whole of 'Exeunt' and the beginning of an epilogue, crossed out and never subsequently completed. It reads: *A year afterwards, Ursula in Italy received a letter from Gudrun in Frankfurt am Main. Since the death of Gerald in the Tyrol, when Gudrun had gone away, ostensibly to England, Ursula had had no news of her sister.*

'I met a German artist who knew you,' Gudrun said 'and he gave me your address. I was silent for so long because there was nothing I could say. I have got a son—he is six months old now. His hair is like the sun shining on the sea, and he has his father's limbs and body. I am still Frau Crich—what actually happened is so much better, to account for one's position, than a lie would be. The boy is called Ferdinand Gerald Crich. As for the past—I lived for some months with Loerke, as a friend. Now I am staying [sentence incomplete] [E441c].

I send you also a story, re-written from MS I got a week or two back, from Italy—stuff done before the war—called 'The Mortal Coil'. It is a first-class story, one of my purest creations [Moore 480]. See October 1913.

NOVEMBER 1916   At Higher Tregerthen.

SUMMARY   At the beginning of the month Lawrence probably wrote 'Samson and Delilah' [C43 A23]. Lawrence intensively revised the novel 6–20, then he rested: *Now I am not doing any work, we need books to read. . . . This is a kind of interval in my life, like a sleep. One only wanders through the dim short days, and reads, and cooks, and looks across at the sea. I feel as if I also were hibernating, like the snakes and the dormice* [Moore 486].

6 NOV.   Lawrence sent Pinker a story which he thought might be suitable for *Strand.* He asked for it to be sent back when typed, together with 'The Mortal Coil', for revision. It was probably 'Samson and Delilah'—*a story which I don't much care for* [Moore 504]. *Strand* required very lightweight stories. The only Lawrence story published there was 'Tickets Please'.

7 NOV.   To Catherine Carswell: *I finished my novel—save the last chapter,*

which, a sort of epilogue, I shall add on later. I hated the typing, so took to scribbling in pencil. Then there was a lot of the original draft that I couldn't have bettered. Pinkers are typing it out for me [Moore 482]. Pinker sent back a top-copy and a carbon, which became shuffled as Lawrence and Frieda revised them:

Charles Ross: 'The revisions of the "original" duplicates were done in stages. Lawrence first made a preliminary run-through in both, changing a few words or a sentence here and there. Next he returned to the beginning and made extensive and often wholesale revisions, which, Frieda copied into the corresponding duplicate portions' [Ross, 201].

13 NOV.   To Pinker: *The novel I will send on in a week's time: not longer. Then I will send a batch of poems, for the American magazines. Then I have another short story on hand, which I shall finish when I've sent off the novel. ... The novel will have an epilogue—a small last chapter. But that, I don't want to write until the whole is sent in to the printer: and heaven knows when that will be* [Huxley 378].

The only poems to appear in American magazines during the following year were 'Autumn Rain' in *Egoist*, February 1917, and 'Resurrection' in *Poetry*, June 1917 [C42 and 47]. The short story was probably 'The Horse Dealer's Daughter' which Lawrence sent to Pinker under its original title 'The Miracle' on 12 January 1917 [Huxley 380]. Lawrence had probably begun this story in the first week of 1916.

20 NOV.   Today I have sent off the MS of my new novel Women in Love. *Can I tell you how thankful I am to have the thing done, and out of the house!* [Moore 485].

21 NOV.   Lawrence sent a copy to Catherine Carswell: *Ask Don* [a barrister] *if he thinks any part libellous—e.g. Halliday is Heseltine, the Pussum is a model called Puma, and they are taken from life* [Priest 263]. He says that no other character is, but his next letter to Catherine Carswell begins: *I heard from Ottoline Morrell this morning, saying she hears she is the villainess of the new book* [Moore 488].

Lawrence followed some of Donald Carswell's suggestions. [See Davis.] Nevertheless Lawrence was obliged to make changes when, after the publication of the book by Secker in 1921, Heseltine threatened legal action. See October 1921.

DECEMBER 1916   At Higher Tregerthen.

SUMMARY   *I have been in Cornwall for twelve months now, never out of it, so I feel a stranger to the world. I find myself divested of all my friends, and much more confident and free, having no connections anywhere. Why should one seek intimacies—they are only a net about one. It is one's business to stand quite apart and single, in one's soul* [Irvine, 8]. Lawrence wrote 'Bits' [CP E49].

2 DEC.   To Catherine Carswell: *I am glad you liked the novel—thanks for the suggestions. Gudrun's coat was supposed to be that pale and lovely bluish green which is a painter's emerald green—really a beautiful shade. Is that still common? You might just put Thomas Bannerman instead of Sholto—or Balfour—any ordinary Scotch name. Gerald and his 'as usual' is sarcastic if anything. I can't understand his persistence in 'dressing'. But good to cross him out* [Huxley 382]. Gudrun's coat, at the beginning of the novel as we have it, is *of a strong blue colour.*

11 DEC.   Lawrence sent Pinker the manuscript of a tiny book of poems called *All of Us* (later *Bits*), which he described as tours-de-force, but perhaps the war literature people were looking for. In March 1918 Lawrence offered them to Beaumont, who rejected them and was offered *Bay* instead. A year later Lawrence recovered the MS from Pinker in order to send it to Harriet Monroe, who published twelve of the thirty poems in the July 1919 *Poetry* [C67] under the title 'War Films'.

JANUARY 1917 At Higher Tregerthen.

SUMMARY *I want to go to America. It is necessary now for me to address a new public. It is no use my writing in England for the English any more. I want to go to New York and write a set of essays on American literature, and perhaps lecture. It is no use my sitting cooped up here any longer. I feel I shall burst* [Huxley 394].

Lawrence finished 'The Horse Dealer's Daughter' and began to prepare *'Look! We Have Come Through!'* [A10]. According to Catherine Carswell, who was in close touch with Lawrence at the time, 'during January he had re-composed the first part of *Women in Love*' [Carswell 83].

9 JAN. *I have got in my head a set of essays, or lectures, on Classic American literature. But I can't write for America here in England* [Huxley 394]. The essays were begun in August.

*12 JAN. To Pinker: *I send you the MS of another story—'The Miracle'— which is beautiful and ends happily* [Huxley 380]. This story, published in 1922 as 'The Horse Dealer's Daughter', had probably been begun in January 1916.

29 JAN. *I am doing out a last book of poems: real poems: my chief poems, and best. This will be the last book of poems I shall have, for years to come. I have reaped everything out of my old notebooks now. I think I shall call this: Poems of a Married Man* [Moore 499]. In fact Lawrence was to reap another collection from his notebooks in the summer of 1918—disingenuously called *New Poems*.

FEBRUARY 1917 At Higher Tregerthen.

SUMMARY The authorities refused to endorse Lawrence's passport for America. He completed *'Look! We Have Come Through!'*. *As a sort of last work, I have gathered and shaped my last poems into a book. It is a sort of final conclusion of the old life in me—'and now farewell', is really the motto* [Moore 498].

*5 FEB. *'Look!' very nearly ready* [Moore 498]. In the same letter Lawrence says: *I feel it is really a question of to be or not to be*. Section VI of 'Manifesto' begins: *To be, or not to be, is still the question*. Lawrence may have revised or extended the poem at this time, but it was probably written earlier, since the third line says that the wheat of Canada is *ripening now*.

18 FEB. Lawrence sent *'Look!'* to Catherine Carswell, with the title *Man*

and Woman [Carswell 83].

23 FEB. *It is spring coming here: already the birds singing and the silveriness in the air. I wish to God it was spring in the world of people* [Irvine, 14]. 'Craving for Spring' begins: *I wish it were spring in the world.* A letter of the same date to Dollie Radford [Moore 502] develops the theme of the poem.

MARCH 1917   At Higher Tregerthen.

SUMMARY   Lawrence completed 'The Reality of Peace' [C45 46 48 50 and *Phoenix*].

*7 MARCH   *I have seven short articles—little essays—called 'The Reality of Peace'* [Huxley 401]. That Lawrence mentioned these essays to several other correspondents, with great enthusiasm, during the next few days, suggests that he had just written them. When he sent them to Pinker on 19 he said: *I intend to follow them up with more such chapters, to make a book* [Huxley 402]. The first three and the seventh were published in the *English Review*. Lawrence later told McDonald that 'The Whistling of Birds' [C63] was also one of this series [*Centaur* 37]. The other two, and the subsequent book *At the Gates*, are lost.

12 MARCH   *I have been painting a picture of the death of Procris, which fills me with great delight* [Moore 507].

APRIL 1917   At Higher Tregerthen until 14, then at Ripley until 19, at 5 Acacia Road, London until 25, at Hermitage, Berkshire, until 27, then back to Zennor.

SUMMARY   *We are busy gardening, and I am writing short essays on philosophy. The pure abstract thought interests me now at this juncture more than art. I am tired of emotions and squirmings and sensations. Let us have a little pure thought, a little perfect and detached understanding* [Moore 508].

13 APRIL   Lawrence had sent back the corrected proof of the first instalment of 'The Reality of Peace'.

19–25   ... *'Frost Flowers', written in Cornwall at the end of the bitter winter of 1916–17* [CP 28]. But the poem begins: *Here among all these folk in London.* Lawrence's visit to London beginning 19 April was his first since December 1915.

78

MAY 1917   At Higher Tregerthen.

SUMMARY   *There is no writing and publishing news. Philosophy inter-*
ests me most now—not novels or stories. I find people ultimately boring:
and you can't have fiction without people. So fiction does not, at the
bottom, interest me any more. I am weary of humanity and human things.
One is happy in the thoughts only that transcend humanity [Moore 514].
Lawrence presumably continued with *At the Gates.*

11 MAY   *Yesterday I began to type out the 'Peace' articles—I wanted*
another copy—and I was recasting the second one. But suddenly I felt
as if I was going dotty, straight out of my mind, so I left off [Huxley
408].

JUNE 1917   At Higher Tregerthen, except for a visit to London about 19,
and to Bodmin, for medical reexamination 23.

SUMMARY   *I am doing philosophy only: very good, I think, but a slow*
job. Still, I beat it out [Moore 515]. *At the Gates.*

JULY 1917   At Higher Tregerthen.

SUMMARY   *I think there ought to be some system of private publication*
and private circulation. I disbelieve utterly in the public, in humanity, in the
mass. There should be again a body of esoteric doctrines, defended from the
herd [Moore 520]. *At the Gates* finished.

27 JULY   *I have just written a tiny book of philosophy—called philosophy*
because I don't know what else to call it. It might be called mysticism
or metaphysic, though unjustly [Moore 519–20].
      Lawrence later tells Pinker that his little book of philosophy is
called *At the Gates.* The title may relate to a phrase in the letter of 27
July already quoted. *I want to come to America, bodily, as soon as the*
war stops and the gates are opened. The word 'bodily' implies that he
felt himself to be already there metaphysically. *At the Gates* may well
have provided the philosophical springboard for *Studies in Classic*
American Literature, which immediately followed it.
      To Pinker: *Tell Huebsch, if he gets the MS of the new novel,*
Women in Love, *that this MS needs correcting from the English copy,*
and needs a tiny foreword, which this other has [Moore 520]. Pinker

79

never sent Huebsch a copy. But this letter implies that Lawrence had been doing recent revision. [See Ross, 205–9.] Neither the American nor the English *Women in Love* was published with a foreword. The Foreword published separately in 1936 [A74] is apparently a later version written in September 1919.

AUGUST 1917   At Higher Tregerthen.

SUMMARY   Lawrence probably extended *At the Gates*. He began his long-planned *Studies in Classic American Literature* [A25].

3 AUG.   Chatto and Windus, about to publish *'Look!'*, requested that two poems, 'Song of a Man Who is Loved' and 'Meeting Among the Mountains', should be omitted, and that a number of lines in other poems should be changed. *The lines I will alter, though for some of them it is a great pity, spoiling the clarity and precision of the expression. I will look after my bad taste in 'Eve's Mass' and 'Candlemass'. Strange are the ways of man, strangest of all, the publishers.* Do *convince them that the 'Song of a Man who is Loved' is beautiful, necessary, and innocuous as a sprig of mignonette. If they still persist, make them say* what *they object to. For I cannot believe that this poem shall be omitted* [Moore 521].

   The publishers insisted that Lawrence should not be allowed to mix religion and love; he could not save 'Song of a Man who is Loved', and had to change the titles of 'Eve's Mass' to 'Birth Night' and 'Candlemass' to 'Valentine's Night'.

   At Catherine Carswell's suggestion, Lawrence removed from *'Look!'* one of his love letters to Frieda which he had intended to include.

*24 AUG.   Lawrence told Eder that he had finished *At the Gates*.

27 AUG.   Lawrence told Pinker that he had finished it, and that it would make about 140 pages, which is hardly 'tiny'. This implies that Lawrence had done more work on it this month.

30 AUG.   To Pinker: *You will see that it is based upon the more superficial 'Reality of Peace'. But* this *is pure metaphysics, especially later on: and perfectly sound metaphysics, that will stand the attacks of technical philosophers. Bits of it that might be very unpopular, I might leave out* [Huxley 414].

   To Amy Lowell: *I am doing a set of essays on 'The Transcendental Element in American (Classic) Literature'. It sounds very fine and large, but in reality is rather a thrilling blood-and-thunder, your-money-or-your-life kind of thing: hands up America!—No, but they are very keen essays in criticism—cut your fingers if you don't handle them carefully.—Are you going to help me to hold up the* Yale Review *or the* New Republic *or some such fat old coach, with this ten-barrelled pistol of essays of mine, held right in the eye of America? . . . Tis a chef-d'oeuvre of soul-searching criticism* [Damon 422]. It seems that at this stage Lawrence was planning ten essays. There were eventually twelve, but two each on two writers.

SEPTEMBER 1917   At Higher Tregerthen.

SUMMARY   *Now I am doing a set of essays on 'The Mystic Import of American Literature'. I hope the title doesn't seem ludicrous: perhaps I shall find a better.—These were begun in the hopes of making money: for money is a shy bird.—But I am afraid they have already passed beyond all price* [Moore 526]. Lawrence also probably did further work on *At the Gates*.

15 SEPT.   *I am writing a set of essays on 'The Transcendental Element in Classic American Literature'—beginning with Crèvecoeur* [Moore 524].

22 SEPT.   Lawrence tells Pinker that he is getting on with the proofs of *'Look! We have Come Through!'*

23 SEPT.   To Koteliansky: *I am finishing correcting proofs of a book of poems which Chatto and Windus are bringing out next month. I have written into its final form that philosophy which you once painfully and laboriously typed out, when we were in Bucks. . . . I have written it four times since then* [Moore 526].

Lawrence apparently thought of *At the Gates* as directly descended from 'A Study of Thomas Hardy', via 'The Crown' and 'Goats and Compasses'. Pinker submitted it to Chatto and Windus, who rejected it on 8 October. On 14 December Philip Heseltine wrote to Robert Nichols from Ireland: 'Did you read D. H. Lawrence's recent essays in the *English Review* ["The Reality of Peace"]? At my instigation one of the partners of a big publishing firm here has secured the MS of the whole book from which they were taken—and it is, in my opinion, as, also in his, the supreme utterance of all modern philosophy' [Nehls 1, 452].

The firm was Maunsel of Dublin, the partner Joseph Hone, with whom Lawrence also discussed the possibility of Maunsel publishing

Women in Love [Moore 532]. Since the other partners were all 'commercialists and bigoted Catholics', Heseltine proposed that several well-known people familiar with Lawrence's work should write to the firm to plead for the speedy publication of *At the Gates*. It was never published and the MS is lost, though it still existed as late as February 1920 if the 'At the Gates' Lawrence includes in a list of short stories is the same work [Tedlock 89].

OCTOBER 1917   At Higher Tregerthen until 15, then at 32 Well Walk, Hampstead, until 20, then at 44 Mecklenburgh Square, London.

SUMMARY   On 12 the Lawrences were ordered to leave Cornwall within three days. *I cannot even conceive how I have incurred suspicion—have not the faintest notion. We are as innocent even of pacifist activities, let alone spying of any sort as the rabbits in the field outside. And we must leave Cornwall, and live in an unprohibited area, and report to the police. It is very vile. We have practically no money at all—I don't know what we shall do* [Moore 527].

29 OCT.   I don't do any work—none at all—only read and see people [Moore 530].

NOVEMBER 1917   At 44 Mecklenburgh Square, London.

SUMMARY   Lawrence probably began *Aaron's Rod* [A21]: *I began it in the Mecklenburgh Square days* [Moore 655]. He also wrote 'The Limit to the British Novelist'.

5 NOV.   To Wilbur L. Cross: *I have written the article you asked me for, for the* Yale Review, *in answer to 'British Novelists Ltd.' J. B. Pinker, my agent, will forward it to you: it is called 'The Limit to the British Novelist'. I hope you will get it in time, and will print it* [Moore 531].
  On 8 October Lawrence had replied to Cross' invitation: *God knows whether I shall find it in my heart to write 40 or 50 MS pages about contemporary English novelists; which I suppose means Wells, Bennett, Galsworthy, Compton Mackenzie, and Gilbert Cannan. They all bore me, both in spirit and in the flesh. By this time, they are such vieux jeu that all the game's gone out of it. . . . I will see if I can get up any feeling about contemporary English novelists—I don't care a rush for any of them, save Thomas Hardy, and he's not contempor-*

ary, and the early *Conrad, which is also looming into distance* [Moore 527]. The article was not printed in the *Yale Review*, or anywhere else, and has disappeared.

*28 NOV.   Lawrence told Pinker that he was revising *Women in Love.*

DECEMBER 1917   At 13b Earl's Court Square, London, until 18, then at Hermitage, near Newbury, Berkshire, until 28, then at Grosvenor Road, Ripley, Derbyshire.

SUMMARY   *My book, 'Look, We have Come Through' is out about a fortnight: as usual the critics fall on me: the* Times *says 'the Muse can only turn away her face in pained distate'. Poor Muse, I feel as if I had affronted a white-haired old spinster with weak eyes. But I don't really care what critics say, so long as I myself could personally be left in peace. This, it seems, cannot be. People write letters of accusation, because one has a beard and looks not quite the usual thing: and then one has detectives at one's heels like stray dogs, not to be got rid of. It is very hateful and humiliating and degrading* [Damon 438]. Lawrence wrote nothing, unless he tinkered with *Aaron's Rod.*

JANUARY 1918 At Ripley until about 11, then at Chapel Farm Cottage, near Newbury, Berkshire.

SUMMARY *I'm not writing anything—only sit learning songs, which I find a great amusement. I can read well enough to learn a song nicely in about a quarter of an hour—so I have already got off twenty or thirty. I don't know why it amuses me so much more than reading or writing* [Moore 539]. Lawrence resumed work on *Studies in Classic American Literature.*

28 JAN. *I am writing a set of essays for America* [Moore 537].

FEBRUARY 1918 At Hermitage, nr. Newbury, Berkshire.

SUMMARY *I am at the dead end of my money, and can't raise the wind in any direction. Do you think you might know of somebody who would give us something to keep us going a bit. It makes me swear—such a damned, mean, narrow-gutted, pitiful, crawling, mongrel world, that daren't have a man's work and won't even allow him to live* [Moore 541]. Lawrence continued to work on *Studies* and *Aaron's Rod.*

2 FEB. *I am finally going through a set of studies in* Classic American Literature, *which of course rejoice my soul, but which no doubt would give the Americans—or the English—fits and convulsions of wrathful disgust if ever they went so far as to read them* [Moore 538].

20 FEB. *I am in the middle of an essay on Edgar Allen, and have lost my copy* [Moore 542]. 'Edgar Allen Poe' was the sixth of the eight essays to be published in *The English Review*. *Going through* suggests that he was revising it, not writing it.

21 FEB. *I am doing some philosophic essays, also, very spasmodically, another daft novel. It goes very slowly—very slowly and fitfully. But I don't care* [Moore 543]. The novel, *Aaron's Rod*, continued to go slowly and fitfully. Lawrence did not finish it until May 1921.

*25 FEB. To Koteliansky, who had undertaken to type the essays: *I send you the first part of the essays. I am afraid there is much more to follow. It troubles me that I have made so many alterations, you will have difficulty in reading. . . . If you see anything that would be best left out, from the publishing point of view, do leave it out* [Moore 594].

26 FEB. Lawrence returned to Beaumont the proofs of 'Labour Battalion' and 'No News' for *New Paths* [B7].

84

MARCH 1918 At Chapel Farm Cottage, Hermitage, Berkshire.

SUMMARY *I go on working because it is the one activity allowed to one, not because I care. I feel like a wild cat in a cage—I long to get out into some sort of free, lawless life* [Moore 548]. Lawrence continued to work on the *Studies* and *Aaron's Rod*.

12 MARCH *I ebb along with the American essays, which are in their last and final form. In them, I have got it all off my chest. I shall never write another book of philosophy—or whatever it is—when these are done* [Moore 545–6]. The essays were to be revised or rewritten in 1919, 1920 and 1922.

*17 MARCH *I have begun a novel now—done 150 pages, which is as blameless as Cranford. It shall not have one garment disarranged, but shall be buttoned up like a Member of Parliament. Still I wouldn't vouch that it is like* Sons and Lovers; *it is funny. It amuses me terribly* [Moore 549].

Lawrence was still describing *Aaron's Rod* as 'proper' in June 1919. An *Aaron's Rod* which was so blameless, and which did not draw on Lawrence's subsequent Italian experiences, must have been very different from the novel we know. Unfortunately, no holograph material seems to have survived.

APRIL 1918 At Chapel Farm Cottage, Hermitage, Berkshire, except for 5–12 at Ripley.

SUMMARY *In some blind and hypnotic fashion I do a few bits of poetry—beyond that, I am incapable of everything—except I dig and set potatoes, and go walks with Frieda* [Moore 550].
Lawrence prepared both *Bay* [A12] and *New Poems* [A11]. He also read with great satisfaction the first volume of Gibbon's *Decline and Fall of the Roman Empire*, an interest which led directly to his undertaking, three months later, to write *Movements in European History*, in which he frequently plagiarizes Gibbon.

*1 APRIL Lawrence received from Lady Ottoline Morrell a bundle of old poetry MSS she had kept for him. From these and two notebooks retrieved from Cornwall [Huxley 429] he made *Bay*.

18 APRIL *I have made a little book of poems that Beaumont asked me for—all smallish, lyrical pieces. I have been doing poetry for a few weeks now—I want to make a second little book. But it is exhausting*

to keep it up. The first book has 18 poems, it more or less refers to the war, and is called Bay. *I don't know if Beaumont will really do it. The second would be different—I would call it* Chorus of Women, *or something like that* [Moore 549–50]. Beaumont published *Bay*, only two hundred copies, in November 1919. *Chorus of Women* was published as part of *New Poems* in October 1918.

MAY 1918 At Mountain Cottage, Middleton-by-Wirksworth, Derbyshire.

SUMMARY *I feel queer and desolate in my soul—like Ovid in Thrace. And the world is such a useless place. But I set potatoes and mow the grass and write my never-to-be-finished* Studies in Classic American Literature. *I am reading Gibbon* [Moore 553].

JUNE 1918 At Mountain Cottage, Middleton-by-Wirksworth.

SUMMARY Lawrence finished *Studies* and put together *New Poems* [A11]. *I have finished up all the things I am writing at present—have a complete blank in front of me—feel very desperate, and ready for anything, good or bad. I think something critical will happen this month, finally critical. If it doesn't I shall bust* [Moore 558].

1 JUNE   To Catherine Carswell, whose son had just been born: *In the English Review today there'll be a little 'War Baby' poem, which I wrote for you—at least, with you in mind—and the infant, of course* [Moore 554].

3 JUNE   *I am writing a last essay on Whitman—then I have done my book of American essays—salt on America's tail, if only America would stay still long enough to have her tail sprinkled* [Moore 556]. Lawrence had now written twelve essays. Eight of them appeared in *The English Review* between November 1918 and June 1919 [C55 56 57 58 60 61 64 65]. 'Whitman' was not published until July 1921 [C83]. All these early published versions are collected in Arnold. The essays were revised in September 1919 and June 1920 and completely rewritten in November and December 1922.

18 JUNE   *I have just gathered a new MS of a book of poems—*Coming Awake*—so named after the first poems. I have worked at some of them for a long time—many years—but many are new, made this*

spring [Damon 462]. Lawrence had decided to combine two smaller books—*In London* and *Choir of Women*. The book was published in October as *New Poems*.

JULY 1918   At Mountain Cottage, Middleton-by-Wirksworth.

SUMMARY   Lawrence began *Movements in European History* [A17]. Vere Collins (who had known Lawrence since 1915 and who worked for the London branch of the Oxford University Press): 'Struck by the knowledge he showed of history, I suggested to him that he might consider the idea of writing an elementary text-book for junior forms in grammar, or upper forms in primary schools, of European history. . . I suggested that Lawrence should not attempt to write a formal, connected, text book, but a series of vivid sketches of movements and people. He suggested *Movements in European History* for the title' [Nehls 1, 471].

3 JULY   *The Oxford Press said I might do a school book, of European History. If only I could get books of reference, I would. I feel in a historical mood, being very near the end of Gibbon. The chief feeling is, that men were always alike, and always will be, and one must view the species with contempt. . . . and find a few individuals . . . to* rule *the species* [Moore 561].

11 JULY   *I have done the first essay of the European History* [Cushman, 25].

26 JULY   To Nancy Henry of the Oxford University Press: *I send you the first three chapters. They are perhaps rather long. The others, some of them, will be much shorter. I wanted to make a serious reader that would convey the true historic impression to children who are beginning to grasp realities. We should introduce the deep, philosophic note into education: deep, philosophic reverence. I've no doubt your people won't like this style. I shan't mind if they don't want me to go on* [Huxley 450].

Lawrence agreed to publish under an alias, and chose Lawrence H. Davison. The second edition of 1925 carried his real name. [See Boulton, Introduction to the Oxford University Press edition of 1971, and Cushman, 21–32.]

AUGUST 1918   At Mountain Cottage until 12, then at 5 Acacia Road, St John's Wood, London, until 17, then to Mersea Island, Essex, for three

days, then to Chapel Farm Cottage, Hermitage, until 26, then to The Vicarage, Upper Lydbrook, Ross-on-Wye, for a tour of the Forest of Dean with Carswells.

SUMMARY   Revising *Studies in Classic American Literature.*

3 AUG.   To Pinker: *I am sending you the first of the* Studies in Classic American Literature. *There are six or seven more—these I will send in about a week's time. Do you read this essay on 'The Spirit of Place'. You will find one MS complete—the other lacking the last eight pages* [Moore 562].

If these are the eight essays which were shortly to appear in the *English Review*, then Lawrence did not send his essays on Dana, Melville and Whitman. We know that he had written the Whitman in June, and that there were twelve essays by 27 January 1919 [Moore 577], and that Lawrence was prepared to see them all appear in *The English Review*. When, in September 1919, Lawrence wanted to send the complete MS of *Studies* to Huebsch, he found he had no suitable text to send of three of the essays, presumably those on Dana and Melville (possibly also Whitman, if he was thinking of the Melville as one essay), and asked Koteliansky to write out fair copies of these on smallish sheets *so that they can make one MS—with the* English Review *pages* [Zytaruk 191–2].

It seems that Lawrence had recently extended 'The Spirit of Place'.

*23 AUG.   *If Ely really decides to have the history I shall work hard at it when I get back. I have got more typed MS of the essays—am revising* [Delany, 197]. G. H. Ely was the head of the Juvenile and Elementary Schools department of the Oxford University Press.

SEPTEMBER 1918   At Mountain Cottage, Middleton-by-Wirksworth.

SUMMARY   Lawrence worked on *Aaron's Rod*, the revision of *Studies* and the proofs of *New Poems*. *I am slowly working at another novel: though I feel it's not much use. No publisher will risk my last, and none will risk this, I expect. I can't do anything in the world today—am just choked* [Damon 482].

13 SEPT.   To Secker: *I return the proofs. I took out 'Late in Life'—also two last verses from 'Everlasting Flowers'* [Secker 11].

Lawrence had apparently been asked to get the book down to sixty-four pages. 'Late in Life' has never been published. It is in the

Ferrier *Variorum* [poem 329]. *CP* prints the earliest version of it, called 'Love Comes Late' [859]. 'Everlasting Flowers' has twelve stanzas in both *New Poems* and *Collected Poems*. The only surviving MS—'From the Italian Lakes' [MS26]—also has twelve stanzas, but the last two are different:

We have lost them all, and the darkness
Alone is left, of all
The wonderful things I had for you.
—So the fall

Of the latch through the night rings final.
And on opposite sides of the door
We are each shut out from the other now
For ever more.

24 SEPT.   *At the moment I am going over my American essays, which are coming back from the typist. The history can wait a bit* [Huxley 455].

*26 SEPT.   To Catherine Carswell: *About the essays, I crossed out the 'Children' passages. Who am I to dictate when hope does or doesn't lie?* [Carswell 102].

On 16 July Lawrence had written to Catherine Carswell: *Children and childbearing do not make spring. It is not in children, the future lies. The Red Indian mothers bore many children, and yet there are no Red Indians. It is the truth, the new perceived hope, that makes spring. And let them bring forth that, who can: they are the creators of life. There are many enceinte widows, with a new crop of death in their wombs. What did the mothers of the dead soldiers bring forth, in childbed?—death or life?* [Moore 468]. It seems that there were originally passages corresponding to this in the essays. There would have been many opportunities: Lawrence accuses both Crèvecoeur and Fenimore Cooper of lying about 'Children'.

OCTOBER 1918   At Mountain Cottage until 7, then to 32 Well Walk, Hampstead, until 22, then to Chapel Farm Cottage, Hermitage, Berkshire.

SUMMARY   Lawrence wrote *Touch and Go* [A14].

16 OCT.   Lawrence corrected the proofs of the first of the *Studies in Classic American Literature* to appear in the *English Review*, 'The Spirit of Place' [C55].

*28 OCT.   Lawrence told Lady Cynthia Asquith that he had written a play, fired by his last sparks of hope in the world. In July 1919 Douglas

Goldring proposed to Lawrence that *Touch and Go* should be the first play to be performed by his People's Theatre Society, and the first to be published in his series *Plays for a People's Theatre*. On this understanding Lawrence let him have the play and its preface free. But Goldring was thwarted by a reactionary majority on his theatre committee. *Touch and Go* was not produced then, or, to my knowledge, since. The first play to appear in the series was Goldring's own *The Fight for Freedom*, which Lawrence despised. *Touch and Go* was the second, in May 1920.

†30 OCT. *I couldn't write the Educational stuff—I tried so hard—it wouldn't work in me—no go* [Carswell 111]. At his medical examination on 26 September Lawrence had been graded C3, which meant that he could be called up for light duties. Feeling that he would be more likely to avoid this if he had some regular employment, Lawrence got an introduction from Donald Carswell to G. S. Freeman, editor of *The Times Educational Supplement*, who encouraged him to submit some articles on education.

NOVEMBER 1918   At Chapel Farm Cottage until 14, except for a visit to London 11, for an Armistice party at Montague Shearman's, then at Mountain Cottage, except for a visit to London and Berkshire 23–6.

SUMMARY   Lawrence wrote 'The Blind Man' [C72 A23], 'The Fox' [C92 93 95 96 A24] and 'Tickets Please' [C62 A23], and began his education essays (*Phoenix*).

*9 NOV.   Lawrence told Catherine Carswell that he was doing 'The Blind Man'.

*21 NOV.   *I've not done 'The Fox' yet—but I've done 'The Blind Man'—the end queer and ironical. I realise* how *many people are just rotten at the quick. I've written three little essays, 'Education of the People'* [Moore 566]. For the background to 'The Blind Man' see Carswell 105–6.

23 NOV.   Lawrence told Pinker that he had written three short stories, two of which were very good. The third was 'Tickets Please', then called 'John Thomas'. During this month Lawrence had made several vists to a dying friend in Eastwood, and had probably travelled between Ripley and Eastwood by tram.

'The Fox' was cut for magazine publication in July 1919 and revised and extended in November 1921. This first MS version was published in *Miscellany*. For background see Nehls 1, 463–7.

DECEMBER 1918   At Mountain Cottage except for a visit to Ripley for Christmas.

SUMMARY   Lawrence returned to work on his European history, and wrote a fourth education essay. *I wish I need never write another line of any sort, for publication, in my life. I've had enough. If only I had a small income, I'd chuck writing altogether. I'm really sick of it. The necessity to earn something is all that drives me—and then I earn nothing, so I might as well keep still* [Zytaruk 153].

6 DEC.   *I am struggling with a European History for Schools, and cursing myself black in the face* [Moore 567].

*10 DEC.   Lawrence had finished his set of education essays, but they were rejected by Freeman: Very interesting, but too deep, rather matter for a book than for a supplement [Moore 568 574].

20 DEC.   *I'm supposed to be doing that little European History and earning my living, but I hate it like poison, and have struck. Why work?* [Moore 569].

JANUARY 1919   At Mountain Cottage, Middleton-by-Wirksworth, Derbyshire.

SUMMARY   Lawrence continued to work on *Movements in European History*, and probably wrote 'Wintry Peacock' [C84 B10 A23].

1 JAN.   *I am doing the history—it will take about a month or six weeks, I suppose* [Moore 574].

15 JAN.   Lawrence sent Pinker a story. It was almost certainly 'Wintry Peacock'. There was deep snow at Middleton at this time. A letter of 9 Feb. to Katherine Mansfield echoes the opening paragraph of the story [Moore 578].

*17 JAN.   *Two more chapters now, and then revision* [Zytaruk 158].

23 JAN.   *I have only one more chapter. Every chapter, I suffer before I can begin, because I do loathe the broken pots of historical facts. But once I can get hold of the thread of the developing significance, then I am happy, and get ahead. I shall need to revise rather carefully. But you'll see, when you get these 4 last chapters, the book does expand nicely and naturally. I am rather pleased with it. There is a clue of developing meaning running through it: that makes it real to me. I hope if you think of any other book I could do, you will propose me for it* [Huxley 466].

FEBRUARY 1919   At Mountain Cottage until the middle of the month, when Lawrence became a victim of the influenza epidemic and was taken to his sister's at Ripley.

SUMMARY   Lawrence finished *Movements in European History*.

3 FEB.   To Nancy Pearn: *I send you here the last four chapters* [Huxley 467]. For the Epilogue, see September 1924.

MARCH 1919   At Grosvenor Road, Ripley, until the middle of the month, then back at Mountain Cottage.

SUMMARY   *I am a wretched object like a drowned ghost creeping downstairs to tea* [Irvine 14]. During his convalescence Lawrence wrote two pieces for the revived *Athenaeum*, now under Murry's editorship, and copied some reproductions.

*6 MARCH   To J. M. Murry: *I am very pleased about the* Athenaeum—*I do* *hope you will enjoy it and that it will be successful. Thank you for asking me to contribute—that pleases me, too. I should like to do it. But you must tell me exactly what you would like me to do, and I will try to be pleasant and a bit old-fashioned. I don't mind if I am anonymous—or a* nom de plume. *When it is to begin? Tell me particulars as soon as you can—so that I can think about it while I am still not well, and make little ideas. That amuses me* [Moore 579].

11 MARCH Murry vaguely asked me to contribute to the Athenaeum—but he doesn't tell me what he wants, nor when he wants it. I feel fearfully mistrustful of him—feel sure we shall be let down [Zytaruk 164].

14 MARCH I have been trying to write for the Athenaeum. *Why is it such a cold effort to do these things?* [Moore 581]. 'The Whistling of Birds' [C63] appeared in the *Athenaeum* on 11 April, but was probably not written at this time, since Lawrence later described it to Edward McDonald as part of the 'Reality of Peace' series. [*Centaur* 37].Other pieces, including 'Adolf', and possibly its companion piece 'Rex', were rejected: *I heard from Murry, very editorial—he sort of 'declines with thanks' the things I did for him. He will publish one essay next week—too late to ask for it back—and that is the first and last word of mine that will ever appear in the* Athenaeum [Moore 584].

'Adolf' and 'Rex' were published in the *Dial* [C73 and 77] and collected in *Phoenix*. In December Lawrence sent Murry further pieces, which were again rejected. When Murry became editor of *The Adelphi* in 1923, Lawrence again contributed, and many of his pieces subsequently appeared there.

20 MARCH Lawrence wrote to Gertler asking for a book of reproductions to copy, preferably Uccello: *I am an irritable sort of convalescent. It would make me happy to paint* [Huxley 474].

25 MARCH Tell Gertler I got his postcards and the book. Tomorrow I will start. I copied a Teniers in the meantime—very nice.—But painting is not my art—only an amusement to me [Zytaruk 168].

APRIL 1919 At Mountain Cottage, Middleton-by-Wirksworth.

SUMMARY Lawrence revised *Movements in European History. I have not written anything these last few months—not since I have been ill. I feel I don't want to write—still less do I want to publish anything. It is like throwing one's treasures in a bog* [Damon 493].

1919

3 APRIL *I have set to, revising my history. It will take about three weeks—pray God not longer—and then I hope speedily to receive the £50. There is a sum for you!* [Moore 585].

17 APRIL *I have got only two more chapters of the history before me. When these are done, I have nothing on hand at all, can turn tramp or bolshevist or government official, any of those occupations one takes up in one's leisure. . . . I am afraid of becoming bored at last* [Zytaruk 175].

*22 APRIL Lawrence told Catherine Carswell that he was just finishing the History.

*23 APRIL Lawrence had received from Gertler a book of reproductions, and some postcards, including Uccellos, to copy. On 23 he told Gertler he had done two pictures, not Uccellos.

MAY 1919 At Chapel Farm Cottage, Hermitage, Berkshire.

SUMMARY *Now the weather is warm I am quite happy—dolce far niente. The world is very lovely, full of flowers and scents. One can be out most of the day* [Moore 587]. Lawrence wrote 'Fannie and Annie' [C87 A23] and 'Monkey Nuts' [C97 A23].

14 MAY Lawrence sends Pinker 'Fannie and Annie', offering to write a different ending if Pinker does not like it.

20 MAY Lawrence sends Pinker a second story, which must be 'Monkey Nuts' since 18 June he thanks Pinker for the return of the MS of 'Monkey Nuts'. Lawrence also asks Pinker for the MS of *Touch and Go*, saying that he would like to look at it again.

JUNE 1919 At Chapel Farm Cottage, Hermitage, Berkshire.

SUMMARY Lawrence wrote the preface to *Touch and Go* [*Phoenix* 2], possibly 'You Touched Me' [C71 A23], and resumed work on *Aaron's Rod*.

8 JUNE Lawrence told Huebsch that he was doing a proper novel which he hoped to finish before leaving for America in August.

18 JUNE Lawrence wrote to Beaumont that he had altered 'Guards!: A Review in Hyde Park 1913', the first poem in *Bay*, in the hope of making it plain. Ferrier MS32 may well be this revised MS.

Lawrence promised Pinker to get more stories done. He may well have kept this promise with 'You Touched Me', which was accepted by *Land and Water* in November.

94

JULY 1919   At Chapel Farm Cottage until 28, except for a few days at the beginning of the month in London and at Otford, Kent, then at Myrtle Cottage, Pangbourne, Berkshire.

SUMMARY   Lawrence probably worked on *Aaron's Rod* during this otherwise barren month.

10 JULY   To Pinker: *I send 'The Fox' by return. I wish I could have cut more—but I simply can't, without mutilating the story* [Huxley 481]. The request for the shortening of the story had come from *Hutchinson's Story Magazine*, which published it in November 1920. Brian Finney: 'Out of a story of some 9,000–9,500 words, Lawrence cut only about 650 words and altered the wording of a few more sentences' [Finney 3].

AUGUST 1919   At Pangbourne until 29, then at Chapel Farm Cottage.

SUMMARY   *I have been editing, for a Russian friend of mine, a rather amusing, not very long translation of a book of philosophy by one of the last of the Russians, called Shestov. It is by no means a heavy work—nice and ironical and in snappy paragraphs* [Secker 12]. Lawrence also wrote 'Poetry of the Present' [C69 70 A11b *Phoenix CP*] as an introduction to the American edition of *New Poems*.

*2 AUG.   To Koteliansky: *I have done a certain amount of the translation* [Zytaruk 184].

*8 AUG.   *I have done 71 of the Shestov paragraphs—more than half* [Zytaruk 185].

*10 AUG.   Lawrence has done part I and asks Koteliansky for part II, for Shestov's introduction, and for a small introduction by Koteliansky himself. He suggests making selections from Shestov to offer to *The Nation* or *The New Statesman*. *I don't want my name printed as a translator. It won't do for me to appear to dabble in too many things. If you don't want to appear alone—but why shouldn't you?—put me a nom de plume like Richard Haw or Thomas Ball. Also, when it comes to payment, in mere justice my part is one-third* [Zytaruk 186].

In *All Things Are Possible* [A13] Lawrence is given credit only for the Foreword. Koteliansky's English was not good enough for him to work unaided; he had already collaborated on several translations with J. M. Murry. Zytaruk 184–91 and Secker 13–15 together give a very full picture of Lawrence's contribution to the translating, editing, and marketing of this volume.

*12 AUG.   *I have done also 'The Russian Spirit'* [Zytaruk 187].

28 AUG.   On 29 August Lawrence told Thomas Moult that he had finished the preface to *New Poems* the previous day.

*29 AUG.   *I have finished Shestov. . . . Let me have the 'Preface' as soon as possible: also everything you know about Shestov, and I'll write a tiny 'Introduction', and we'll approach the publishers* [Zytaruk 189].

SEPTEMBER 1919   At Grimsbury Farm, near Newbury, Berkshire, until 15, then back at Chapel Farm Cottage.

SUMMARY   The Shestov MS sent to Secker was entirely in Lawrence's hand. He also sent his Foreword. He wrote the Foreword to *Women in Love* [A74 and *Phoenix 2*], and revised that novel. He also revised *Studies in Classic American Literature*, and possibly finished the first draft of *Aaron's Rod*.

7 SEPT.   Lawrence corrected the proofs of *Bay*.

To Seltzer, who was to publish *Women in Love* in November 1920: *I wanted moreover to go through the MS once more. . . . Please be careful with the MS as it is the most complete one:—I am forwarding it to you by the next mail. . . . Would you like me to write a short Foreword?—And which title do you prefer,* Women in Love, *or* The Sisters [Seltzer 3].

12 SEPT.   The Foreword to *Women in Love* bears this date. Seltzer used it in his publicity leaflet, but not in the book.

15 SEPT.   To Secker: *You can put 'Edited by D. H. Lawrence', or leave it out, as you like. I find Shestov's 'Preface' long and tedious and unnecessary. You could leave it out if you thought fit, and put in the little 4-page Foreword I enclose* [Secker 13]. For all their joint labours on this book Lawrence and Koteliansky were paid £20 [Secker 15].

In a memoir written in 1955 Cecily Lambert Minchin recalled that Frieda returned to Chapel Farm Cottage alone, leaving Lawrence at Grimsbury Farm 'to finish his book which he spent most of the day writing in one room—*The Lost Girl*, I believe it was. Anyway the manuscript was sent on for us to type, or rather Miss Monk typed and I read it to her, some weeks later' [Nehls 1, 505].

It was certainly not *The Lost Girl*, the unfinished MS of which Lawrence was unable to secure until the following spring. Lawrence was certainly revising *Women in Love* at this time, but the MS sent to

Seltzer had Lawrence's 1919 revisions in reddish-brown ink [Ross, 206–7]. If it was a novel, it must therefore have been *Aaron's Rod*. Certainly Lawrence had already spent a lot of time working on *Aaron's Rod*. Yet when he mentions it again, in July 1920, he says he has got it one-third done, and speaks of it as *my new novel*. Certainly the *Aaron's Rod* we know contains a great deal of Lawrence's post-1919 Italian experience. It is quite possible, therefore, that he finished the first draft in September 1919, discarded it, and started again in June or July 1920. No holographs of *Aaron's Rod* have surfaced.

30 SEPT.　To Huebsch: *I have finished the* Classic American *essays—end up with an essay on Whitman* [Moore 595]. Lawrence claims that *no one in the world* has seen the Whitman essay. He also says that the essays contain a *new science of psychology* which the professional psychologists are trying to steal from him. The essays are, he says, *the result of five years of persistent work*. It is not known how much revision Lawrence did at this time. The essays were to be revised again in 1920 and rewritten in 1922 before publication. The intermediate stages have not survived.

OCTOBER 1919　At Chapel Farm Cottage, except for 14–16 in Hampstead, and a trip to the Midlands the following week.

SUMMARY　Lawrence wrote 'Democracy' [*Phoenix*]. His energies for the rest of this month went into negotiations with publishers, obtaining Frieda's passport and visa and seeing her off to Germany 15, visiting his sick sister the following week, and, though ill himself, making his arrangements to go to Italy.

6 OCT.　Lawrence sent four little essays on 'Democracy' to *The World*.

10 OCT.　Lawrence sent Huebsch the 'completed' MS of *Studies in Classic American Literature*. What Lawrence sent was in fact pages from the *English Review* of the eight essays they had published, presumably revised, and fair copies made in longhand by Koteliansky of the remaining essays. Lawrence had still not rewritten the unpublished part of his Hawthorne essay as 'Hawthorne's *Blithedale Romance*'. Twelve essays were written, and there were to be twelve in the book, but 'The Two Principles' [C65] was not to be included.

NOVEMBER 1919   At Chapel Farm Cottage until 4, then at 5 Acacia Road, St John's Wood, London, until 14, then to Italy. There Lawrence stayed first at Sir Walter Becker's villa, Val Salice, near Turin, 15–17, 18–19 at Lerici. On 19 Lawrence reached Florence (Pensione Balestri, 5 Piazza Mentana).

SUMMARY   In Florence Lawrence wrote 'David' [*Phoenix*].

*26 NOV.   *Here I sit in my room over the river, which is swollen with heavy rain, and yellow. The horses and mules, as they cross the bridge, have nice grey bonnets on their heads, and the carters are hidden under big green umbrellas* [Moore 599].

At the beginning of 'David' Lawrence writes: *The Arno, having risen with rain, is swirling brown. . . . Morning in Florence. Dark, grey and raining, with a perpetual sound of water. Over the bridge, carriages trotting under great ragged umbrellas* [Phoenix 60].

DECEMBER 1919   At Pensione Balestri, Florence until 9, then in Rome until 13. At Picinisco until 22, then to Capri.

SUMMARY   Lawrence seems to have done nothing this month but correct the proofs of *All Things Are Possible*.

3 DEC.   *I am going to do various small things—on Italy and on Psychoanalysis—for the periodicals* [Moore 599]. Lawrence wrote nothing on Italy beyond 'David' at this time, but wrote *Psychoanalysis and the Unconscious* in January.

*6 DEC.   *I sent Murry an essay from here* [Zytaruk 200]. Probably 'David'. Lawrence must have sent Murry other contributions for the *Athenaeum* at this time, since in a letter to Murry of 30 January he refers to the returned articles. These rejections led to a violent split between Lawrence and Murry, which never really healed.

20 DEC.   To Secker: *I have done the Shestov proofs, please correct from my corrections, Koteliansky will miss a thousand things. . . . I have only corrected misprints, and changed about ½ doz. words—except one little paragraph, which was wrong* [Secker 18].

27 DEC.   *I am waiting for MS of a novel three parts done,* Mixed Marriage, *which I left in Germany before the war. This would make a perfect selling novel when I've finished it* [Secker 19]. The MS arrived in February 1920. After attempting to continue it, Lawrence abandoned it, and began again.

98

JANUARY 1920   At Palazzo Ferraro, Capri, except for a three-day excursion down the Amalfi coast at the end of the month.

SUMMARY   Lawrence was hampered by the Italian postal strike: *I sit dearly waiting for a MS which is in the post, and which will lie in the post till Doomsday, along with my Christmas parcels, my sweetcake and my nice mincepies from my sister. . . . So—dolce far niente. Here I sit at the top of my palace, and do nothing, sweet nothing, except go out to lunch, or walk from one end of the island to the other* [Moore 616].
In the second half of the month Lawrence wrote *Psychoanalysis and the Unconscious* [C202 A18].

16 JAN.   *The MS which is now in the post, coming from Germany, has lain in Bavaria since early 1914. It is a novel, two-thirds finished—quite unlike my usual style—more eventual—I am very keen to see it. I thought if I finished it, it would be quite* unexceptionable, *as far as the censor is concerned* [Moore 616].
As usual, Lawrence was not able to maintain for long the 'unexceptionable' character of the novel. Though *The Lost Girl* did not cause trouble with the censor, it did with the circulating libraries.

25 JAN.   Lawrence has finished correcting the proofs of *Movements in European History* [Moore 617].

29 JAN.   To Huebsch: *I'm going to send you six little essays on Freudian Unconscious* [Moore 618].

FEBRUARY 1920   At Palazzo Ferraro, Capri, until 26, except for a trip to the Abbey of Montecassino 19–21. Then to Sicily, house-hunting.

SUMMARY   The long-waited MS of *The Insurrection of Miss Houghton* arrived at last, and Lawrence began work on it at once.

12 FEB.   *MS—began novel* [Tedlock 89]. This proved to be a false start. On 22 March Lawrence was to write to Mackenzie: *I scrapped all the novel I did in Capri* [Mackenzie 171].

MARCH 1920   After house-hunting for several days with the Brett Youngs, Lawrence discovered the Fontana Vecchia, Taormina, and moved in 8 March.

SUMMARY   *Perhaps I shall write here—if only I could care again* [Mackenzie 170]. Lawrence worked solidly at *The Lost Girl* [A16].

1920

9 MARCH   *I am doing* Mixed Marriage—*it should be more popular—one withdraws awhile from the battle* [Seltzer 7].

*11 MARCH   Lawrence told Marsh that he had done the proofs of the history.

*15 MARCH   *I've begun to try to work—begun a novel—don't know if it will ever end* [Huxley 501].

*22 MARCH   *I scrapped all the novel I did in Capri—have begun again, got about 30,000 words, I believe, done since I'm here. Rather amusing. But as for me, I may come to a full stop any moment—you never know* [Mackenzie 171].

*25 MARCH   *I am doing a novel—amuses me—perhaps I shall even finish it* [Moore 625].

*31 MARCH   *I've done about, I should think, about 50,000 words of a rather comic novel, which runs out of my control and jumps through the port-hole into the unknown ocean, and leaves me on deck painfully imploring it to come home* [Sagar 2, 96].

   I have done 50,000 words of a novel which amuses me but perhaps won't amuse anybody else. I am going to give it to Mary [Cannan] *to criticize. I feel that as she sits in her room at Timeo she will represent the public as near as I want it. So like an 'aristo' before Robespierre I shake in my superior shoes* [Douglas 355].

APRIL 1920   At Fontana Vecchia, Taormina, Sicily, until about 22. Then to Syracuse for a few days; then at Randazzo and Bronte for three days, returning 27.

SUMMARY   Lawrence continued to work on *The Lost Girl.*

*5 APRIL   *I have done half my new novel—quite amusing. . . . It is as proper as proper need be* [Zytaruk 207].

9 APRIL   *My novel is page 245 and I like it so much, it does so amuse me. I want to wind it up about page 400 MS* [Mackenzie 178]. The MS at Texas is in fact 450 pages, 431 in Lawrence's faulty numbering. This letter makes clear what has been becoming increasingly evident, that Lawrence was speaking literally when he said he had 'begun' a novel, that not only had he scrapped what he had written in Capri, but what he had written before the war also, the two hundred pages of *The Insurrection of Miss Houghton,* which have not survived.

*29 APRIL   *I hope to finish my novel next week. It is called* The Lost Girl—*or maybe* The Bitter Cherry. . . . *It is I think an amusing book,*

100

and I don't think it is at all improper, quite fit for Mudies. I wish it could be serialised [Secker 24].Mudie's did not agree with him. Either his judgement of what they would think fit was at fault, or the passages they objected to had not yet been written.

MAY 1920 At Fontana Vecchia, Taormina 17. The Lawrences took a trip to Malta, intending to stay two days, and were kept there for ten by a steamer strike.

SUMMARY Lawrence finished *The Lost Girl* [A16] and immediately began *Mr Noon* [A71 and *Phoenix* 2]. He probably wrote 'The Mosquito' [C81 A27]. *I should like to talk once more South Seas. That interests me finally. I have to poke myself to be interested in novels and plays. . . . But after my novel I am holidaying for one month. Then I should like to start again with another I have in mind. I feel as if I were victualling my ship, with these damned books. But also somewhere they are the crumpled wings of my soul. They get me free before I get myself free. I mean in my novel I get some sort of wings loose, before I get my feet out of Europe* [Mackenzie 179].

5 MAY Lost Girl *finished* [Tedlock 90].

6 MAY *I don't know what I shall do, my novel finished, myself out of work. Suppose I shall run hopelessly to seed one way or another* [Sagar 2, 98].

7 MAY To Lady Cynthia Asquith: *I've actually finished my new novel. The Lost Girl: not morally lost, I assure you. That bee in my bonnet which you mention, and which I presume means sex, buzzes not over-loud. I think* The Lost Girl *is quite passable, from Mudie's point of view* [Moore 628]. In the event the circulating libraries—Smith's, Mudie's and Boot's—did not find it passable, and four passages were slightly expurgated. See October.

'Began Mr Noon' [Tedlock 90].

17 MAY On the way to Malta the Lawrences spent the first night at the Grand Hotel, Syracuse: *It is a rather dreary hotel—and many bloodstains of squashed mosquitoes on the bedroom walls. Ah, vile mosquitoes!* [Introduction to *Memoirs of the Foreign Legion*, 68]. 'The Mosquito' is signed Siracusa.

*30 MAY To Richard Aldington: *Here is the other sketch for* The Dial *if it'll suit them* [Joost 37]. *The Dial* had accepted 'Adolf' and apparently asked to see the companion piece, 'Rex', which they also accepted. It may have been written at the same time as 'Adolf' (see March 1919). Lawrence has a diary entry for 20 June: *Sent Richard 'Rex', to go with 'Adolf', for the* Dial [Tedlock 90]. Perhaps the letter of 30 May, which was written on the back of the MS of 'Rex', was not actually sent until 20 June.

JUNE 1920   At Fontana Vecchia, Taormina.

SUMMARY   There is no further mention this month of *Mr Noon*. Lawrence probably wrote three or four poems for *Birds, Beasts and Flowers*. He revised *Studies in Classic American Literature* and *The Lost Girl*, and extended the 'Education of the People' essays into a small book.

1 JUNE   *I shouldn't wonder if my skin went black and my eyes went yellow, like a negro's* [Damon 538]. In 'Tropic' we find the lines:

> *Behold my hair twisting and going black.*
> *Behold my eyes turn tawny yellow*
> *Negroid.*

'Tropic' is the first poem in the earliest surviving *Birds, Beasts and Flowers* MS [Tedlock 87]. It is followed by 'Peace' and 'Southern Night', which may have been written at the same time. They form a group quite distinct from the rest of *Birds, Beasts and Flowers*.

5 JUNE   *I have just been going through the complete MS of my* Studies in Classic American Literature [Seltzer 11]. Perhaps the revision of the Crèvecoeur essay inspired the writing of 'Humming Bird' [C80 A27]. In *Birds, Beasts and Flowers* 'Humming Bird' is signed 'Española', which is a village near Taos, New Mexico, where there are indeed humming birds. But the poem was first published, in an identical text, in May 1921, when Lawrence had never heard of Española and never seen a wild humming bird, or probably even a live one. His knowledge of them and interest in them derived entirely from his reading. In the first version of the Crèvecoeur essay, written in 1917, Lawrence had quoted Crèvecoeur's passage about humming birds in full, and commented: *We have read various descriptions of humming birds. W. H. Hudson has a good one. But this one gives a curiously sharp, hard bit of realisation, something surely intrinsic, a jewel-sharpness and refraction inherent in the little soul of the creature. . . . He sees their dark, primitive, weapon-like souls.*

In the book version this has become: *I have read about humming-birds elsewhere, in Bates and W. H. Hudson, for example. But it is left to the American Farmer to show me the real little raging lion. He sees how they start and flash their wings like little devils, and stab each other with egoistic sharp bills.* In the poem the humming bird is seen (through the wrong end of the telescope of time) as *a jabbing, terrifying monster.*

12 JUNE *I have the carbon copy, and am correcting it. There is not much to alter* [Secker 27]. When Lawrence got *The Lost Girl* back from his typist, Miss Wallace in Rome, he immediately sent the holograph MS to Secker and the top copy to Seltzer.

15 JUNE *Began 'Education of the People'* [Tedlock 90].

16 JUNE Letter of 26 June: The Studies in Classic American Literature *I finished revising ten days ago* [Priest 321].

17 JUNE [The Lost Girl] *is fully corrected, and with the few alterations in the actual text, only in one place I have made a serious change—about two pages. But that is serious. I'm just finishing a little book* Education of the People, *which Stanley Unwin asked me for last year, 30,000 words* [Secker 28].

In his next letter to Secker (24 June) Lawrence expanded on his *only long serious alteration* in The Lost Girl: *It comes in the chapter where Alvina meets Cicio and Mr Tuke at Leeds, and Alvina talks to Cicio—Chapter XI—in the hotel at night* [Secker 28].

Lawrence had already sent his revised carbon to Herbert Foss, editor of *Land and Water,* who had said that the *Queen* would like to see it for serialising. Nothing came of this, and Lawrence asked Secker to obtain this carbon and use it to correct the proofs of *The Lost Girl,* which was set up from the original MS. As usual Lawrence's idea of what constituted serious alterations did not coincide with his publisher's; though by 18 September Lawrence himself had somewhat changed his tune: *Yes, please do correct the proofs in the office, but do them from the typed MS which* The Queen *had. You will* at once *see my handwritten corrections over the type. Don't fail—as there are a few rather important alterations later on. And remember the proper way to spell Cicio is with three c's—Ciccio* [Secker 32].

Secker found 'considerable alterations' on the carbon. It has unfortunately disappeared. But a comparison between the MS from which Secker had originally set up and the published text reveals substantial revision, especially of the chapter called 'The Wedded Wife'. Lawrence was too late to get the spelling of Ciccio corrected. Stanley Unwin did not publish *Education of the People,* which was not published until *Phoenix.*

JULY 1920   At Fontana Vecchia, Taormina.

SUMMARY   Lawrence continued with *Aaron's Rod*, and, possibly, *Mr Noon*. He wrote 'Snake' [C82 B11 A27].

10 JULY   *I have begun another novel—amusing it is.—But oh, the days are so hot just now—one lounges them away* [Seltzer 13].

13 JULY   *I'm working with ever-diminishing spasms of fitfulness at a novel which I know won't go forward many more steps. It's like when you feel your motor-car breaking down—you poke its vitals and proceed 100 yards—then all u.p.* [Sagar 2, 99].

18 JULY   *Yes, I have another novel in hand. I began it two years ago. I have got it ⅓ done, and it is very amusing. But it stands still just now, awaiting events. Once it starts again, it will steam ahead* [Secker 31].

This is clearly *Aaron's Rod*. But on the same day Lawrence wrote to Seltzer: *I have begun another novel: such a queer mad affair* [Seltzer 14]. Can he be speaking of the same novel? In September Lawrence is to describe *Aaron's Rod* to Mackenzie as *my novel—the new one*. It is new as opposed to the old one—*The Lost Girl*—which had monopolised Lawrence for some time, but also, I suggest, because he had just begun it again, scrapping, as in the case of *The Lost Girl*, most of the old material. In two years Lawrence must have written more than a third of the novel, however sporadic his work on it.

26 JULY   *Receive galleys of* Women in Love *from Seltzer* [Tedlock 91].

30 JULY   *It has been hot blazing sun for week after week, day after day, and so hot lately it was too much. I have lived for weeks in a pair of pyjamas, and nothing else* [Nehls 2, 47].

The poem 'Snake' begins:
A snake came to my water-trough
On a hot, hot day, and I in pyjamas for the heat,
To drink there.

Later it refers to *the day of Sicilian July*. In no other July was Lawrence in Sicily.

AUGUST 1920   The Lawrences left Sicily 2 for Anticoli and Monte Cassino. On 6–9 they were in Rome; 12 they left Anticoli for Florence, and were in Milan by 16. From there Frieda went to Germany and Lawrence went walking with the Whittleys round Lake Como. By 24 Lawrence was in Venice, where he remained until the end of the month.

SUMMARY   Lawrence corrected proofs of both *Women in Love* and *The Lost Girl*.

10 AUG.   To Secker: *I have first batch of* W. in L. *proofs, will let you have them corrected and exact, and you can print from them* [Secker 31].

30 AUG.   To Seltzer: *I send you corrected proofs of* Lost Girl—*will let you have the rest as soon as I get them from Secker* [Seltzer 14].

31 AUG.   To Secker: *I sent you off the proofs I had received (2 lots) the other day* [Secker 32].

SEPTEMBER 1920 At Villa Canovaia, San Gervasio, Florence, until about 28, then to Venice.

SUMMARY   Lawrence, alone in Florence, wrote a little more of *Aaron's Rod*, 'America, Listen to Your Own' [C74 and *Phoenix*], and a dozen poems for *Birds, Beasts and Flowers*.

Rosalind Thornycroft Popham: 'While still in Sicily, Lawrence had hoped to come to Florence, and said he would like to take on the Canovaia in spite of the lack of windows. Eventually he did come, and he stayed there two or three weeks before going on to Venice where later Frieda joined him en route from Germany. While he was there he wrote "The Evangelistic Beasts", the tortoise poems, "The Pomegranate", "The Peach", and "The Figs". Sometimes he came to Fiesole where I was now living, climbing by a steep track up through the olives and along the remains of Fiesole's Etruscan walls, and arriving rather jauntily, carrying something peculiar and humerous—a salamander or a little baby duck as a pet for the children. . . . It was here several other poems were suggested—"Cypresses", for example. I remember very well meeting with the Turkey Cock, the swart grape, and the sorb apple, and how Lawrence spoke of these things as we were walking among the farms and country lanes above Fiesole' [Nehls II, 49–50].

The poems written this month were: 'St Matthew' [C106], 'St Mark' [C79], 'St Luke' [C79], 'St John' [C79], *Tortoises* [A19], 'Pomegranate' [C78], 'Peach', 'Figs', 'Cypresses' [C111], 'Turkey Cock' [C99], 'Grapes', 'Medlars and Sorb-Apples' [C75], 'The Revolutionary' [C76].

12 SEPT.   To Compton Mackenzie: *What is this I hear about Channel Isles? The Lord of the Isles. I shall write a skit on you one day* [Mackenzie 190]. When, six years later, Lawrence wrote 'The Man Who Loved Islands', Mackenzie threatened legal action.
   My novel jerks one chapter forward now and then. It is half done.

But where the other ½ is coming from, ask the Divine Providence [Mackenzie 190].

26 SEPT. *My novel—the new one—has stuck half way, but I don't care. I may get a go on him at Taormina. If not, I think I can sort of pimp him picaresque* [Sagar 2, 101]. A letter of 7 October clearly identifies this novel as *Aaron's Rod*.

OCTOBER 1920 At Venice until 14, then back to Taormina via Florence and Rome, arriving 20.

SUMMARY   On his return to Taormina Lawrence wrote 'Sicilian Cyclamens' [A27].

7 OCT.   I am still stuck in the middle of Aaron's Rod, *my novel. But at Taormina I'll spit on my hands and lay fresh hold* [Gallup 258].

20 OCT.   *Proofs of* Women in Love *from Secker* [Tedlock 91]. Lawrence rebuked Secker for having broken up *Women in Love* into 'a thousand little chapters' [Secker 34]. He found his thirteen chapters had been split up into thirty-one.

25 OCT.   *Valley full of cyclamens; poem to them among other vers libre* [Mackenzie 192].

26 OCT.   *Secker asks for a rewritten version of p. 256* Lost Girl [Tedlock 91]. The objection had come from *Smith's and Mudie's* [Seltzer 15]. Lawrence had written: *White, and mute, and motionless, she was taken to her room. And at the back of her mind all the time she wondered at his deliberate recklessness of her. Recklessly, he had his will of her—but deliberately, and thoroughly, not rushing to the issue, but taking everything he wanted of her, progressively, and fully, leaving her stark, with nothing, nothing of herself—nothing.*
   This he now changed to: *White, and mute, and motionless, she let be. She let herself go down the unknown dark flood of his will, borne from her old footing forever.* This expurgation is still to be found in the Heinemann Phoenix edition.

NOVEMBER 1920 At Fontana Vecchia, Taormina.

SUMMARY   *Am not working—too unsettled yet, and this autumn-winter is my uneasy time. Let the year turn* [Secker 35]. Lawrence did much proof-correcting, wrote a new chapter for *Movements in European History*, and possibly returned to *Mr Noon*.

4 NOV. *Sent poem MS* Birds, Beasts and Flowers *to Miss Wheelock to type* [Tedlock 91]. Lawrence already had his title, though only half the poems eventually contained in this volume were yet written. *Correct final proofs of* Movements in European History [Tedlock 91].

7 NOV. *Thank you for all the proofs of* Women in Love. *I went through them. There are only very slight incorrections* [Seltzer 15].

10 NOV. *Enclosed proofs of* W. in L. *up to page 320* [Secker 34].

16 NOV. *I've been swotting Ital. history: having finished proofs of the hist. for the Oxford Press, they ask me for another chap. on Italian unification. Have read all up, now proceed to write* [Moore 636]. The chapter is the penultimate one, 'Italy', which ends with an expression of Lawrence's 1920 disillusion with Italy: *And so Italy was made—modern Italy. Fretfulness, irritation, and nothing in life except money: this is what the religious fervour of Garibaldians and Mazzinians works out to—in united, free Italy as in other united, free countries. No wonder liberty so often turns to ashes in the mouth, after being so fair a fruit to contemplate. Man needs more than liberty.*

I'm copying a very amusing picture—Lorenzetti's—Anacorete nelle Tebaidi—thousands of amusing little monks doing things in the Thebaid: like it very much: success so far [Moore 636]. See January 1921.

We shall be coming north in the spring—have promised to go to Germany—perhaps do a book on Venice as John Lane asked me—perhaps Sardinia—who knows? [Moore 636]. John Lane worked for the Bodley Head publishing house.

22 NOV. *Am doing no serious work, but painting a picture* [Moore 637]. *Herewith the last, final, and concluding proofs of* Women in Love, *508 pages* [Secker 35].

*29 NOV. *I did more than half of* Aaron's Rod, *but can't end it: the flowering end missing, I suppose—so I began, a comedy which I hope will end* [Sagar 2, 102]. Lawrence presumably meant that he had returned to *Mr Noon*. See December.

30 NOV. *I return proof of Chap. VII. Have altered it a bit, enough, I think. If enemies want to fasten, they'll fasten anywhere* [Secker 36]. The alterations were not enough. After threats of legal action by Philip Heseltine, this chapter, 'Totem', and others, had to be altered a bit more. See October 1921.

DECEMBER 1920   At Fontana Vecchia, Taormina.

SUMMARY   Lawrence continued to work on *Mr Noon*, and wrote 'Bare Fig-trees' [A27] and 'Bare Almond Trees' [A27].

12 DEC.   *Probably between* Women in Love *and* The Rainbow *best insert another incensorable novel—either* Aaron's Rod, *which I have left again, or* Mr Noon, *which I am doing* [Secker 37].

JANUARY 1921   At Fontana Vecchia, Taormina, except for an excursion to Sardinia 4–13.

SUMMARY   Lawrence continued to work on *Mr Noon,* and wrote 'Almond Blossom' [C90 A27] and 'Hibiscus and Salvia Flowers' [A27].

1 JAN.   *Finished my anchorites picture after Lorenzetti disappointed after all. p. 374 MS of* Noon [Tedlock 91]. This picture was given to Mary Cannan [Moore 640].

5 JAN.   *Am busy with* Mr Noon [Seltzer 17].

14 JAN.   *Have been away in Sardinia—rather fascinating. Think of going and writing a sketch book of Sardinia in the early summer. I think I may finish* Lucky Noon—*the new novel—next month* [Secker 37].

27 JAN.   *It is very lovely here just now with Almond Blossom in clouds* [Sagar 2, 103]. In the poem 'Almost Blossom' we have:
> *See it come forth in blossom*
> *From the snow-remembering heart*
> *In long-nighted January.*

31 JAN.   *Wrote 'Hibiscus and Salvia Flowers* [Tedlock 92].

FEBRUARY 1921   At Fontana Vecchia, Taormina.

SUMMARY   Lawrence set aside *Mr. Noon* in order to write *Sea and Sardinia* [A20]. He also wrote 'Purple Anemones' [A27].

4 FEB.   Lawrence sent Secker five amendments (requested by Secker) to *Women in Love.* They amounted to only a dozen words.
The MS of 'Purple Anemones' bears this date [Tedlock 100].
Am writing a little itinerary of the trip. Novel having a little rest, it being a bit of a strain. But end in sight [Secker 38]. This suggests that Lawrence was at this stage expecting *Mr Noon* to be a much shorter novel than it later became. See June 1921.

*12 FEB.   *I have nearly done a little travel book: Diary of a* Trip to Sardinia [Moore 641].

22 FEB.   *Post first part* Mr Noon *to Mountsier: also end of* Sardinia *to Miss Wheelock* [Tedlock 92]. The MS sent to Mountsier survives. [Tedlock 48]. It is a 142-page carbon copy with extensive revision in Lawrence's hand. It consists of twelve chapters. Part I was published from this MS in 1934 [A71]. Miss Wheelock was at this time doing all Lawrence's typing in Palermo.
It is unlikely that Lawrence ever in fact returned to *Mr Noon.* There

is no evidence that he touched it before 12 June, when he wrote to Secker: *I will finish* Lucky Noon *before Christmas, God being with me. But it will be rather impossible only funny. It is 3-parts done, nearly the first two vols—up to 1913. Second part ends 1914. Third part ends 1919. But third part not yet begun. Part I you have seen. Part II, which is 3 times as long, or more, is about ½ done. MS in Palermo* [Secker 42]. This exactly describes the surviving 450-page holograph, which ends in the middle of a sentence in chapter 17. The unpublished 278 pages of the holograph is half of part II.

MARCH 1921   At Fontana Vecchia, except for 11–14 in Palermo.

SUMMARY   Lawrence wrote 'The Ass' [A27], and put the finishing touches to *Sea and Sardinia.*

2 MARCH   'The Ass' bears this date [Tedlock 100].

7 MARCH   *I am just finishing a little* Diary of a Trip to Sardinia: *light and sketchy* [Moore 645]. Since Lawrence had recorded in his diary (3 March) that Miss Wheelock had *received all Sardinia MS.* [Tedlock 92], he must have been revising the typescript of the early chapters.

*16 MARCH   *I am correcting the MS of my* Diary of a Trip to Sardinia [Moore 646]. This typescript is at Texas, with Lawrence's interlinear revisions in black ink. There were further changes before publication of two sections in the *Dial*, and extensive changes before publication as *Sea and Sardinia* in December.

APRIL 1921   At Fontana Vecchia until 9, then leaves for Palermo, Rome and Capri. In Capri at least 15–19. Then to Rome and Florence (22–3). By 27 in Baden-Baden.

SUMMARY   *I shall try to finish* Aaron's Rod *this summer, before finishing* Mr Noon II, *which is funny, but a hair-raiser. First part inno-cent—*Aaron's Rod *innocent* [Secker 38].

22 APRIL   *The title for the Sardinia book Mountsier objected to. I suggested others:* Sardinian Films, *for example* [Moore 649].

MAY 1921   At Ludwig Wilhelmstift, Baden-Baden, Germany.

SUMMARY   Lawrence finished *Aaron's Rod* [A21]. 'The Evening Land' [C99 A27] is signed Baden-Baden, and was probably written on this visit.

2 MAY   Lawrence told Gilbert Cannan that he was trying to go on with *Aaron's Rod*, but did not know if he would succeed.

*8 MAY   To the Brewsters: *I am finishing* Aaron. *And you won't like it* at all. *Instead of bringing him nearer to heaven, in leaps and bounds, he's misbehaving and putting ten fingers to his nose at everything. Damn heaven. Damn holiness. Damn Nirvana. Damn it all* [Moore 653].

12 MAY   Lawrence told Curtis Brown that *Aaron's Rod* was two-thirds done.

*16 MAY   *Here I have got* Aaron's Rod *well under weigh again, and have the end in sight. Nothing impossible in it at all* [Secker 40].

27 MAY   *I have nearly finished my novel* Aaron's Rod, *which I began long ago and could never bring to an end. I began it in the Mecklenburgh Square days. Now suddenly I had a fit of work—sitting away in the woods. And save for the last chapter, it is done. But it won't be popular* [Moore 655]. Lawrence was at 44 Mecklenburgh Square, London, in October and November 1917.

You will be glad to hear that I have as good as finished Aaron's Rod, *that is, it is all done except the last chapter—two days' work. It all came quite suddenly here. But it is a queer book* [Secker 41]. On 1 June Lawrence told Curtis Brown that he had just finished the novel.

JUNE 1921   At Ludwig Wilhelmstift, Baden-Baden, for a few days, then at Hotel Krone, Ebersteinburg, Baden-Baden.

SUMMARY   Lawrence began *Fantasia of the Unconscious* [A22] and rewrote Koteliansky's translation of Bunin's *The Gentleman from San Francisco* [C88 B9].

1 JUNE   Lawrence told Curtis Brown that he had made notes for a second book on psychoanalysis, to be called *Psychoanalysis and the Incest Motive*.

3 JUNE   To Seltzer, from whom Lawrence had just received his copies of *Psychoanalysis and the Unconscious*: *I want you to tell me fairly soon if this sells enough to make it worth while my going on with the next little volume, which continues the development of the theory of the Unconscious. I have begun it, and it should be as interesting, if not*

more, than the first book' [Seltzer 20].

7 JUNE   Lawrence tells Jan Juta that he goes off into the woods each morning to write a sequel to his psychoanalysis book. Lawrence apparently finished the first draft of *Fantasia* this month. The earliest MS, in the John E. Baker collection, is dated June 1921. It contains an epilogue not used in the published version, but printed in *Priest* 337–8. Seltzer published a longer epilogue, and Secker no epilogue at all.

16 JUNE   To Koteliansky: *Yesterday 'The Gent. from S. Francisco' and the pen: very many thanks. Have read 'The Gent.'—and in spite of its lugubriousness, grin with joy. Was Bunin one of the Gorki-Capri crowd?—or only a visitor? But it is screamingly good of Naples and Capri: so comically like the reality: only just a trifle too earnest about it. I will soon get it written over: don't think your text needs much altering* [Moore 656].

Lawrence goes on to suggest that the *Dial* might print the story, which it did, in January 1922. The text was probably revised by Leonard Woolf before publication by the Hogarth Press in May 1922. [See Zytaruk 2, 51–5.].

JULY 1921   At Ebersteinburg until 10. Then Lawrence walked across the Black Forest, arriving Contance 15 and Zell-am-See 20 (Villa Alpensee, Thumersbach).

SUMMARY   Lawrence started to plan *A History of Painting for Children.*

2 JULY   To Curtis Brown: *I have written to de Grey* [of the Medici Society] *that I want title altering to* A History of Italian Painting for Children. *I don't see how one Dürer can represent Germany, and Chardin or Lancret, France, and the awful Rembrandts, the mere Terborch and Van der Goes, Holland. And I won't say a word about the pictures which are not included. The supply of illustrations is too unsatisfactory for a child's list of painting. Whereas there is a fair representation of Italy. And the subject is quite big enough* [Moore 657].

4 JULY   *I am supposed to write* A History of Italian Painting, *for Children—for the Medici Press. Don't know whether I shall ever get it done* [Moore 659].

30 JULY   To Seltzer: *Perhaps when I am cajoled into a good mood, I will write you a Tyrol story—short novel—like 'Wintry Peacock'. Very many thanks for sending the 'Wintry Peacock' proofs* [Seltzer 25].

'Wintry Peacock' appeared in the *Metropolitan* in August. The proofs are heavily revised. The reference to a Tyrol story suggests that Lawrence was already thinking of 'The Captain's Doll'. See October.

AUGUST 1921   At the Villa Aplensee, Thumbersbach, Zell-am-See, until 25, then at 32 Via dei Bardi, Florence.

SUMMARY   *No work doing here: impossible to work in this country: no wits left, all gone loose and scattered. I shan't be sorry to come back to Italy again: but feel Europe is a bit empty altogether. Only the States are worse, I'm sure* [Nehls 2, 68].

At Zell-am-See Lawrence wrote 'Fish' [C94 A27]. He also sent Seltzer a foreword to *Aaron's Rod*, which seems not to have survived, and began to revise that novel.

7 AUG.   Lawrence heard from Curtis Brown that his proposal was not acceptable to the Medici Society: *About the Medici Society—I was sorry to have to make that sudden change. But I couldn't know what lay before me till I had really started to plan the book. And when I had dimly made my plan, I found that the Medici supply of pictures for Holland, Germany, France and Spain was just quite hopelessly inadequate. One* can't *write about pictures unless the pictures are there* [Moore 660].

Lawrence acknowledged the receipt of the typescript of *Aaron's Rod* from Curtis Brown.

14 AUG.   Lawrence told Curtis Brown that he would not be able to return the typescript for some time, since he must go through it carefully. He did not in fact return it until 23 November. By 8 October, however, Lawrence had sent another corrected typescript to Mountsier for Seltzer. Lawrence returned to Curtis Brown proofs for the *English Review*, which published 'Medlars and Sorb Apples' and 'Pomegranate' in the August number, and 'The Revolutionary' in the September.

SEPTEMBER 1921   At 32 Via dei Bardi until 21, then with Brewsters on Capri for a few days. Back at Fontana Vecchia by the end of the month.

SUMMARY   Lawrence began his Venice story, and wrote 'Bat' [C98 A27] and 'Man and Bat' [A27].

1 SEPT. *I find it lovely and cool, and am writing a story about Venice. Later I want to write one about Florence and this house: modern, of course* [Moore 662]. See October.

17 SEPT. Lawrence sent Curtis Brown 'Bat' and 'Man and Bat' [Moore 663].

19 SEPT. Lawrence received from Insel-Verlag the first page-proofs of the German translation of *The Rainbow*.

OCTOBER 1921   At Fontana Vecchia, Taormina, Sicily.

SUMMARY *When I gather myself together I want to get to work. I only did two poems all the summer—'Fish' and 'Bat'. But I did* Harlequinade of the Unconscious. *I am thankful to be at rest for the moment—but feel more than ever come loose from all moorings* [Damon 576–7].

Lawrence continued the Venice novel, revised *Fantasia of the Unconscious*, wrote forewords to *Fantasia* and *Aaron's Rod*, re-wrote 'The Horse Dealer's Daughter' and began 'The Captain's Doll' [A24b].

Secker had published *Women in Love* in June. Philip Heseltine claimed to be libellously portrayed in the character of Halliday in 'a chapter' [Secker 131]. Lawrence returned to Taormina to find the offending pages waiting for him:

8 OCT. *I enclose the altered pages. The Pussum* [Minnie Lucie Channing, Heseltine's mistress, later wife, known as Puma] *I have made a blue-eyed fair-haired little thing. Halliday black and swarthy: the manservant an arab: the flat a house in St John's Wood. For this last item,* please correct in a previous chapter. *Please go through it all carefully, to see there are no discrepancies* [Secker 44].

Secker did not go through it carefully enough. These alterations were made fairly consistently in two early chapters, 'Creme de Menthe' and 'Totem', but were not made at all in the later chapter 'Gudrun at the Pompadour', in which Halliday and Pussum reappear (in the novel as we have it, with different coloured hair and eyes!). This corrupt text has been reprinted ever since, except in the Modern Library edition, which went back to the 1920 Seltzer text. Heseltine was not satisfied with the alterations, but eventually accepted them with £50 damages. See Branda, 314–9, for a fuller account.

I have begun a proper story *novel—in the Venetian lagoons: not pretty pretty—but no sex and no problems: no love, particularly. It won't go in England at all. But I am held up at the moment going over*

the MS of The Child and the Unconscious—*which follows*
Psychoanalysis and the Unconscious. *I like it much better. . . . I have
written a foreword answering the critics: rather funny. . . . I will
collect my short stories for a volume. . . . With all this the Venice story
doesn't look like getting ahead very fast* [Seltzer 26]. The Texas
typescript of *Fantasia of the Unconscious* has extensive interlinear
revision, and twenty-four holograph pages inserted at various points.
The foreword is dated 8 October 1921. It is called 'An Answer to
Some Critics' and has never been published, despite Lawrence's plea to
Seltzer: Do *print the introduction to the* Fantasia [Seltzer 28]. The
collection of stories was to be *England, My England* [A23]. The
Venice novel is heard of only once more. 10 November: *I started a
novel in the Venice lagoons. If I didn't get so disgusted with everybody
and everything I'd finish it* [Secker 45].

By this date Lawrence had sent Mountsier a revised typescript of
Aaron's Rod, probably the one now at the University of Texas [Secker
26].

*18 OCT.   Lawrence has *just finished correcting Fantasia* [Moore 665].
22 OCT. *I am sending you today . . . a small introduction to* Aaron's Rod
[Seltzer 27]. This is different from the one sent from Zell-am-See
[Seltzer 26]. Neither has survived.
25 OCT.   *I am not very busy: just pottering with short stories* [Moore 668].
Lawrence goes on to ask Donald Carswell for information about Scots
military dress: *I want a man in those tight trews in a story.* The story is
'The Captain's Doll'.

*I have only been reading Giovanni Verga lately. He exercises quite
a fascination on me, and makes me feel quite sick at the end. But
perhaps that is only if one knows Sicily.—Do you know if he is
translated into English?—*I Malavoglia *or* Mastro-don Gesualdo—*or*
Novelle Rusticane, *or the other short stories. It would be fun to do
him—his* language *is so fascinating.* Lawrence was to translate
Mastro-don Gesualdo in February 1922, *Little Novels of Sicily* in
March and April 1922, and *Cavalleria Rusticana and Other Stories* in
August 1922 and August and September 1927.
26 OCT.   *Corrected proofs of 'Fannie and Annie' for Hutchinsons. . . .
Have written over 'The Miracle' . . . called now 'The Horse Dealer's
Daughter'. Have nearly finished story: 'The Captain's Doll'* [Tedlock
93].

NOVEMBER 1921   At Fontana Vecchia, Taormina.

SUMMARY   Lawrence finished 'The Captain's Doll' and revised 'The Fox' and several of the stories for *England, My England. I am getting my short stories into order, and settling up my MSS. I want to get all straight. I want to feel free to go away from Europe at any minute. I am so tired of it. It is a dead dog which begins to stink intolerably. Again I entertain the idea of going to America* [Moore 673].

2 NOV.   *I . . . suddenly wrote a very funny long story called 'The Captain's Doll', which I haven't finished yet. But I have just got it high up in the mountains of the Tyrol, and don't quite know how to get it down without breaking its neck* [Moore 670].

7 NOV.   *Send MS of 'The Captain's Doll' to Mrs Carmichael* [Tedlock 94].

10 NOV.   *I am getting together my short stories for a book* [Secker 44].

[Verga] *is extraordinarily good—peasant—quite modern—Homeric —and it would need somebody who could absolutely handle English in the dialect, to translate him. He would be most awfully difficult to translate. That is what tempts me: though it is rather a waste of time, and probably I shall never do it. Though if I don't, I doubt if anyone else will—adequately, at least* [Moore 674]. The adequacy of Lawrence's Verga translations is discussed by Cecchetti, 333–44.

13 NOV.   *Write 'Fox' ending. . . . Had 'The Primrose Path' from Garnett* [Tedlock 94]. 'The Primrose Path' had been typed by Douglas Clayton in July 1913. This typescript survives at Texas, with interlinear corrections in black ink. It has Edward Garnett's name and address at the top of the first page, and Curtis Brown's stamp. There are only minor differences between this revised typescript and the text in *England, My England.* Lawrence's diary records sending 'The Primrose Path' to Mrs Carmichael to be typed on 24 November and again on 1 December, and receiving it back from her and sending it to Curtis Brown 12 December. One would thus expect the Carmichael typescript to incorporate the revisions on the Clayton typescript. But the only other surviving typescript, which is not a carbon of the Clayton typescript, and of which Texas has both the top copy and a carbon, is slightly different, but does not incorporate the interlinear revisions, which were incorporated into the printed text. It seems, therefore, that these revisions were done onto the original Clayton typescript after Lawrence had received it back from Mrs Carmichael. The Original holograph MS also survives, at Nottingham.

15 NOV.   Lawrence had received from Donald Carswell the information he

needed about Scots military dress, for 'The Captain's Doll': *About the trews, that is all I want to know. Very good. I've done the story and can just correct it where it needs* [Moore 675].

16 NOV. *Finish Masaccio picture* [Tedlock 94].

   I have brought the short stories up to scratch, ready for a volume: and written a long short story 'The Captain's Doll', which I think is interesting, and put a long tail to 'The Fox', which has a bobbed short story. Now he careers with a strange and fiery brush [Moore 678].

   Brian Finney: 'Lawrence used the original manuscript version, and not the first published version of this story, when revising and elongating it to about three times its original length. From the point in the story when March fails to agree to Henry's proposal of marriage onwards represent the new second part Lawrence added to his original story to convert it to the length of a novelette' [Finney 3].

23 NOV. Lawrence returned the typescript of *Aaron's Rod* to Curtis Brown, heavily revised.

26 NOV. To Seltzer: *About Aaron: I haven't got any type-written corrected MS, so don't quite know how it stands. I have only my handwritten MS—which luckily I haven't yet burned. If you really must modify Argyle . . . you can do so at your discretion, by just lifting a word or two. I'll go through the Marchesa MS tonight.*

   Argyle was modelled on Norman Douglas, who had a reputation for being foul-mouthed. Lawrence added a post-script: *I have looked through the original MS. It is no good, I can't alter it. But if you like to follow the typescript, which I have often written over, in the scenes you mention, and if you like to leave out what is written over, I don't think you need fear the public much. And if you like to leave out a sentence or two, or alter a phrase or two, do so. But I can't write anything different. Follow the original typescript* [Seltzer 28–9]. See December and January.

   To Seltzer: *'The Fox' and 'The Captain's Doll' are so modern, so new: a new manner. Then I will send seven or so other stories, shorter.—I don't want to start anything serious now before I leave* [Seltzer 29].

   On 1 December Lawrence was to send to Seltzer, via Mountsier, 'Samson and Delilah', 'Hadrian' (published as 'You Touched Me'), 'The Horse Dealer's Daughter', 'Monkey Nuts', 'The Blind Man' and 'Fannie and Annie'. 'The Primrose Path' and 'Tickets Please' went to the typist on the same day. No typescripts of any of these stories except 'The Primrose Path' seem to have survived.

DECEMBER 1921   At Fontana Vecchia, Taormina.

SUMMARY   Lawrence wrote 'The Ladybird' [A24] and re-wrote 'England, My England'. He spent Christmas and the rest of the month in bed with influenza.

7 DEC.   *I am finishing the third of three little novelettes* [Secker 45]. *'England, My England' I am working on* [Moore 680].

12 DEC.   *There remains now only 'England, My England' . . . which I am re-writing. Also the novelette—'The Ladybird'—which is nearly ready* [Moore 680]. Though this letter is dated 7, the postscript reveals it was held back for five days.

17 DEC.   *Of the three novelettes, all are finished* [Secker 46]. 'England, My England', which Lawrence promised to send in about ten days, was probably also with the typist. The three novelettes—'The Ladybird', 'The Fox' and 'The Captain's Doll'— were published by Secker in March 1923 as *The Ladybird*, and by Seltzer in November 1923 as *The Captain's Doll*.

29 DEC.   *I am making some modifications in* Aaron's Rod, *for Seltzer* [Secker 46]. Apparently Seltzer had persuaded Lawrence since 26 November to take a more active part in the 'modification' of *Aaron's Rod*.

118

JANUARY 1922   At Fontana Vecchia, Taormina.

SUMMARY For the first half of the month Lawrence was ill with influenza. He began his translation of Verga's *Mastro-don Gesualdo* [A28], wrote his introduction to Maurice Magnus' *Memoirs of the Foreign Legion* [B14] and, possibly, 'He-goat' and 'She-goat' [A27].

'He-goat' and 'She-goat' were written before Lawrence left Taormina, probably in December or January. On 2 November Lawrence has written that his she-goat was overdue. In the poem he says:

Yet she has such adorable spurty kids, like spurts of black ink.
And in a month again is as if she had never had them.

9 JAN. *I have finished writing for a bit, thank God. I am sick of the sight and thought of manuscripts. But to amuse myself on shipboard and so on I shall probably go on with a translation of the Sicilian novel* Mastro-don Gesualdo, *by Giovanni Verga* [Seltzer 30]. Lawrence did not wait for embarcation, since by 8 February he was *nearly half-way through* [Moore 691].

14 JAN. *The typed MS of* Aaron's Rod *came today. I again tried altering it. I can modify the bits of Argyle's speech. But the essential scenes of Aaron and the Marchesa it is impossible to me to alter* [Seltzer 32]. Argyle was based on Norman Douglas, a sample of whose speech can be seen below.

The Texas typescript of *Aaron's Rod* does not correspond to the published text, and the significant changes are almost all in the Argyle speeches and in the scenes between Aaron and the Marchesa. Either Lawrence made these changes on another typescript or on the proofs, or someone else made them. From Argyle's speeches we lose not only such fruity little Douglasisms as: *Seems I've grown in the arsal region* or: *Damned filthy methylated spirit they sell. I asked the man if he peed in it*, but lengthy passages such as:

'I don't know what cock-bird committed adultery with the holy dove, before it laid the Easter egg, I'm sure. But there must have been one you know. There must have been one. Ha! Ha! Ha!—I'd give a lot to have seen him at it. Soul is born of—believe me. Of nothing but —.'

We cannot print the word used by Argyle, though it is a quite common one, often chalked on walls by little boys.

The love-making of Aaron and the Marchesa is very heavily cut. Three consecutive paragraphs are missing:

But afterwards her fingers traced him and touched him with a strange fine timidity, and a strange, strange, curiosity. And he felt

119

somewhere beyond himself—as it were ship-wrecked. He was acutely sensible to the delicate, inordinate curiosity of her finger-tips, and the stealth, and the innermost secrecy of the approach of her power.—Nay, nay, was this the woman he had known as Cleopatra, with the rouge on her lips and the fard on her face, and the elegant, frightening Paris gown?

He slept for a very little while, and woke suddenly, and his desire had an element of cruelty in it: something rather brutal. He took his way with her now, and she had no chance now of the curious opposition, because of the way he took her. And afterwards, she clung suddenly to his breast, and curled her head there, as if hiding, and as if suddenly convulsed with shyness or shame of what had been: but still pleased. And so curled, with her head on his breast and her hair tangling about his throat, it was she who slept now. And after a long while, he slept too.

And when he woke, and still the desire came back, with something dogged in its persistence, she seemed to wince a little. But perhaps she was pleased too. But this time she took no part, really.

27 JAN. *Sent* Dregs *and Magnus Memoir to Mountsier* [Tedlock 95]. Dregs was Maurice Magnus' own title for *Memoirs of the Foreign Legion*. On 12 February Lawrence wrote: *I did such a 'Memoir of Maurice Magnus' to go in front of his horrid Legion book* [Moore 692].

Before proceeding with this book, Lawrence had received from Magnus' executor Norman Douglas a carte blanche: 'Whoever wants it may ram it up his exhaust pipe. . . . By all means do what you like with the MS. . . . Pocket all the cash yourself' [23 December 1921]. Thus Douglas' later accusations against Lawrence were completely unjustified. See F2 and C138 [reprinted in *Phoenix* as 'The Late Mr Maurice Magnus: A Letter'].

FEBRUARY 1922   At Fontana Vecchia until 20. At Palermo 20–3, 23–6 at Naples. On 26 embarked on the Osterley for Ceylon.

SUMMARY *I am filling in my time translating a Sicilian novel.* Mastro-don Gesualdo, *by Giovanni Verga: he died last month. It is so good. But I am on thorns, can't settle* [Moore 692].

8 FEB.   *Nearly half-way through* [Moore 691].
15 FEB.   *Sent half Gesualdo to Mrs Carmichael* [Tedlock 95]. Lawrence

had been reading and thinking about translating Verga since October 1921.

MARCH 1922   The Osterley arrived in Kandy, Ceylon, 13.

SUMMARY   Achsah Brewster: 'Generally we sat on the north verandah in the morning. . . . Lawrence sat curled up with a school-boy's copy-book in his hand, writing away. He was translating Giovanni Verga's short stories from the Sicilian. Across the pages of the copy-book his hand moved rhythmically, steadily, unhesitatingly, leaving a trail of exquisite, small writing as legible as print. No blots, no scratchings marred its beauty. When the book was finished, he wrapped and tied it up, sending it off to the publisher. All of this went on in the family circle. Frieda would come for consultation as to whether the rabbit's legs should be embroidered in yellow or white. The pen would be lifted a moment then go on across the page. Sometimes Lawrence would stop and consult us about the meaning of a word; considering seriously whatever comments were offered, [Brewster 250].

Lawrence must have finished *Mastro-don Gesualdo* in March, since his Introductory Note, which follows the translation in the holograph, is dated Kandy, March 1922. He then began *Little Novels of Sicily* [A30]. Wrote 'Elephant' [C104 A27].

*7 MARCH   *I spend the day talking small-talk with Australians on board—rather nice people—and translating* Mastro-don Gesualdo *and having meals—and time passes like a sleep* [Moore 696].

23 MARCH   The Perahera described in the poem 'Elephant' took place.

*25 MARCH   *I don't believe I shall ever work here* [Huxley 541].

APRIL 1922   At Ardnaree, Kandy, Ceylon until 22, then at Braemore, Bullers Road, Colombo, until 24, then on board the RMS Orsova, heading for Freemantle, Western Australia.

SUMMARY   *I merely translate Giovanni Verga—Sicilian—*Mastro-don Gesualdo *and* Novelle Rusticane—*very good—to keep myself occupied* [Moore 702]. Lawrence wrote 'Apostrophe of a Buddhist Monk' [Brewster 50 CP].

17 APRIL   *Of course one doesn't work here at all—never would* [Zytaruk 241].

1922

*22 APRIL   To Curtis Brown: *I expect Mountsier will send you shortly the first half of another Verga translation, of the* Novelle Rusticane:—*short stories of Sicily. I suggest as title the title of one of the stories 'Black Bread'* [Huxley 544].

MAY 1922   The Orsova arrived at Freemantle 4. At Leithdale, Darlington, until 18. Then on board the Malwa, arriving Sydney 27. On 29 the Lawrences took up residence at Wyewurk, Thirroul, New South Wales until August.

SUMMARY   *Tell them I have sent my Muse into a nunnery while I took a look at the world* [Damon 606].
At the end of the month Lawrence began *Kangaroo* [A26].

17 MAY   The proofs of 'Fish' for the *English Review* [C94] were sent to Lawrence, but it is not known whether he corrected them.

*20 MAY   *I am not thinking of any work* [Brewster 53].

†29 MAY   *I've got a* Heimweh *for Europe: Sicily, England, Germany.* [Moore 706].

    I've got a burning bitter nostalgia for Europe, for Sicily, for old civilisation and for real human understanding [Huxley 548].

    He longed for Europe with hungry longing. . . . It was May—end of May—almost bluebell time, and the green leaves coming out on the hedges. Or the tall corn under the olives in Sicily. . . . Or Bavaria with gentian and yellow globe flowers, and the Alps still icy [Kangaroo 14].

    Since Lawrence mentions this nostalgia for Europe twice in letters of this day, and nowhere else, it seems likely that he wrote the corresponding passage in *Kangaroo* within a day or two.

JUNE 1922   At Wyewurk, Thirroul, New South Wales, Australia.

SUMMARY   Lawrence wrote more than half of *Kangaroo* [A26].

3 JUNE   To Mabel Dodge: *I have started a novel and if I can go on with it, I shall stay till I've finished it—till about end of August. But if I can't work I shall come on to America* [Luhan 23].

9 JUNE   To Thomas Seltzer: *I have begun a novel, and it seems to be going well—pitched in Australia. Heaven knows if anybody will like it—no love interest at all so far—don't intend any—no sex either. . . . I should like very much to write an American novel, after this Australian one:*

122

on something the same lines [Seltzer 35].

11 JUNE To Seltzer: *I think I'm calling my new novel* Kangaroo. *It goes so far—queer show—pray the gods to be with me, that I finish by August* [Setlzer 36].

20 JUNE *Am stuck in my novel* [Luhan 25].

*21 JUNE Frieda Lawrence: 'L. has written a novel, gone at it full tilt to page 305, but has come to a stop and kicks' [Luhan 25]. At this stage Lawrence was six pages into chapter 9.

To Seltzer: *I have done more than half of the novel: the Lord alone knows what anybody will think of it: no love at all, and attempt at revolution. I do hope I shall be able to finish it: not like Aaron, who stuck for two years, and Mr Noon, who has been now nearly two years at a full stop. But I think I see my way* [Seltzer 39].

JULY 1922 At Wyewurk, Thirroul, New South Wales.

SUMMARY Lawrence finished *Kangaroo* and wrote 'Kangaroo' [A27]. *There is a great fascination in Australia. But for the remains of a fighting Conscience, I would stay. One can be so absolutely indifferent to the world one has been previously condemned to. . . . If I stayed here six months I should have to stay for ever—there is something so remote and far off and utterly indifferent to our European world, in the very air. I should go a bit further away from Sydney, and go 'bush'.—We don't know one single soul—not a soul comes to the house. And I can't tell you how I like it. I could live like that for ever: and drop writing even a letter: sort of come undone from everything* [Moore 712].

3 JULY *Have nearly written* Kangaroo [Tedlock 96].

9 JULY *I was in Sydney, and the consul will give the visas all right* [Luhan 27]. According to the penultimate page of the penultimate chapter (probably the last chapter in the version written in Australia) of *Kangaroo*, it was on this visit to Sydney that Lawrence fed peppermints to the kangaroos at Sydney Zoo. The poem contains the line: *There, she shan't have any more peppermint drops.* Since 9 July was a Sunday, the visit must have been a few days earlier.

I have nearly finished my novel here—but such a novel! Even the Ulysseans will spit at it [Moore 712].

15 JULY Lawrence finished *Kangaroo* [Seltzer 40].

24 JULY *Having done my novel I am out of work until we sail—but we have only a fortnight longer here* [Brewster 59].

1922

AUGUST 1922   At Thirroul until 9, then to Sydney, to embark 10 on the *Tahiti* for San Francisco. On 15 at Wellington, New Zealand, 20 at Raratonga, 22 at Tahiti.

SUMMARY   Four of the *Cavalleria Rusticana* [A39] stories—the title story, 'The She-Wolf', 'Fantasticalities' and 'Jeli the Shepherd'—are in a notebook which has a similar watermark to the third *Kangaroo* notebook, and has a Sydney address in the front. After the translation comes 'Journey to the Southwest'—the first thing Lawrence wrote in Taos. In September Lawrence suggested that Leonard Woolf should ask Curtis Brown to let him see the MS of *Cavalleria Rusticana* [Moore 716]. The remaining stories were not translated until 1927. It seems almost certain, therefore, that these four were done on board the *Tahiti*. [See Tedlock 272–3].

SEPTEMBER 1922   The *Tahiti* arrived at San Francisco 4. The Lawrences left for Lamy 8, spent a night in Santa Fe, and arrived in Taos, New Mexico 11, Lawrence's thirty-seventh birthday. On 14 Lawrence was taken on a five-day trip to the Jicarilla Apache Reservation.

SUMMARY   *It is all an experience. But one's heart is never touched at all—neither by landscape, Indians, or Americans. Perhaps that is better so. Time, I suppose, that one left off feeling, and merely began to register.—Here, I register* [Moore 720].

Lawrence wrote 'Indians and an Englishman' [C102 and *Phoenix*] and 'Taos' [C103 and *Phoenix*] and began a projected novel based on the life of Mabel Luhan. The first chapter is published as 'The Wilful Woman' in *The Princess and Other Stories*, Penguin 1971.

20 SEPT.   According to Mabel Luhan [52] Lawrence wrote 'Indians and an Englishman' immediately after his return from the Apache trip. The MS he left with her contained also the first six paragraphs of 'Certain Americans and an Englishman' [Luhan 58].

22 SEPT.   To Seltzer: *Could you send me too that Herman Melville book*—Herman Melville, Poet and Mystic.—*I will go over the* Studies in C.A. Literature *again.* [Seltzer 43].
Lawrence wrote the first chapter. 'Journey to the Southwest', of his projected novel [Luhan 58ff].

†23 SEPT.   *So you are mise en scène. . . . I have done your 'train' episode and brought you to Lamy at 3 in the morning* [Moore 724]. This letter asks Mabel for detailed notes of her experiences. Frieda lost no time in

124

making impossible the intimate co-operation between Lawrence and
Mabel which this project would have entailed. Apparently Lawrence
produced no more than the few sketchy notes printed by Tedlock [53].
29–30 'Taos' describes the San Geronimo Festival which took place on
these days.

OCTOBER 1922   At Taos, New Mexico, U.S.A.

SUMMARY   Lawrence wrote his review of Ben Hecht's *Fantazius Mallare*
[C101 Moore 725], revised *Kangaroo*, wrote at least two poems, and
'Certain Americans and an Englishman' [C100].

4 OCT.   To Harriet Monroe, editor of *Poetry: If there is time make the tiny
alterations at the end of 'Turkey Cock'* [Huxley 559]. 'Turkey Cock'
appeared in the November number of *Poetry*.

12 OCT.   Lawrence sent his first contribution to *The Laughing Horse*. His
outspoken review of *Fantazius Mallare* caused its editor, Ray Chans-
lor, to be expelled from the University of California. [See Roberts
264.]

16 OCT.   To Seltzer: *Have gone through* Kangaroo—*many changes—it is
now as I wish it. I want to* keep in *the war-experience piece: and I
have made a new last chapter* [Seltzer 44].

19 OCT.   *I have done two poems here: my first in America* [Damon 622].
Five of the poems in *Birds, Beasts and Flowers* are signed Taos, and
were therefore written before Lawrence left Taos on 1 December.
They are 'Eagle in New Mexico', 'The Red Wolf', 'Men in New
Mexico', 'Autumn in Taos' and 'Spirits Summoned West'. 'Autumn in
Taos' is likely to be one of the earliest, since it describes the yellow
aspen leaves which would be gone by late October. The other was
probably 'Eagle in New Mexico', which Mabel dates three months
before 15 January 1923 [Luhan 102].

25 OCT.   Lawrence's letter to Willie Hopkin about the death of his wife
Sallie ends with the following postscript: *England seems full of graves
to me*. This is also the first line of 'Spirits Summoned West'.

30 OCT.   *It has been the Bursum Bill till we're sick of it. I've done an article*
[Moore 727]. Lawrence's article on the Bursum Bill is 'Certain
Americans and an Englishman'.

NOVEMBER 1922   At Taos.

SUMMARY   Lawrence probably wrote two or three of the poems listed in October, and rewrote *Studies in Classic American Literature* [A25].

19 NOV.   *I am busy with Studies in Classic A. Lit.—you'll like them much better, I think: much sharper, quicker* [Seltzer 47].

*28 NOV.   *I've nearly done Studies. It is the American Demon indeed. Lord knows what you'll think of them. But they'll make a nice little book: much shorter* [Seltzer 48].

DECEMBER 1922   At Del Monte Ranch, Questa, New Mexico.

SUMMARY   Lawrence finished his revision of *Studies in Classic American Literature*, and probably wrote 'Blue Jay' [A27]. *It is good fun on this ranch—quite wild—Rocky Mts—desert with Rio Grande Canyon away spreading below—great and really beautiful landscape—looking far, far west. We ride off to the Rio Grande to the hot springs, and bathe—and we chop wood and wagon it in, and all that. But there's no inside to the life: all outside. I don't believe there ever will be any inside to American life—they seem so dead—till they are all destroyed* [Moore 733].

5 DEC.   *Have done all* Studies *except the last two. . . . Will finish in a week (Deo volente)* [Seltzer 52].

17 DEC.   *Am not writing here* [Moore 733].

JANUARY 1923 At Del Monte Ranch, Questa.

SUMMARY Lawrence revised *Little Novels of Sicily*, and began to prepare *Birds, Beasts and Flowers* for publication. He wrote 'Bibbles' and 'Mountain Lion'.

4 JAN. To Seltzer: *I enclose the last words of* Kangaroo: *the last page. . . . I am going through the Verga MS—Black Bread—the short sketches. . . . Yesterday William killed a steer—and that young Pips would not be kept away—became shamefully sick—got well spanked—and so has gone to live with the Danes. There let her stay. She's got no loyalty. To me, loyalty is far before love. Love seems usually to be just a dirty excuse for disloyalties* [Seltzer 54–5]. On 1 February Lawrence was to tell Seltzer *there is a poem to Bibbles.* Pips is another name for Bibbles.

23 JAN. *Am busy doing the Birds, Beasts. They will soon be done* [Seltzer 60]. Lawrence was also concerning himself about the jacket design, and is probably responsible for the one used.

FEBRUARY 1923 At Del Monte Ranch, Questa.

SUMMARY Lawrence wrote 'Surgery for the Novel, or a Bomb' [C105 and *Phoenix*] and 'Model Americans', a review of Stuart Sherman's *Americans* [C107 and *Phoenix*], and finished the preparation of *Birds, Beasts and Flowers*.

1 FEB. Lawrence sent Seltzer 'Surgery for the Novel' which he had just finished [Seltzer 62, 64].

10 FEB. *Sent Seltzer MS of Birds, Beasts, and galleys of Capts Doll.* [Tedlock 96].

16 FEB. *Sent proofs of Ladybird to Seltzer* [Tedlock 96].

25 FEB. *Sent proofs of Sherman article to* Dial [Tedlock 96].

MARCH 1923 At Del Monte Ranch, Questa until 18. Left Santa Fe 20. El Paso 21; Mexico City 23 (Hotel Monte Carlo).

SUMMARY Lawrence wrote 'American Eagle'.

14 MARCH To Seltzer: *I send you the last poem I shall write in the US this time: 'The American Eagle'* [Seltzer 79].

APRIL 1923 At Hotel Monte Carlo until 27, except for trip to Puebla, Tehuacan and Orizaba 13–21. Then at Zaragoza 4, Chapala, Mexico until July.

SUMMARY Lawrence wrote 'Au Revoir, U.S.A.' [C114 *Phoenix*]. *I should never be able to write on this continent—something in the spirit opposes one's going forth* [Seltzer 89].

8 APRIL Frieda Lawrence: 'We saw a big bullfight—A wild and low excited crowd 4 bands, then a nice young bull and the men with their mantles dodging it so quickly, the bull jumped the barrier and the attendants jumping so cleverly was fun—but then oh horrors, blind-folded horses led up to it by picadores who prick the bull with lances, the bull of course thinks it's the horse that hurts him, and with his horns he goes for the horse—I know no more, I fled and Lawr white with rage followed me—My last impression—a smell of flesh and blood and a heap of bowels on the ground—vile and degraded the whole thing—Very interesting an old pre-Aztec place with temples and pyramids and terrible carvings—Xexalcoatl the God of sacrifice human hearts his speciality' [Seltzer 87–8]. It seems to have been some weeks before Lawrence wrote up the bull-fight as the beginning of *Quetzalcoatl*. See 26 May. The visit to Teotihuacan is recorded in 'Au Revoir, U.S.A.'

*9 APRIL *I feel I would like to settle down and do a novel here* [Seltzer 86].

MAY 1923 At Zaragoza 4, Chapala, Mexico.

SUMMARY Lawrence began *The Plumed Serpent* [A33] as *Quetzalcoatl*. *Mexico is queer: very savage underneath. It still is unsafe to live in the country: and not very safe anywhere. Somebody tried to get in here last night. It seems to me Mexico will never be safe. I have my ups and downs of feeling about the place. It will end, I suppose, in my staying as long as it takes me to write a novel—if I can write a novel here* [Seltzer 93].

2 MAY *I shall begin a novel now, as soon as I can take breath* [Seltzer 91].

9 MAY To Seltzer: *I just sent you the first lot of* Studies *proofs: as far as the end of Poe. . . . I'd like the revisions made. There are one or two serious alterations in the first essay, that are important to me. . . . I have made two false starts at a novel here. Shall make a third start tomorrow* [Seltzer 93].

*22 MAY *The enemy almost gets us down sometimes. Am having a hard*

128

fight myself. The enemy of all the world. Doesn't want me to write my novel either. Pazienza! [Seltzer 94].

26 MAY   *I hope my novel will go all right. If it does, I ought to finish it—in its first rough form—by the end of June. . . . I am having the first slight scene of my novel—the beginning of a bull-fight in Mexico City—typed now, and will send it in two days' time. It is complete in itself* [Moore 743].

30 MAY   Frieda Lawrence: 'Lawrence is writing a novel already 250 pages—he sits by the lake under a tree and writes.'

*31 MAY   *I have already written ten chapters* [Moore 744].

JUNE 1923   At Chapala.

SUMMARY   Lawrence almost finished *Quetzalcoatl*.

*8 JUNE   *Novel more than half done* [Seltzer 96].

*10 JUNE   Frieda Lawrence: 'Lawr— is at page 350 of a most surprising novel—Lawr— says it will take Thomas all his time to publish it—I think it is the most splendid thing he ever did' [Seltzer 96].

   I like my new novel best of all—much. But it's perhaps too different for most folks: two-thirds done [Seltzer 97].

15 JUNE   To Thomas Seltzer: *All right, I'll go over the Whitman essay again. . . . The novel has gone well. Shall I call it* Quetzalcoatl? *Or will people be afraid to ask for a book with that name.—I've done 415 MS pages—except about another 100. It interests me, means more to me than any other novel of mine. This is my real novel of America. But you may just hold up your hands with horror. No sex* [Seltzer 99].

27 JUNE   *The novel is nearly finished—near enough to leave. I must come to New York—and go to England* [Priest 373]. *Quetzalcoatl* ends at page 469. The last chapter is very like the last chapter of *The Plumed Serpent*, with the loading of the spangled bull into the boat, and the new-born ass-foal, but with nothing of the last eight or nine pages. It seems not quite finished. The MS ends: *Under these trying circumstances Kate tried to get on with her packing.*

JULY 1923   At Chapala until 9, then via Laredo, San Antonio, New Orleans and Washington to New York, arriving 19

SUMMARY   *I expect we shall arrive in New York on Wednesday. I shall stay long enough to correct all proofs and get my MS typed—then I suppose we shall go on to Europe. I am not very keen even on going to England. I think what I would like best would be to go back to Mexico. If we were a few people we could make a life in Mexico. Certainly with this world I am at war* [Huxley 572].

26 JULY Lawrence sent corrected galley proofs of *Kangaroo* to Curtis Brown, and promised the proofs of *Birds, Beasts and Flowers* in a couple of days. The proofs of *Masto-don Gesualdo* were still to be done.

AUGUST 1923 In New York until 21, then to Buffalo until 27. Arrived Los Angeles 28.

SUMMARY Lawrence finished his proof-correcting marathon, revised Koteliansky's translation of Gorky's *Reminiscences of Andreyev*, and wrote 'A Spiritual Record' [C110 and *Phoenix*].

7 AUG. *I've been very busy doing proofs here: of* Kangaroo, *my novel: and* Birds, Beasts and Flowers: *poems: and* Mastro-don Gesualdo, *the Verga novel. . . . Now I shall have a breathing space* [Moore 749].

*13 AUG. To Koteliansky: *I got your MS from the* Dial *today. They accept it, and I am going through it at once* [Zytaruk 258].

17 AUG. *I went through your Gorky MS and returned it to* Dial. *I made the English correct—and a little more flexible—but didn't change the style, since it was yours and Katherine's. But the first ten pages were a bit crude* [Zytaruk 259].

Maxim Gorky's *Reminiscences of Leonid Andreyev* was published in 1924 both in the *Adelphi* and the *Dial* as translated by Katherine Mansfield and S. S. Koteliansky. Both Katherine Mansfield and Lawrence had in fact gone over Koteliansky's original translation. [See Zytaruk xxix–xxx.]

*30 AUG. *I want to do the article for Canby, and if I can, put together Miss Skinner's Australian novel—which is good, if only threaded* [Seltzer 107]. Henry Seidel Canby was the editor of the *New York Evening Post Literary Review*. Two days earlier Lawrence had received from him a review copy of *A Second Contemporary Verse Anthology*. His review appeared there 29 September.

SEPTEMBER 1923 In Los Angeles until 25, then to Palm Springs and Guaymas.

SUMMARY Lawrence began *The Boy in the Bush* [A29] and wrote 'The Proper Study' [C113 and *Phoenix*].

2 SEPT. To Mollie Skinner: *I have read* The House of Ellis *carefully—such good stuff in it: but without unity or harmony. I'm afraid as it stands you'd never find a publisher. Yet I hate to think of it all wasted. I like the quality of so much of it. But you have no constructive power.—If you like I will take it and recast it, and make a book of it* [Moore 751]. For Mollie Skinner's account of her relationship with Lawrence see her *The Fifth Sparrow*.

*15 SEPT. Lawrence received the MS of Frederick Carter's *Dragon of the Apocalypse*, and began to go through it, improving the punctuation and style, and trying to make it less obscure, in an effort to help Carter to find a publisher.

17 SEPT. To J. M. Murry: *I asked Seltzer to send you on an article I posted him, which the NY.* Nation *wanted—to send it you immediately it was typed—'The Proper Study'. I'm afraid I wrote it more with the* Adelphi *in mind than the* Nation [Moore 753]. The essay appeared in the *Adelphi* in December, but not in the *Nation*.

*24 SEPT. To Adele Seltzer: *Also I posted in the parcel the first part of the* Boy in the Bush, *the Western Australia novel* [Seltzer 111]. This was Lawrence's title for the novel Mollie Skinner had called *The House of Ellis*.

OCTOBER 1923 Left Guaymas for Navojoa, Sonora, 1. At Minas Nuevas, near Alamos, 3–4. Left Navojoa, 5. At Mazatlan, 6–9; 10–14 at Tepic, Nayarit; 16 at Hotel Garcia, Guadalajara.

SUMMARY *I think I shall go ahead with that, the Boy, to finish it before I try* Quetzalcoatl *again, because this is much more important to me, my* Quetzalcoatl. *The Boy might be popular—unless the ending is a bit startling.—I sometimes feel that, when these two books are off my hands, I shall give up writing for a time—perhaps a few years. I get so tired of the continual feeling of canaillerie one gets from the public and from people* [Seltzer 115].

*20 OCT. *I'll see if I can write a few little sketches for* Vanity Fair [Seltzer 116]. About this time Lawrence began the notebook described by

Tedlock [134–6] containing essays and notes for essays all beginning 'On . . .'. Two of these essays, 'On Human Destiny' [C117 and *Phoenix 2*] and 'On Being a Man' [C121 and *Phoenix 2*] appeared in *Vanity Fair*. 'On Being Religious' [C116 and *Phoenix*] was published in *The Adelphi* in February 1924. One complete essay in the notebook 'On Taking the Next Step' remains unpublished, though the ending is printed by Tedlock [206]. The notes also contain the germ of the later essay 'Books' [*Phoenix*]. The essays were written up for publication in December.

NOVEMBER 1923   At Hotel Garcia, Guadalajara, until 16, then to Mexico City (Hotel Monte Carlo) until 21. Sailed on the Toledo from Vera Cruz 22, for England. At Havana, Cuba, 25.

SUMMARY   Lawrence finished *The Boy in the Bush*.

1 NOV.   To Mollie Skinner: *I have been busy over your novel, as I travelled. The only thing was to write it all out again, following your MS almost exactly, but giving a unity, a rhythm, and a little more psychic development than you had done. I have come now to Book IV. The end will have to be different, a good deal different. . . . Your hero Jack is not quite so absolutely blameless an angel, according to me. You left the character psychologically at a standstill all the way: the same boy at the beginning and the end. I have tried, taking your inner cue, to make a rather daring development, psychologically. You may disapprove* [Moore 760]. Mollie Skinner wept, but acquiesced.

10 NOV.   *The Australian novel is very nearly done* [Moore 762].

15 NOV.   To Mollie Skinner: *I finished the novel yesterday. . . . I think quite a lot of it* [Huxley 585].

Idella Purnell: 'He drew me a number of very fine cover designs for *Palms*, several of which I used' [Nehls 2, 268]. Lawrence also contributed to the Christmas 1923 number of *Palms* [C115 Nehls 2, 268–9] a short piece called 'A Britisher Has a Word with Harriett Monroe'–an answer to Miss Monroe's piece 'The Editor in England' in the October *Poetry*.

DECEMBER 1923   Lawrence was in London by 14, at 110 Heath Street, Hampstead. On 29 he went to spend the New Year with his family in the Midlands.

SUMMARY   Lawrence wrote 'On Coming Home' [C240 and *Phoenix 2*], wrote or rewrote (see October) 'On Being Religious' [C116 and *Phoenix*].

24 DEC.   *I am doing a series of articles for the* Adelphi. *The February number will contain a very caustic article by me, against England: 'On Coming Home'. Also another article, the first of a series: 'On Being Religious'.—I want to write further 'On Being a Man'—and: 'On Writing a Book'—and 'On Reading a Book'. Probably I shall expand it to six essays* [Seltzer 127].

In the event 'On Coming Home' proved too caustic for Murry, who rejected it. It was never published until 1958. He did, however, print 'On Being Religious' in the February number, 'On Human Destiny' in March, and 'On Being a Man' in September. The two projected book essays were combined in 'Books'.

JANUARY 1924   At 110 Heath Street, Hampstead, London, until 23, except for a visit to Frederick Carter at Pontesbury, Shropshire, 3–5. Then at Hotel de Versailles, Paris.

SUMMARY   Lawrence wrote 'On Being a Man' [C121, A53, *Phoenix 2*], 'Dear Old Horse, A London Letter' [C120, Moore 767], 'A Paris Letter' [C139 and *Phoenix*] and probably 'Jimmy and the Desperate Woman' [C125 A41], 'The Last Laugh' [B15 A41] and 'Books' [*Phoenix*].

9 JAN.   Lawrence sent his London Letter to the *Laughing Horse*.

*11 JAN.   Lawrence made stylistic alterations in Frederick Carter's essay 'The Ancient Science of Astrology' before submitting it to *The Adelphi*, where it appeared in April.

13 JAN.   To Mollie Skinner: *I have got the complete typescript of* The Boy in the Bush *now, and am going through it* [Moore 772].

*22 JAN.   Lawrence sent Curtis Brown *The Boy in the Bush*, also an article, probably 'On Being a Man'.

To Mabel Luhan: *Yes, I liked 'Fairytale'. And your poems do amuse me* [Moore 772]. One of the poems Mabel sent Lawrence at this time was 'The Ballad of a Bad Girl' [Luhan 137]. Lawrence did a drawing 'The Bad Girl in the Pansy Bed' illustrating this poem in *The Laughing Horse*, May 1924.

27 JAN.   *It's a queer thing to be in the Tuileries on a Sunday afternoon and watch the crowd drag through the Galleries* ['Paris Letter']. The letter was already sent to Willard Johnson by 1 February.

*29 JAN.   Lawrence wrote to Catherine Carswell that he was *trying to amuse myself by writing stories* [Carswell 215]. The stories he probably began at this time were 'Jimmy and the Desperate Woman' and 'The Last Laugh'.

* 31 JAN.   To Kot=eliansky: *I send back the proofs. . . . I was trying to write a couple of stories, keep myself going* [Moore 773–4]. The proofs may have been of 'On Being Religious', which appeared in *The Adelphi* in February.

FEBRUARY 1924   At Hotel de Versailles, Paris, until 6. At Ludwig-Wilhemstift, Baden-Baden, until 19. Back at the Hotel de Versailles 21. In London, Garland's Hotel, Pall Mall, by 26.

SUMMARY   Lawrence wrote 'The Border Line' [C123 A41], his review of Dr John Oman's *The Book of Revelation* [*Adelphi*, April 1924, and *Phoenix 2*], and 'Letter from Germany' [C216 and *Phoenix*].

134

2 FEB. *Keep myself amused here dodging round a bit and trying to write a story* [Moore 774]. That the three short stories Lawrence was working on while in Europe were 'Jimmy and the Desperate Woman', 'The Last Laugh' and 'The Border Line' is revealed when he sends these three to Curtis Brown on 4 April.

15 FEB. Lawrence sent his review of Oman's book to Murry.

19 FEB. Lawrence sent his 'Letter from Germany' to *The New Statesman*.

MARCH 1924   Left London for New York 5 on RMS Aquitania. Arrived 11. Left New York 18 for Taos. Arrived 22.

SUMMARY   At the end of the month Lawrence probably began to rewrite his three recent short stories before sending them to 'Spud' Johnson to be typed.

APRIL 1924   At Taos.

SUMMARY   *F. has got her little ranch here: and I think we shall stay till late autumn—therefore I shan't get the* Quetzalcoatl *novel done this year. I don't feel much like working at anything just now* [Seltzer 132]. Lawrence wrote 'Indians and Entertainment' [C126 A37], 'The Dance of the Sprouting Corn' [C122 A37], 'O! Americans!' [C221 A80], and also, possibly, 'The Overtone' [A63].

Brett dates the conception of *David* in this month: 'As we plod along, you say suddenly to Ida [Rauh]: "Ida, what kind of play do you like best?" Ida, surprised, replies: "Oh, I like stories from the Bible best". You say: "Do you know the story of David's wife, Michel?" "No," says Ida. "After David came back from the wars, Michel said, 'I'll never live with you again,' and she never did. Do you like that story, Ida?" Ida says, laughing: "Yes, I think it's perfect." and you reply with a laugh, saying, "I'll write a play about it for you"' [Brett 60].

4 APRIL   To Seltzer: *I am busy doing a few short stories—I wish they'd stay shorter. But they are the result of Europe, and perhaps a bit dismal* [Seltzer 131]. The only new story Lawrence could have written at this time is 'The Overtone'. On this same date Lawrence sent 'Jimmy and the Desperate Woman', 'The Last Laugh' and 'The Border Line' to Curtis Brown. At least the last two had been re-written.

10 APRIL Lawrence sent to Secker his jacket design for *The Boy in the Bush.* It was not used [Secker 57].

20 APRIL Lawrence sent 'Indians and Entertainment' to Curtis Brown, already typed.

'O! Americans!' contains the lines:

> Today is Easter Sunday: Christ Risen! Two days ago was Good
>> Friday: Christ Crucified!
> On Good Friday the big white men of the Indian Bureau and big
>> white men from Washington drove out to the pueblo,
>> summoned the old Indian men, and held a meeting
>> behind closed doors [CP 777].

The only Easter Sunday Lawrence was in Taos was 20 April 1924.

23 APRIL *This is the Wednesday after Easter, after Christ risen and the corn germinated. They dance on Monday and on Tuesday. Wednesday is the third and last dance of this green resurrection* ['Dance of the Sprouting Corn'].

MAY 1924 Went to Lobo from Taos, to build up the ranch 5 [Tedlock 98].

SUMMARY *Naturally I don't write when I slave building the house—my arms feel so heavy, like a navvy's, though they look as thin as ever* [Seltzer 137]. Lawrence wrote the first version of 'Pan in America' [*Phoenix*].

2 MAY To Seltzer: *I send you here the design for the book-jacket. I took Brett's design and worked it out in the two colours myself—think it is very effective, don't you? I am sending by the same post the duplicate of Secker's proofs for* The Boy in the Bush. *There are a few alterations—not much* [Seltzer 133]. Seltzer used the Brett/Lawrence jacket design for *The Boy in the Bush.*

*12 MAY To Mabel Luhan: My article—'Pan in America'—will, I think, have to have two parts. I'll see if I can finish first half this evening, and send it to Spoodle to type [Moore 788].

The article was to be completely rewritten, probably the following month, by which time Lawrence had been able to develop a relationship with the pine tree outside his door, which gave him the splendid central section of the later version. In this early version there is only the purely theoretical passage: *Then, in those days, when the world was still Pan, one man would find, perhaps, one particular tree that was his friend and his giver. Or perhaps a whole tribe would find one tree—or one grove of trees.*

*14 MAY   To Mabel Luhan: *I haven't finished the article yet—too many things to do, till late evening. But I had said the things you wrote about the Indians, differently. At present I feel a trifle discouraged, don't want to write* [Luhan 200].

JUNE 1924   At Lobo Ranch.

SUMMARY   *As for myself, I am a wandering soul. I want to go down to Old Mexico at the end of September, and my wife will go with me. It means abandoning this place, which is a pity. We should probably come back next April. I haven't been doing much work since last autumn. The winter, and the visit to Europe, was curiously disheartening. Takes one time to get over it* [Moore 793]. Lawrence wrote 'The Woman Who Rode Away' [C131–2 B20 A41], and probably the final version of 'Pan in America', and 'Altitude' [C222 *CPlays*]. He began 'St Mawr' [A31].

*5 JUNE   To Mabel Luhan: *I began to write a story* [Luhan 215]. Shortly afterwards Lawrence showed the completed story to Mabel. It was 'The Woman Who Rode Away', which she described as 'that story where Lorenzo thought he finished me up' [Luhan 238].

18 JUNE   Lawrence told Nancy Pearn that he would soon send her a couple more stories, one finished, one being done again. The latter was presumably 'St Mawr', known to have existed in two versions [Powell 12] until the MSS were burned with Aldous Huxley's house.

19 JUNE   *We are down in Taos for a day or two. . . . Clarence Thompson is a young New Yorker staying here—nice boy—and there is a Mrs Sprague. Always somebody at Mabel's, when one descends from the hills* [Seltzer 138].
   Willard Johnson: 'He scribbled the opening lines on the back of a candy box one evening in Mabel Luhan's living room, with several friends present offering suggestions as to who the characters should be and what they should do and say. It was an amusing game, and few of those who played it knew until many years later that the next day Lawrence finished this first scene and began a second' [Tedlock 122]. The play was 'Altitude', in which both Clarence Thompson and Mrs Sprague appear as characters. 'Spud' Johnson, who is also a character, does not make clear whether or not he was actually present. If he was, the occasion cannot have been the weekend of 19 June, but must have been some other such gathering at Mabel's in the summer of 1924.

JULY 1924   At Lobo Ranch.

SUMMARY   *We sit here very quitely, with the sun and the thunderstorms, the trees and the horses. I go on slowly with my second long-short story—a queer story. Frieda of course admires her 'place' all the time* [Secker 58].

7 JULY   To Martin Secker: *Here are the revised proofs of the Magnus Introduction* [Secker 58].

AUGUST 1924   At Lobo Ranch but for the ten-day trip to Hopi country.

SUMMARY   Lawrence finished 'St Mawr' and wrote 'The Hopi Snake Dance' [C127 A37].

8 AUG.   *I've nearly got to the end of my second 'novelette'—a corker* [Secker 59].

21 AUG.   In the De Vargas Hotel in Santa Fe, on the way home from the snake dance which Lawrence had seen on 16, he showed Mabel Luhan 'Just Back from the Snake Dance—Tired Out' [C124 Moore 802]: 'He had written a dreary terre a terre account of the long road to the Hopi village and of the dance, a mere realistic recital that might have been done by a tired, disgruntled business man. It had no vision, no insight, no appreciation of any kind. . . . I had not taken him to the Snake Dance to have him describe it in this fashion.'

Next morning Lawrence said: *I know you didn't like that article of mine. I'll try and do another one.* The following day he wrote: *I'll write a sketch for the Theatre Arts, and draw one, too, if I can: not for the Horse to laugh at* [Luhan 267–8]. The first sketch appeared in *The Laughing Horse* in September, the second longer and altogether more serious piece in *Theatre Arts Monthly* in December, but without a drawing.

26 AUG.   The notebook in which 'The Hopi Snake Dance' is the first entry bears this date.

30 AUG.   Sends Curtis Brown 'The Hopi Snake Dance' [Huxley 610].

SEPTEMBER 1924   At Lobo Ranch.

SUMMARY   Lawrence wrote 'The Bad Side of Books' [B16 and *Phoenix*], the Epilogue to *Movements in European History* [A17b], began 'The Princess' [C128–30 A31], and wrote 'Climbing Down Pisgah' [*Phoenix*], acknowledged by Curtis Brown 2 October. Also 'Change of Life' [A80].

138

I SEPT.   The MS of 'The Bad Side of Books' bears this date.

13 SEPT.   To Martin Secker: *Yes, the novelette 'St Mawr' is finished and Brett is typing it out. It's good—a bit bitter—takes place in England, then moves to this ranch—some beautiful creation of this locale and landscape here. But thank God I don't have to write it again. It took it out of me* [Secker 60]. Brett says that Lawrence's pronunciation of St Mawr was *Seymour*, a surname which derives from the Norman French de St Maur. The story tells us that Lewis, the groom, who has come with St Mawr from Wales, pronounces it *with a Welsh twist*. 'Mawr' is Welsh for 'big' or 'great'.

The Oxford Press are doing a new edition of Movements in European History *and want illustrations and an epilogue. The epilogue, all right* [Centaur 15]. By the time Lawrence received the pictures he had asked for from McDonald, on 28, the Epilogue, *which will make them hesitate*, was already written [*Centaur* 16].

*19 SEPT.   To Mabel Luhan: *I wish there could be a change . . . Perhaps the only thing that will really help one through a great change is discipline, one's own deep, self-discovered discipline, the first 'angel with a sword'* [Moore 809]. This is Lawrence's response to Mabel's poem 'Change' [Luhan 157–9] and includes a half-quotation from his own rewriting of it 'Change of Life':
Past saluting swords of the angels [CP 770].

30 SEPT.   To Curtis Brown: *I am sending you today the MS of the novelette 'St Mawr' which I have finished this summer. It works out more than 60,000 words, I believe. With 'The Woman Who Rode Away' and another story of out here that I am doing, called 'The Princess', it will make a book. . . . If you think it better, 'St. Mawr' can be called 'Two Ladies and a Horse'* [Moore 810]. For an account of the origin of 'The Princess' see Carswell 201–4 (reprinted in my introduction to *The Princess and Other Stories*, Penguin, 1971).

This dating of 'Climbing Down Pisgah' might seem at first glance to be at odds with the order of texts in the 'Hopi Snake Dance' MS [Tedlock 184–5]. The sixteen pieces in that notebook are listed by Tedlock in the order in which they appear in the book, which is not the order of composition. Lawrence started at the front with 'The Hopi Snake Dance', 'Introduction to Bibliography' and 'The Princess'. Before he had finished 'The Princess', and of course not knowing how many more pages he would require for it, he wanted to write 'Climbing Down Pisgah', and so jumped to p. 158, leaving himself just three pages to the end of the notebook. The piece occupies five and a half, so that he was obliged to use both sides of the end paper and half the inside back cover. By the time he came to write his Preface to *Black Swans* he had finished *The Princess*, but started immediately after it the *Mornings in Mexico* essays. Probably not knowing at that stage whether he would write any more, he jumped to the back again for the Preface, to p. 155, again leaving himself only three pages. He required four, so had to go back to 154 for the fourth. In January Lawrence had decided there would be no more *Mornings*, and so began 'Resurrection' on the first blank page [118] and thereafter used the pages consecutively through to 'Beyond the Rockies' in Jan. 1926. Pages 147–153 are blank.

OCTOBER 1924   At Lobo Ranch until 11. Left Taos 16, left Santa Fe, 18; 20 at El Paso, 22 Mexico City (Hotel Monte Carlo).

SUMMARY   Lawrence finished 'The Princess'.

8 OCT.   *Finished 'The Princess'* [Tedlock 99].

NOVEMBER 1924   At Hotel Monte Carlo, Mexico City until 8. From 9 to 18 at Hotel Francia, Oaxaca, then at 43 Avenue Pino Suarez, until February 1925.

SUMMARY   *We are way down here in the South of Mexico—marvellous sunshine every day, but rather stupid people. F. and I are moving into a house tomorrow, but Brett will stay on in the hotel. I suppose we shall be here a month of two: though I'm wishing I'd gone to Europe instead of coming here. Sometimes I hanker for the Mediterranean, and long to get away from the American continent altogether. However, I'll try first if I can get any work done. If I can't, I shall sail* [Moore 820]. Lawrence resumed work on *Quetzalcoatl*.

19 NOV.   The first notebook of the second draft of *Quetzalcoatl* has this date at the front.

DECEMBER 1924   At 43 Avenue Pino Suarez, Oaxaca, Mexico.

SUMMARY   *We are settled in a house down here, and I am doing my Mexico book. This is a marvellous climate—roses, bananas, lilies—the madonna lilies wild on the mountains. The little town of Oaxaca is lonely, away in the south and miles from anywhere except the Indian villages of the hills. I like it, it gives me something. When one once gets over the peculiar resistance Mexico offers always* [Secker 53–4].

Lawrence continued with *Quetzalcoatl* and also wrote four chapters of *Mornings in Mexico* [A37], and Preface to *Black Swans* [Phoenix 2].

*7 DEC.   *I am working at my novel which is just beginning to digest its own gall and wormwood* [Nehls 2, 389].

*18 DEC.   *I am doing one or two little articles which will probably suit* Vanity Fair [Moore 824]. These were *Mornings in Mexico*, 'Friday Morning', published as 'Corasmin and the Parrots' [C134], 'Saturday Morning', published as 'The Gentle Art of Marketing in Mexico' [C140], 'Sunday Morning', published as 'Sunday Stroll in Sleepy Mexico' [C147] and 'Monday Morning', published as 'The Mozo' [C151].

Only the first of these could have been written by 18. According to Brett (192–4) *The Road to Mitla* was painted at about this time.

20 DEC.   'Market Day' begins: *This is the last Saturday before Christmas.*

21 DEC.   The walk to Huayapa took place on this day.

24 DEC.   The Preface to *Black Swans* ends: *Tonight is Christmas Eve, and who knows what sort of a child the Virgin is going to bring forth, this time!* [Phoenix 2, 296].

'The Mozo' also contains the sentence: *This, then, is a pretty Christmas Eve.* But the essay later relates the behaviour of Rosalino for several days after the walk to Huayapa, up to and including Christmas Day. If Lawrence broke off 'The Mozo' on Christmas Eve in order to write the Preface to *Black Swans*, this would explain why he turned to the end of the notebook to do so.

31 DEC.   The second *Quetzalcoatl* notebook bears this date at the front. In the first notebook, Lawrence had done 381 pages and reached the beginning of chapter 13.

SUMMARY   Lawrence finished *Quetzalcoatl*. He also wrote 'Resurrection' [*Phoenix*] and 'See Mexico After' [*Phoenix*].

10 JAN.   To Curtis Brown: *I am getting ahead with the Mexican novel. If heaven is with me, I should finish it this month. I had a good deal done from last year.—It will probably make you open your eyes—or close them: but I like it very much indeed* [Moore 826].

   To Luis Quintanilla: *And the little article came. I was a bit sad, because it was sad and rather bitter: in fact very: with undigested spleen. Is that how you really feel about them. . . . I couldn't help writing out your little article again* [Moore 825]. The article was 'See Mexico After' by Luis Quintanilla. 'Resurrection' must have been written shortly before this, since it comes between the Preface to Black Swans and 'See Mexico After' in the MS notebook (see December).

12 JAN.   To Luis Quintanilla: *I find even my article barely covers its rancour, rancor, and is a bit bewildering. There must be a terrible bitterness somewhere deep down between the U.S.A. and Mexico, covered up. When one touches it, it scares one, and startles one. . . . I have done a lot of my novel again—I had the biggest part done last year. It is good, but scares me a bit also* [Nehls 389].

16 JAN.   *Did my* Quetzalcoatl *novel down here. It scares me a bit. But it's nearly done* [Damon 669].

29 JAN.   *I have finished* Quetzalcoatl, *or at least, am in the last chapter. It is a long novel. I feel, at the bottom of my heart, I'd rather not have it published at all* [Secker 62]. On the same day Lawrence told Curtis Brown that the novel was finished.

FEBRUARY 1925   At 43 Avenue Pino Suarez until 14. Then Lawrence, who had been struck down with malaria on 4 and had almost died, was moved to the Francia Hotel. On 25 in Tehuacan; 26 in Mexico City (Hotel Imperial).

SUMMARY   Immediately before his illness Lawrence seems to have been planning a number of short stories [Tedlock 56–7]: 'The Flying Fish' or 'The Weather Vane', 'The Wedding Ring', 'The Dog', and 'The Woman Out of the Water'. Against the heading 'Suggestions for Stories' in the notebook, Lawrence later added in pencil—*never carried out! DHL*. In fact the first of them was later partially written. See March. The 'Suggestions for Stories'

142

are neatly written in ink. The next two items in the 'Hopi Snakedance' notebook are in pencil, and probably date from the time of Lawrence's illness. They are the unpublished philosophical fragment 'Man is essentially a soul. . .' and 'Noah's Flood' [*Phoenix* and *CPlays*], also unfinished. On 3 March Lawrence wrote to Ida Rauh describing in detail the scheme he had worked out for the play, but when he was able to return to drama it was a scheme he had mentioned to Ida Rauh the previous November which captured his attention—to write about King David.

MARCH 1925   At the Hotel Imperial, Mexico City, until 25. After a two-day fight and after putting rouge on his cheeks, Lawrence got across the border at El Paso and arrived at Santa Fe 29.

SUMMARY   In Mexico City Lawrence's condition was for the first time positively diagnosed as tuberculosis. *I went and got malaria, plus grippe, so badly in Oaxaca, that I was a month in bed and can still hardly crawl through the days. . . feeling done in by this dirty sickness* [Nehls 2, 396]. Nevertheless, Lawrence began *David* [A34], corrected the proofs of 'St. Mawr', and wrote 'The Flying Fish' [*Phoenix*].

*19 MARCH   Lawrence told Ida Rauh that he had begun a play.

†23 MARCH   To Secker: *The proofs of 'St. Mawr' came. I am returning them today* [Secker 52].

LATE   Achsah Brewster: 'One afternoon he sat holding a child's copy-book saying that he was going to read us an unfinished novel he had started on the way back from Mexico when he was very ill, and written down by Frieda from his dictation. It was called "The Flying Fish" with the old haunting symbolism of *pisces*. As he read it, it seemed to reach an ever higher more serene beauty. Suddenly he stopped, saying: "The last part will be regenerate man, a real life in this Garden of Eden." . . .

'The enduring beauty of "The Flying Fish" made us ask at various times if he had not finished it, to which he would reply, that we must not urge him to finish it. "I've an intuition I shall not finish that novel. It was written so near the borderline of death, that I never have been able to carry it through, in the cold light of day" ' [Brewster 288]. Lawrence's original scheme for the story is printed by Tedlock [57].

APRIL 1925   At Kiowa Ranch, as Lawrence had now decided to call it, Questa, New Mexico.

SUMMARY   *Am much better, but must be careful all summer—lie down a great deal. When the wild cold winds come, I just go to bed. In the wonderful sunny days—they are six out of seven—I putter about and lie on a camp bed on the porch. I don't work yet* [Moore 839]. Lawrence continued with *David*, and wrote 'Accumulated Mail' [B18 and *Phoenix*].

*14 APRIL   Lawrence told Ida Rauh he had done six scenes of *David*.
18 APRIL   Lawrence sent 'Accumulated Mail' to Mrs Knopf.

MAY 1925   At Kiowa Ranch.

SUMMARY   *I am much better: and hope to get to England in the autumn. Meanwhile I am just 'ranching'* [Seltzer 151].

*7 MAY   Lawrence finished *David*.

JUNE 1925   At Kiowa Ranch.

SUMMARY   *We sit here on our own little ranch, up to the eyes in doing nothing. I spent all the golden evening riding though the timber hunting the lost cow: and when at last I got her into the corral, I felt more like killing her than milking her. . . . I don't do any work since we are here—except milk the black-eyed Susan and irrigate the field—when there's any water. I never felt less literary* [Moore 843].

Lawrence revised *Quetzalcoatl* and wrote several essays on the novel: 'Art and Morality' [C133 and *Phoenix*], 'Morality and the Novel' [C135 *Phoenix*], 'The Novel' [A32 and *Phoenix 2*], 'Why the Novel Matters' [*Phoenix*] and 'The Novel and the Feelings' [*Phoenix*].

5 JUNE   Lawrence told Mrs Knopf that he had been through *Quetzalcoatl* and would do a few things to it.
10 JUNE   *I've revised the MS. of my Mexican novel—which I wanted to call* Quetzalcoatl. *But the publisher wept at the sound of it: and pleaded for a translation:* The Plumed Serpent [Moore 843–4].
29 JUNE   To Mr Jester: *I am sending you here a little article on 'The Novel', as you asked me, for the small book of essays. Let me know if it is too antiseptic for you. I think it's amusing* [Centaur 21].
       The book was *Reflections on the Death of a Porcupine* [A32]. 'The

Novel' is one of a set of essays on the novel which Lawrence wrote shortly after finishing the first draft of *David,* and in the same notebook. The mechanical numbering of that notebook gives us the likely order of composition. Apparently *David* originally ended on p. 98. Page 100 has a fragment of an essay on art; 101 an abandoned beginning of 'Art and Morality'; 102–6 an early unpublished version of 'Art and Morality'; 107–11 an early unpublished version of 'Morality and the Novel'; 112–16 the published version of 'Art and Morality'; 117–21 the published version of 'Morality and the Novel'; 122–3 are blank; Pages 125–31 have 'The Modern Novel' (later 'The Novel'). Pages 132–8 were torn out and used to insert in *David* in place of original pages there [Tedlock 123–4]. By 11 July 'Art and Morality' and 'Morality and the Novel' were already in the hands of Curtis Brown [Moore 846].

Two other essays on the novel—'Why the Novel Matters' and 'The Novel and the Feelings' may well also date from this period. They are on leaves from the same notebook as each other, but not from the *David* notebook [Tedlock 168–9].

JULY 1925   At Kiowa Ranch.

SUMMARY   All the essays in *Reflections on the Death of a Porcupine* [A32 and *Phoenix* 2] with the exception of 'The Crown' (1915) and 'The Novel' (see June), were written in July and early August 1925.

15 JULY   To Mr Jester (Centaur Press): *If you could send me a few of the essays, like the one on 'Love', I think I would rather revise them a good deal: perhaps re-write them. That would amuse me just now. I don't very much want to re-publish half-baked sort of stuff. I'd like to make a complete little book, with more or less a central idea, an organic thing. . . . I don't like those volumes of oddments men bring out. Real oddments should remain odd, and uncollected* [Centaur 21].

In April Lawrence had agreed that the Centaur Press might publish a volume of his uncollected essays [*Centaur* 18], and had sent several, including, apparently, 'Love' [*Phoenix*] (see October 1917). 'Love' he re-wrote beyond recognition. In the holograph it is still called 'Love', but in the typescript Lawrence changed the title to ' . . . Love Was Once a Little Boy'. This letter suggests that Lawrence had not yet written 'Reflections on the Death of a Porcupine' (which describes events of *the last days of June*), or 'Him with His Tail in His Mouth', or 'Blessed Are the Powerful' or 'Aristocracy'.

AUGUST 1925 At Kiowa Ranch.

SUMMARY Lawrence finished the essays for *Reflections*, including the revision of 'The Crown', for which he wrote an introductory note.

12 AUG. Lawrence told Mr Jester that he had done a little introductory note for 'The Crown'. That note says: *I alter 'The Crown' only a very little [Phoenix 2 364]*, which is not strictly true. There are minor changes in the first three sections, and major ones in the last three. Lawrence also said that he would send the complete text of *Reflections* in a few days. On 25 Lawrence told Secker that he had *Sent them the prepared ms. last week: I didn't care for the old essays, so they are all new, except the first, called 'The Crown'. . . . They're essays written here, and the porc. was one I shot here* [Secker 64].

SEPTEMBER 1925 At Kiowa Ranch until 10, then via Denver to New York, arriving 13. Sailed 21 on SS Resolute, arriving Southampton 30.

SUMMARY *We've just sat tight and considered the lily all summer. I am quite well. It grieves me to leave my horses, and my cow Susan, and the cat Timsy Wemyss, and the white cock Moses— and the place,* [Moore 849].

21 SEPT. Lawrence sent Mrs Knopf the proofs of 'Accumulated Mail' [B18].

OCTOBER 1925 At Garland's Hotel, Pall Mall, London, until 8. Then at Nottingham until 14, and Ripley until 22. Then back to London, 73 Gower Street until 29. Then to Baden-Baden.

SUMMARY Lawrence corrected the proofs of *The Plumed Serpent* and wrote three book reviews.

*9 OCT. To Martin Secker: *Could you send me that monograph by Shane Leslie on Frederick Rolfe, as soon as possible? I am doing the review on* Hadrian the Seventh, *and I should like a few facts* [Secker 65].
*13 OCT. Lawrence sends this review to Nancy Pearn.
*16 OCT. Lawrence is correcting the galley proofs of *The Plumed Serpent* [Moore 859].
20 OCT. To Alfred A. Knopf: *I've sent the proofs of* The Plumed Serpent *back to Secker. . . . I have sent reviews of* Hadrian VII *and of* Saïd the Fisherman *to the* Tribune. . . . *I think my two reviews are rather*

nice. . . . I'm going to do a review now of Origins of Prohibition [Moore 860]. Both reviews appeared in *Adelphi,* neither in the *New York Herald Tribune Books* [C134 C148 and *Phoenix*].

NOVEMBER 1925 At Ludwig-Wilhelmstift, Baden-Baden until 12. Arrived Spotorno 15 (Villa Maria). Moved into Villa Bernarda 23, where the Lawrences lived until April 1926.

SUMMARY *I'm not doing any serious work yet, just bits, that I have promised, and not much of those. Am a bit disgusted with work altogether* [Secker 68]. Lawrence had promised *The New York Herald Tribune* a review of J. A. Krout's *Origins of Prohibition* [C137 and *Phoenix*], and Spud Johnson some contributions for the special D. H. Lawrence number of *The Laughing Horse* [C139].

*17 NOV. To Vere Collins (Oxford University Press): *I'm sending the mauled history by this mail. When I went through it, I was half infuriated and half amused. But if I'd had to go through it, personally, and make the decision merely from myself, I'd have sent those Irish b's seven times to hell, before I'd have moved a single iota at their pencil stroke* [Moore 865]. The Irish edition of *Movements in European History* [A17d] had been censored by the Catholic Church. [See Roberts 51.]

21 NOV. Lawrence sent his review of *The Origins of Prohibition* to Nancy Pearn.

*25 NOV. To Hon. Dorothy Brett: *I'm enclosing two little MSS.—one for Spud* [Moore 869]. These were 'A Little Moonshine with Lemon' [C139 A37] and probably 'Europe Versus America' [C139 and *Phoenix*]. The first written that evening, St Catherine's Day.

DECEMBER 1925 At Villa Bernarda, Spotorno, Italy.

SUMMARY Lawrence wrote 'Smile' [C142 A41], 'Sun' [C145 A35 A41] and 'Glad Ghosts' [C143–4 A36 A41].

†8 DEC. To Hon. Dorothy Brett: *I am sending two more stories. I promised Cynthia Asquith a ghost story for a collection she is making. How will she swallow 'Gay Ghosts'?* [Moore 882 misdated].

12 DEC. To J. M. Murry (editor of *The Adelphi*): *I send back the Molly Skinner article—rewrote the first four pages, and cleared the rest a*

bit. . . . It's quite good, for a sort of 'note' [Moore 869]. Mollie Skinner's 'The Hand' appeared in *The Adelphi* in May 1926. The hand of Lawrence is not evident in it.

*12 DEC.   To Hon. Dorothy Brett: *I had the typing . . . I send you 'Sun'. . . . I'm still struggling with my 'Gay Ghosts'. Alas and a thousand times alack, it's growing long—too long. Damn it! Even 'Sun' is a bit too long* [Irvine 2, 59]. The typing was probably 'Smile', which Lawrence sent to Nancy Pearn a week later. It was published in *New Masses*, June 1926 [Finney 3].

'Sun' exists in two versions. Lawrence's own comments suggest that his original story was expurgated for publication in *New Coterie*, autumn 1926, and the Archer *Sun* [A35a] and 'The Woman Who Rode Away' [A41] and was not printed in its original form until the Black Sun Press edition in October 1928 [A35b]. On 29 April 1928 Lawrence was to write to Harry Crosby: *'Sun' is the final MS, and I wish the story had been printed as it stands there, really complete* [Huxley 730]. It seems more likely, however, that Lawrence was practising a little mild deception on Harry Crosby, and that the original MS corresponded to the first published version, and was subsequently burned by Lawrence. See April 1928.

'Gay Ghosts' became 'Ghost of Silence', and, finally, 'Glad Ghosts'.

*24 DEC.   *I've done ¾ of 'Ghost of Silence' and now have got stuck* [Moore 870].

29 DEC.   To Doroty Brett: *I send you another story, 'Glad Ghosts'. It's finished at last, and, usual woe, is much too long* [Moore 873–4].

JANUARY 1926   At Villa Bernarda, Spotorno.

SUMMARY   *No, no! I'm forty, and I want, in a good sense, to enjoy my life. Saying my say and seeing other people sup it up doesn't amount to a hill o' beans, as far as I go. I want to waste no time over it. That's why I have an agent. I want my own life to live* [Moore 876]. Lawrence wrote *The Virgin and the Gypsy* [A54], 'Mediterranean in January' and 'Beyond the Rockies' [C139 and CP].

*6 JAN.   *We painted two pictures, which would amuse you: quite good. I am correcting final proofs of* David *and find it good* [Moore 877]. For an account of his joint paintings with his step-daughter Barby, see Nehls, 3, 22.

*18 JAN.   *I had a good whack at my gipsy story tonight and nearly finished it over the climax and on the short down slope to the end* [Secker 69].

21 JAN.   To Secker: *Here is the rest of the gipsy story. When it's typed, will you send me the MS so I can go over it* [Secker 69]. No revised typescript has survived, but the published text incorporates exactly the kind of revision Lawrence was in the habit of making on his typescripts, and must have been set up from one. For example, in the first paragraph Lawrence wrote of the vicar as *still full of quiet passion*, then crossed out *quiet* and put *secretive*. But the published text has *furtive*. The whole of the final paragraph of part I is not in the MS. The last phrase of part IV, *by the river* is not in the MS. Lawrence originally wrote *What takes you sniffing round such couples*, then altered *sniffing* to *nosing*. The published text has *creeping*. The MS has: *She wanted to be confirmed by him.* The published text has added: *against her father, who had only a repulsive fear of her.*

FEBRUARY 1926   **At Villa Bernarda, Spotorno, until 22. Then at Hotel Beau Sejour, Monte Carlo, until 25. Then to Capri via Ventimiglia and Rome, arriving 27.**

SUMMARY   *I've left off writing now; I am really awful sick of writing* [Moore 886]. Lawrence wrote 'The Rocking Horse Winner' [B19 A63].

25 FEB.   Lawrence sent 'The Rocking Horse Winner' to Nancy Pearn. It was first published in *Harper's Bazaar*, July 1926 [Finney 3].

149

MARCH 1926 With the Brewsters on Capri. By 11 at Hotel Palumbo, Ravello, Amalfi. Left Ravello for Rome, 22; left Rome for Perugia and Florence, 25; left Florence for Ravenna, 30.

SUMMARY   Lawrence seems to have written nothing this month.

APRIL 1926 Returned to Villa Bernarda, Spotorno, 3. Left for Florence (Pensione Lucchesi), 20.

SUMMARY   *I am 'off' writing* [Moore 895]. Lawrence began to plan *Etruscan Places*. This is the most likely month for his review of Isa Glenn's *Heat* [*Phoenix*], which had been published at the end of March.

4 APRIL   To Martin Secker: *We might go to Perugia, and I might do a book on Umbria and the Etruscan remains. What do you think? It would be half a travel book—of the region round Perugia, Assisi, Spoleto, Cortona, and the Maremma—and half a book about the Etruscan things, which interest me very much. If you happen to know any good book, modern, on Etruscan things, I wish you'd order it for me. I've only read that old work, Dennis'—*Cities and Cemeteries of Etruria. *There will be some lectures in Perugia* [Secker 72].

*18 APRIL   Lawrence tried to persuade Richard Aldington to join him on an Etruscan tour [Moore 901].

26 APRIL   Nancy Pearn sent Lawrence the proofs for the *New Criterion* 'Mornings in Mexico' article [C140].

28 APRIL   *I'm reading Italian books on the Etruscans—very interesting indeed. I'll join Vieusseux's library here—they will have more things* [Secker 73].

MAY 1926 At Pensione Lucchesi, Florence, until 6, then to Villa Mirenda, Scandicci, Florence, which was then the Lawrence home until June 1928.

SUMMARY   Lawrence wrote his Introduction to *Max Havelaar* [B21 and *Phoenix*] and 'Two Blue Birds' [C154 B22 A41], and continued to work on the Etruscans.

3 MAY   *I more or less promised to do a sort of travel book about the old Etruscans and their remains here in Tuscany and Umbria.—So now we have taken a villa about 7 miles out of Florence here, in the country, and I can use that as a centre, when I have to go travelling round to Bologna and Cortona and Volterra and down the Maremma to*

*Tarquinia—quite a number of places in Tuscany and Umbria, where
the best remains are. At present I am supposed to be reading up about
my precious Etruschi!* [Moore 908].

13 MAY   To Nancy Pearn: *I send you a story, 'Two Blue Birds'—probably
to be another tribulation to you* [Huxley 658].

To W. Siebenhaar: *I received the MS of* Max Havelaar *a few days
ago, and read it at once, and did a brief introduction, without waiting
for your essay* [Huxley 658].

26 MAY   To Else Jaffe: *I said to myself I would write perhaps a book about
the Etruscans: nothing pretentious, but a sort of book for people who
will actually be going to Florence and Cortona and Perugia and
Volterra and those places, to look at the Etruscan things. They have a
great attraction for me: there are lovely things in the Etruscan
Museum here, which no doubt you've seen. But I hope you'll come in
the autumn and look at them again with me. Mommsen hated
everything Etruscan, said the germ of all degeneracy was in the race.
But the bronzes and terracottas are fascinating, so alive with physical
life, with a powerful physicality which surely is as great, or sacred,
ultimately, as the* ideal *of the Greeks and Germans* [Lawrence 223].
Lawrence had to wait almost a year before making his Etruscan tour.

JUNE 1926   At the Villa Mirenda, Scandicci, Florence.

SUMMARY   *I haven't done any of the Etruscan book yet: and shan't do it,
unless the mood changes. Why write books for the swine, unless one
absolutely must!* [Moore 923]. Lawrence wrote 'The Man Who Loved
Islands' [C157 A41b], 'Fireworks' [C155 and *Phoenix*] and 'The Nightingale' [C158 and *Phoenix*].

*8 JUNE   I'm busy typing out F[rieda]'s translation of David—be glad you
don't have to do it—every noun in German a capital letter! And
everything to re-translate F's translation—oh, dear! But I've done
three-fourths—I've not been able to go around to my Etruscans at
all—shall have to do it when we come back in September* [Moore
917–18].

14 JUNE   *I have an invitation up to Scotland also—two invitations,
Compton Mackenzie wants me to go to an isle off Lewis, in the Outer
Hebrides* [Moore 918]. Lawrence must have begun his story based on
Compton Mackenzie—'The Man Who Loved Islands'—at about this
time. See below.

1926

23 JUNE *We're doing a fine embroidery——peacock, kid, and deer among the vines!* [Moore 921].

24 JUNE *Then the evening comes cooler, and the nightingale starts singing again. There are many nightingales, in every little wood you can hear half a dozen singing away all day long, except in the hot hours, very lively. The wheat is very fine, and just turning yellow under the olive trees. Today is San Giovanni, the Saint of Florence, and a great festa. So we shall go in to town this evening for dinner, and stay for the fireworks. They will illuminate the town, and everybody will be in full holiday rig* [Moore 921]. Three days later Lawrence sent Nancy Pearn three little articles for *Vogue* or *Vanity Fair*. Two of them were certainly 'The Nightingale' and 'Fireworks'.

25 JUNE Arthur and Lilian Gair Wilkinson: 'Found the author embroidering a panel—a design adapted from an old Etruscan design—in the brightest of colour'. Probably the embroidery reproduced in Huxley [344]. But see September 1928.

27 JUNE Lawrence told Nancy Pearn that he had a story nearly done. He sent her a story 10 July, and 19 July asked her if she had received the Islands story.

JULY 1926 At the Villa Mirenda until 12. At Ludwig-Wilhelmstift, Baden-Baden 13–29. In London 30.

SUMMARY *In the real summer, I always lose interest in literature and publications. The cicadas rattle away all day in the trees, the girls sing, cutting the corn with the sickles, the sheaves of wheat lie all the afternoon like people dead asleep in the heat. E piu non si frega. I don't work, except at an occasional scrap of an article. I don't feel much like doing a book, of any sort* [Moore 923]. Lawrence wrote 'Mercury' [C152 and *Phoenix*].

20 JULY Lawrence reported a storm and torrents of rain on this day. A week later he was still reporting torrents and thunder. 'Mercury' was written at this time.

AUGUST 1926 At 25 Rossetti Gardens, Chelsea, London, until 6. Weekend with the Aldingtons in Padworth, Berkshire. Back in London 8. To Edinburgh 9. By 11 at Newtonmore, Inverness. From there Lawrence 'made an excursion to the west, to Fort William and Mallaig, and sailed up from Mallaig to the Isle of Skye' [Moore 931], arriving 17. Back in

Newtonmore 19. To Mablethorpe, Lincolnshire 21. 28 to Duneville, Sutton-on-Sea, two miles away.

SUMMARY *I am so bored by the thought of all things literary—why not sell cigarettes!* [Zytaruk 294]. Lawrence reviewed *The World of William Clissold* [C146 and *Phoenix*].

20 AUG. *There is still something of an Odyssey up there, in among the islands and the silent lochs: like the twilight morning of the world, the herons fishing undisturbed by the water, and the sea running in, for miles, between the wet, trickling hills, where the cottages are low and almost invisible, built into the earth. It is still out of the world, and like the very beginning of Europe* [Moore 931].

It is difficult to believe that Lawrence wrote 'The Man Who Loved Islands' with no experience of 'Celtic' islands to draw on. Whether he did, in fact, rewrite the story to incorporate his experience of Skye will probably never be known, since no MSS have surfaced. On this date Lawrence sent Nancy Pearn his review of H. G. Wells' *The World of William Clissold*.

SEPTEMBER 1926 At Sutton-on-Sea until 13, then to Ripley. In London 16–28 (30 Willoughby Road, Hampstead). Paris, 29, on the way back to the Villa Mirenda.

SUMMARY *Literary news, none! I'm still feeling dead off writing altogether* [Moore 936]. Lawrence corrected a few proofs.

2 SEPT. To Secker: *I feel, if ever I were going to do an English novel, I'd have to come to England to do it. Perhaps this neighbourhood. But not now* [Secker 76].
8 SEPT. Lawrence sent Nancy Pearn the corrected proofs of the *New Coterie* 'Sun' [C145].
22 SEPT. Lawrence received the proofs of *Glad Ghosts* [A36] and sent them off at once, to Michael Joseph of Ernest Benn Ltd.
27 SEPT. Lawrence received the proofs of his review of *The World of William Clissold* [C146].

OCTOBER 1926 Arrived back at Villa Mirenda 4.

SUMMARY *The days pass so quickly. I do very little work—go out for walks by myself in these hills—and talk a bit with our only neighbours—the Wilkinsons* [Lawrence-Ada 140]. Lawrence wrote 'In Love' [C162 A41], began *The First Lady Chatterley* [A42g] and possibly wrote 'Return to Bestwood' [*Phoenix* 2], 'The Duc de Lauzun' [*Phoenix*] and 'The Good Man' [*Phoenix*]. The opening sentence of 'Return to Bestwood' is: *I came home to the Midlands for a few days, at the end of September.* 'Came' rather than 'went' might suggest that the piece was written there. But Lawrence's 'Getting On', an early draft of 'Return to Bestwood', begins: *I went this autumn once more to the place of my birth.*

6–11 OCT.   The Aldingtons stayed with the Lawrences at the Villa Mirenda. Richard Aldington: 'At this distance of time I am not certain of the dates, but I know that in 1926, in addition to other work. I had engaged to edit about twenty or thirty volumes of 18th-century French memoirs in English. This, by the way, enables me to clear up a little point in Lawrence's bibliography. How did it happen that among his posthumous works there appears a short essay on the Duc de Lauzun? Ingenious theories have been formed to explain it, but the facts are simpler. I arranged with F. S. Flint to translate the duke's memoirs, but for some reason Flint didn't want to write the introduction. I had the book with me on one of the occasions when I stayed with the Lawrences at Scandicci, and I had Lorenzo read the book to see if he cared to write about it. From his breakfast-table homilies on the subject I gathered that he thought Lauzun and the whole French aristocracy and litterateurs of that epoch a collection of lice, and that anything he wrote on the subject would say so. I considered this would be an improper introduction to a public which was pretty languid about the French 18th century anyhow; so I said no more about it, and wrote the essay myself. Apparently Lawrence had already written his essay, for it was among the manuscripts of his I went through in Florence in 1930' [Tedlock 246]. The essay exists in two forms, one called 'The Duc de Lauzun', the other 'The Good Man'.

16 OCT.   To Robert Atkins (who was producing *David* in London): *I enclose the music I have written out for David. It is very simple——needs only a pipe, tambourines, and a tom-tom drum* [Moore 941]. The music was published in *Miscellany*.

   'In Love' must have been written about this time, since on 1 November Lawrence told Nancy Pearn he had sent it a fortnight previously. [See Joost, 105.]

18 OCT.   *I feel I'll never write another novel* [Lawrence 231].

26 OCT.   Lawrence had reached p. 41 of *Lady Chatterley's Lover* [Tedlock 20], which at this stage he thought of as a mere story.

27 OCT.   *I am working at a story—shortish—don't feel like a long effort* [Secker 78–9].

*31 OCT.   Frieda Lawrence: 'Lawrence goes into the woods to write, he is writing a short long story, always breaking new ground, the curious class feeling this time or rather the soul against the body, no I don't explain it well, the *animal* part' [Moore 944]. At this point Lawrence interpolated: *Ooray! Eureka!*

NOVEMBER 1926   At the Villa Mirenda.

SUMMARY   Lawrence continued with and possibly finished *The First Lady Chatterley*, wrote his review of H. M. Tomlinson's *Gifts of Fortune* [C150 and *Phoenix*] and 'Man is a Hunter' [*Phoenix*], and embarked on his major paintings.

9 NOV.   Lawrence sent his Tomlinson review to Nancy Pearn.

11 NOV.   To Maria and Aldous Huxley: *I've already painted a picture on one of the canvases. I've hung it up in the new salotto. I call it the Unholy Family, because the bambino—with a nimbus—is just watching anxiously to see the young man give the semi-nude young woman un gros baiser. Molto moderno!* [Moore 945]. This painting was published in *The Paintings of D. H. Lawrence* [A46] as *A Holy Family*. [See *Phoenix 2*, 603.]

15 NOV.   *I have begun a novel in the Derbyshire coal mining districts—already rather improper. The gods alone know where it will end—if they'll help me out with it. . . . I've painted a nice big picture that our vegetarian neighbours the Wilkinsons are afraid to look at, it's too 'suggestive'. Why do vegetarians always believe that the world was vegetably propagated, even?* [Secker 79–80].

23 NOV.   *The novel goes pretty well—is already very improper—and will apparently be quite short. . . . The bathing men are framed, and hang in Frieda's room* [Secker 81]. The painting was *Men Bathing* [Huxley 472].

24 NOV.   *I have started painting, quite seriously, on my own. Maria Huxley . . . brought me some canvases that her brother had daubed on. . . . I've done a nice biggish picture—that is, I like it—a man and woman in a pink room, and a child looking up—modern. Now I'm going to do a long one, about 1½ yards by ¾ yard—of Boccaccio's story of the gardener and the nunnery. It's rather fun, discovering one can*

paint one's own ideas and one's own feelings—and a change from writing [Moore 949].

*26 NOV.   *My design for my Boccaccio picture is so nice, if only I can get it on the canvas* [Secker 82].

LATE NOV.   Lawrence told Nancy Pearn, 23, that he would try some little sketches. On 1 Dec. he sent her 'Man is a Hunter'.

DECEMBER 1926   At the Villa Mirenda.

SUMMARY   Lawrence began *John Thomas and Lady Jane,* and wrote his review of R. B. Cunningham Graham's *Pedro de Valdivia* [C149 and *Phoenix*] and two poems 'The Old Orchard' and 'Rainbow' [C153 CP]. He finished *Boccaccio Story* and also painted *Fight with an Amazon* [A46].

6 DEC.   *Suddenly I paint away. I'm doing a biggish canvas—about 1½ yards by 1 yard—of Boccaccio's story of the nuns and the gardener: nice improper story, that tells itself. Painting suddenly interests me seriously—to get a certain feel into it* [Irvine 2, 71].
   Novel goes nicely—so does my Boccaccio picture!! [Secker 82].

13 DEC.   Lawrence sends his review of *Pedro de Valdivia* to Nancy Pearn.

14 DEC.   *Lately I've been painting—quite a big picture, my last, . . . of Boccaccio's story of the nuns and the gardener. I'm sure it would amuse you—it does me. Think I'll turn into a painter, it costs one less, and probably would pay better than writing. Though for that matter I'm patiently doing a novel—scene in the Midlands* [Zytaruk 304]. The word 'patiently' probably indicates that Lawrence had now begun the novel again. There is no evidence in the letters to support Tedlock's conjecture that Lawrence was working on the second version of the novel again. The second version was certainly finished in February—*in the two best books* [Moore 970—i.e. E186b].

19 DEC.   *Now it's a lovely sunny day, and I sat out in the wood this morning, working at my novel—which comes out of me slowly, and is good, I think, but a little too deep in bits—sort of bottomless pools. . . . I've finished my Boccaccio picture—quite nice, nuns in frocks like lavender crocuses—and I've done a quick one,* Fight with an Amazon. *I like it best* [Irvine 2, 72].
   Frieda Lawrence: 'Lawrence is becoming a painter he has painted 3 big pictures and 2 little ones—*so fine*' [Irvine 2, 72–3].

28 DEC.   Fight with an Amazon *is nearly done* [Moore 955].

31 DEC.   Lawrence sent 'The Old Orchard' and 'Rainbow' to Curtis Brown.

JANUARY 1927   At the Villa Mirenda.

SUMMARY   Lawrence continued to write *John Thomas and Lady Jane*. He also wrote 'Autobiographical Sketch' [C182 A53 and *Phoenix 2*], and painted *Red Willow Trees* [A46] and *Negro Wedding*. *I seem to be losing my will-to-write altogether: in spite of the fact that I am working at an English novel—but so differently from the way I have written before! I spend much more time painting—have already done three, nearly four, fairly large pictures. . . . Painting is more fun than writing, much more of a game, and costs the soul far, far less* [Lawrence 235].

8 JAN.   *I'm getting on with the novel . . . and am doing a landscape with figures* [Secker 83].

9 JAN.   To Nancy Pearn: *The* Insel Verlag *asked me for a more or less personal article to put in their Almanack, in German. So I did them one* [Huxley 678]. The original title was 'Becoming a Success'.

12 JAN.   *The new novel is getting on. . . . And I did a little picture of a negro wedding—fairly amusing* [Secker 84].

20 JAN.   *The will-to-write seems to be departing from me: though I do write my novel in sudden intense whacks* [Zytaruk 306].
    My men bathing and red willow-trees is nearly done [Moore 960, mistranscribed].

*25 JAN.   *I've just finished my landscape of red willow trees and men bathing. I like it best, now. It is fun to paint* [Moore 959]. *Red Willow Trees* is in the La Fonda Hotel, Taos.

FEBRUARY 1927   At the Villa Mirenda.

SUMMARY   Lawrence finished the second version of *Lady Chatterley's Lover*. He wrote his review of Carl Van Vechten's *Nigger Heaven*, Walter White's *Flight*, Dos Passos' *Manhatten Transfer* and Hemingway's *In Our Time* [C153 and *Phoenix*], 'John Galsworthy' [B24 and *Phoenix*] and probably 'The Individual Consciousness v. the Social Consciousness' [*Phoenix*]. He began 'The Lovely Lady' [B23 A63] and painted *Flight Back into Paradise* [A46], which is in the La Fonda Hotel, Taos.

To Earl Brewster: *I stick to what I told you, and put a phallus, a lingam you call it, in each one of my pictures somewhere. And I paint no picture that won't shock people's castrated social spirituality. I do this out of positive belief, that the phallus is a great sacred image: it represents a deep, deep life which has been denied in us, and still is denied* [Moore 967].

157

1927

6 FEB.   *I am in the thick of another picture:* Eve Regaining Paradise. . . . *I like to paint rather wet, with oil, so the colour slips about and doesn't look like dried bone, as Magnelli's pictures do. And I'm not so conceited as to think that my marvellous ego and unparalleled technique will make a picture. I like a picture to be a picture to the whole sensual self, and as such it must have a meaning of its own, and concerted action. . . .* My new novel is three parts done, and so absolutely *improper in words, and so really* good, *I hope in spirit—that I don't know what's going to happen to it* [Moore 964].

8 FEB.   To Martin Secker: *It won't take me very long, I think, to finish the novel, so it won't be too lengthy—80 to 90 thousand, I suppose. But you'll probably hate it. I want to call it* Lady Chatterley's Lover, *nice and old-fashioned sounding* [Secker 84].

9 FEB.   To Hon. Dorothy Brett: *I've nearly done my novel—shall let it lie and settle down a bit before I think of having it typed. And I challenge you to a pictorial contest. I'm just finishing a nice big canvas, Eve dodging back into Paradise, between Adam and the Angel at the gate, who are having a fight about it— and leaving the world in flames in the far corner behind her. Great fun, and of course a capolavoro! I should like to do a middle picture, inside Paradise, just as she bolts in. God Almighty astonished and indignant, and the new young God, who is just having a chat with the serpent, pleasantly amused, then the third picture, Adam and Eve under the tree of knowledge, God Almighty disappearing in a dudgeon, and the animals skipping. Probably I shall never get them done* [Moore 965]. These exact pictures were never painted, but *Throwing Back the Apple* and *Dance Sketch* have certain features of them.

25 FEB.   Lawrence sent Nancy Pearn his review of four books for *The Calendar.* He told her he had done all he intended to do of his novel for the time being, and that he had nearly done a story for Cynthia Asquith's murder book. This was 'The Lovely Lady'.

28 FEB.   To Nancy Pearn: *I am sending a 'Scrutiny' on John Galsworthy. . . . I'm afraid it is not very nice to Galsworthy—but really, reading one novel after another just nauseated me up to the nose* [Moore 968]. The MS of 'The Individual Consciousness v. the Social Consciousness' if from the same notebook as the Galsworthy essay [Tedlock 169–71].

MARCH 1927   At the Villa Mirenda until 19, then in Rome until 21. At Palazzo Cimbrone, Ravello, 22–28.

SUMMARY   Earl Brewster: *One day, after the promised visit to us in Ravello, Lawrence and I drove out to the end of the Sorrentine Peninsula, returning to Sorrento on foot. . . . From Sorrento we started on our Etruscan pilgrimage, beginning with the museum of the Villa di Papa Giulia in Rome* [Brewster 120, 122].

Lawrence finished 'The Lovely Lady', painted *Fauns and Nymphs* [A46] and began *Resurrection* [A46].

8 MARCH   To Hon. Dorothy Brett: *How are your radishes? Since my* Eve Regaining Paradise *I've not done anything. I began a resurrection, but haven't worked at it. In the Spring one slackens off* [Moore 969]. Brett's painting of Lawrence in Oaxaca—*Feast of the Radishes*—is reproduced in Levy as by Lawrence.

11 MARCH   To Nancy Pearn: *I am sending today the MSS of 'The Lovely Lady', murder story (sic) for Cynthia Asquith* [Huxley 681].

12 MARCH   Lawrence returned the corrected typescript of 'John Galsworthy' to Nancy Pearn.

22 MARCH   To Nancy Pearn: *Tell Secker not to do anything about* Lady Chatterley's Lover. *I must go over it again and am really not sure if I shall publish it—at least this year* [Moore 970].

25 MARCH   The proofs of 'Two Blue Birds' for the *Dial* [C154] were sent to Lawrence.

22–28   Achsah Brewster: 'Eager as a child with a new toy, singing in bursts of happy excitement, he began to paint a picture. It was going to be a crucifixion with Pan and the nymphs in the foreground. It passed through many metamorphoses and ended by being Pan and the nymphs, without the crucifixion. He was very busy over it, and exuberantly happy while he painted. It was one of his largest pictures (30 × 40 inches or more), and he was greatly pleased with the result [Brewster 275]. This painting, *Fauns and Nymphs*, is now in the La Fonda Hotel, Taos. Lawrence returned to this picture in November 1927 and again in April 1928.

APRIL 1927   At Sorrento until about 3, then to Rome until 6. At Cerveteri, 6; 7–9 at Tarquinia; 9 to Montalto di Castro, Vulci and Grosseto. On 10 (Easter Sunday) to Volterra. Back to the Villa Mirenda, 11.

SUMMARY   *I was really happy looking at Etruscan tombs by the coast north of Rome—Cerveteri, Tarquinia etc. No rush there! Even the ass brays slowly and leisurely, and the tombs are far more twinkling and alive than the houses of men* [Centaur 29].

Lawrence wrote *The Escaped Cock* [A50a], 'Making Love to Music' [*Phoenix*], 'Flowery Tuscany' [C159 161 164 and *Phoenix*], his review of Rozanov's *Solitaria* [C156 and *Phoenix*], and probably 'Germans and Latins' [C217 and *Phoenix*] and 'Germans and English' [*Phoenix 2*]. He began *Etruscan Places* [C163 165 166 168 A60].

We have come to the lying in the garden stage, and I go off into the woods to work, where the nightingales have a very gay time singing at me. They are very inquisitive and come nearer to watch me turn a page. They seem to love to see the pages turned [Moore 973–4].

10 APRIL   Earl Brewster: 'My memory is that Easter morning found us at Grosseto [in fact Volterra]: there we passed a little shop, in the window of which was a toy rooster escaping from an egg. I remarked that it suggested a title—The Escaped Cock—a story of the Resurrection. Lawrence replied that he had been thinking about writing a story of the Resurrection: later in the book of that title which he gave to me, he has written: *To Earl this story, that began in Volterra, when we were there together*' [Brewster 124].

12 APRIL   To Nancy Pearn: *I am in a quandary about my novel,* Lady Chatterley's Lover. *It's what the world would call very improper. But you know it's not really improper—I always labour at the same thing, to make the sex relation valid and precious, instead of shameful. And this novel is the furthest I've gone. To me it is beautiful and tender and frail as the naked self is, and I shrink very much even from having it typed. . . . I think perhaps it's a waste of time to write any more novels. I could probably live by little things* [Moore 972].

13 APRIL   To Secker: *I found the proofs of* Mornings in Mexico *and managed to go through them this morning* [Secker 86].

25 APRIL   *I've been doing a story of the Resurrection—what sort of a man 'rose up', after all that other pretty little experience. Rather devastating!* [Lacy 65].

26 APRIL   Lawrence sent 'Making Love to Music' to Nancy Pearn [Tedlock 210].

27 APRIL   To Koteliansky: *I read Rozanov [*Solitaria*] as soon as he came: and wrote a criticism as soon as I'd read him. . . . Now I really want to do a series of* Travel Sketches of Etruscan Places. *I liked my trip to Cerveteri and Tarquinia and Vulci so much, I'd like to jot them down while they are fresh* [Zytaruk 310–11].

160

28 APRIL   *I'm not painting—but wrote a story of the Resurrection* [Brewster 126]. His next letter gave the Brewsters a fuller account: *I wrote a story of the Resurrection, where Jesus gets up and feels very sick about everything, and can't stand the old crowd any more—so cuts out—and as he heals up, he begins to find what an astonishing place the phenomenal world is, far more marvellous than any salvation or heaven—and thanks his stars he needn't have a 'mission' any more. It's called* The Escaped Cock, *from that toy in Volterra* [Moore 975].

29 APRIL   To Scofield Thayer: *I'm sending back the proofs of 'The Man Who Loved Islands' and 'More Modern Love'* [Joost 104]. Lawrence suggests changing the title of the latter to 'In Love?'. The question mark was used in the *Dial* [C162] but has been dropped in all subsequent printings.

To Martin Secker: *I began my essays on the Etruscan things* [Secker 87].

30 APRIL   'Germans and Latins' contains the sentence: *Tomorrow is the first of May* [*Phoenix* 128]. 'Germans and English' probably dates from about the same time. On 12 April Lawrence had told Nancy Pearn that he hoped soon to send her some small things [Moore 972]. He apparently sent 'Flowery Tuscany' since on 2 May she acknowledged its receipt.

MAY 1927   At the Villa Mirenda.

SUMMARY   *I've once more had a bronchial cold plus malaria, but am feeling better. It is summer, and lazy weather. I'm finishing a picture of the* Resurrection, *and doing a few trifles, but nothing much. This is not a working season* [Secker 88].

Lawrence wrote 'None of That!' [A41], 'Things' [C173 A63], his new introduction to Verga's *Mastro-don Gesualdo*, which exists in two versions, one in A28b and *Phoenix 2*, the other in *Phoenix*, his review, of Walter Wilkinsons's *The Peep Show* [C156 and *Phoenix*], and 'The Man Who Was Through with the World' [*Essays in Criticism*, July 1959 and *The Princess and Other Stories*, Penguin 1971]. He also revised 'The Lovely Lady' and finished *Resurrection*, which is at the University of Texas.

5 MAY   Lawrence sent *The Escaped Cock* to Nancy Pearn.

6 MAY   Lawrence sent the corrected proofs of 'The Man Who Loved Islands' to Nancy Pearn.

1927

9 MAY   Lawrence told Jonathan Cape that he had sent the Introduction to *Mastro-don Gesualdo* to Curtis Brown [Delaney 205]. Lawrence had complained to Christine Hughes in a letter of 25 April about the difficulty he was experiencing in finding any material about Verga: *I scour Florence, but Verga had better have been a Hottentot, the Italians would know more about him. I suppose I'll have to invent it out of my own head—povero me!* [Lacy 65].

12 MAY   Lawrence sent his review of *The Peep Show*, and a shortened version of 'The Lovely Lady' to Nancy Pearn. On 25 April Nancy Pearn had suggested that the length of the story, over twelve thousand words, was 'somewhat terrifying', and had passed on some requests from Lady Cynthia Asquith for specific cuts and changes. She had not liked either 'the drainpipe part' or 'the miaowing part'. Lawrence thought her objection to the drainpipe absurd.

13 MAY   *I did paint a bit of my* Resurrection *picture—un poco triste, ma mi pare forte. I got him as impersonal as a queer animal! But I can't finish it* [Moore 976].

27 MAY   Lawrence sent Nancy Pearn 'None of That', telling her that it was founded on fact.

28 MAY   To Lady Cynthia Asquith: *Have your note about 'The Lovely Lady'. Unfortunately I haven't a copy of the briefer version—which you now hold—only of the longer version. And I can't in the least remember the differences between the two. If there's time ask Miss Pearn if she has a copy of the first—and then mark any bit you'd like me to put into your final version—and send both along—and I'll run 'em together. If there's not time, I'll try to put the bit in, if you send me your copy by return* [Finney 246–7].

It seems Lawrence had gone rather too far for Lady Cynthia in shortening the story. It is unlikely that the changes he here offers to make were ever made, since the text in *The Black Cap* [B23] is only just over half the length of the Yale corrected typescript. [See Finney.]

I finished my Resurrection *picture, and like it. It's Jesus stepping up, rather grey in the face, from the tomb, with his old ma helping him from behind, and Mary Magdalen easing him up towards her bosom in front* [Moore 981].

Throughout this spring we find frequent references to the attractions of the hermit life. 12 April: *I only want to retire away into the hills here, and be a hermit* [Centaur 30]. 19 May: *I feel like turning hermit and hiding away the rest of my days away from everybody. But I suppose it is a phase, a sort of psychic change of life many men go through after forty. I wish it would hurry up and get over* [Lawrence-Ada 157]. By 28 May Lawrence seems to have got over it. To Earl Brewster: *So you lie and muse of Cyprus . . . and of bho-trees and winding lanes, silence and the sea, long conversations, disciples, and success. Caro, it's no good. We shall never go to Cyprus, nor to any other happy isle. You will hover round Capri, and I shall go out into the world again, to kick it and stub my toes. It's no good my thinking of retreat: I rouse up, and feel I don't want to. My business is a fight, and I've got to keep it up* [Moore 980].

He may have helped to exorcise his own desire to be a hermit by writing 'The Man Who Was Through with the World', which is on paper torn from the same notebook as *Etruscan Places*. Henry the Hermit is both Lawrence and Earl Brewster. Lawrence's concern for the Brewsters at this time [see letters of 25 and 27 June, Moore 986–7] is also reflected in the story 'Things', which must have been written at this time, since Nancy Pearn returned the original MS to Lawrence on 10 June.

JUNE 1927 **At the Villa Mirenda, except for a day or two with the Aldous Huxleys at Forte dei Marmi between 14 and 21.**

SUMMARY Lawrence finished his Etruscan essays and began *The Finding of Moses* [A46].

6 JUNE To Secker: *I began doing the Etruscan book, have done about 80 pp. mss . . . I might possibly, if the gods wish it, get these* Sketches of Etruscan Places *done by early autumn. . . . It would have to be a book with many full illustrations, a hundred even, and as such it could be a standard popularish, not scientific—book on the Etruscan things and places, and might really sell, for the photographs at least are striking and beautiful. When I've finished Tarquinia, I'll let you see the essays on Cerveteri and Tarquinia* [Secker 89]. Lawrence had just begun chapter 4, the second of the two chapters on the painted tombs of Tarquinia.

9 JUNE *I began the Etruscan essays: have done Cerveteri and Tarquinia so far* [Moore 984].

11 JUNE *. . . painting a smallish picture*—Finding of Moses—*all negresses. It's amazing, because I don't quite know how to do it* [Lawrence-Ada 159–60].

14 JUNE Lawrence sent 'Cerveteri' to Curtis Brown, and told Secker that he had done four more. This means he had now added 'Vulci'.

25 JUNE   To Earl Brewster: *I wrote my essay on Volterra—made me think of you. One day we will really go after more Etruscans together. Meanwhile I think I shall go to Arezzo and Cortona, Chiusi, Orvieto, Perugia with Frieda, towards the end of next week. I'd like to do those places before we leave. With Cerveteri and Tarquinia, Vulci and Volterra, that makes nine of the great cities—the twelve.—But it leaves a whole bookful of little places—Veii, Civita Castellana, Norchia, Vetulonia, Cosa, Populonia, Bieda—we might do those, and make a second vol.—after* [Moore 986]. The gods did not wish it. Bathing in the sea at Forte dei Marmi, a few days before the planned excursion to Etruria, Lawrence brought on a bronchial haemorrhage, and the trip had to be abandoned. For Lawrence the completion of the book was contingent upon seeing these other sites. He continued to plan the trip for another two years, but it was never made.

JULY 1927   At the Villa Mirenda

SUMMARY   *But the Etruscan and all work can sleep with the devil, if only I get well again. I will enjoy myself and forget everything* [Lawrence 243–4]. Lawrence was too ill to work for most of the month, but got ready for publication, with notes, the first two stories from *Cavalleria Rusticana* [A39].

2 JULY   Lawrence told Secker he wanted to do Etruscan essays on Florence and Fiesole.

5 JULY   Nancy Pearn sent Lawrence the proofs of 'The Man Who Loved Islands' for the *London Mercury*.

22 JULY   Lawrence had still done only the six essays, and said: *I shan't be able to do any more of my Etruscans this summer* [Secker 91]. He did, however, add a seventh essay, 'The Florence Museum', probably after his return to Florence in October.

31 JULY   Lawrence told Nancy Pearn that he was sending her the first two stories from Verga's *Cavelleria Rusticana*. These are 'Cavalleria Rusticana' and 'La Lupa', both of which Lawrence had originially translated in August 1922.

AUGUST 1927   At the Villa Mirenda until 4. Then at Hotel Fischer, Villach, Austria, until 29. Then, via Saltzburg to Irschenhausen (Villa Jaffe), near Munich.

SUMMARY   Lawrence wrote his review of *The Social Basis of Conscious-ness* by Trigant Burrow [C160 and *Phoenix*], and continued his translations of Verga.

3 AUG.   Lawrence wrote a very appreciative letter to Trigant Burrow, ending: *I shall write a review of your book if I can* [Moore 994]. He did so immediately, and left it in Florence to be forwarded to Nancy Pearn.
*13 AUG.   To Pino Orioli: *I translate my Verga on rainy days, and I still like him, and still worry you about him* [Moore 997]. Lawrence was asking Orioli for help translating a passage near the beginning (seventh page of printed text) of 'Jeli the Herdsman'.
17 AUG.   To Secker: *I left the ms of* Lady Chatterley *at the Mirenda—one day I'll show it to you privately. I want to write a continuation of it, later* [Secker 93]. Lawrence was to rewrite the novel, but the third version is in no sense a continuation of the second.
22 AUG.   *I bought water-colours here, but so far, have not wet a brush* [Moore 998].
23 AUG.   Lawrence asks Nancy Pearn if the first three Verga stories arrived safely.
26 AUG.   Lawrence returned to Curtis Brown the corrected proofs of 'John Galsworthy'.

SEPTEMBER 1927   At Villa Jaffe, Irschenhausen

SUMMARY   *I don't do much except take walks in the forest, and translate Verga's* Cavalleria Rusticana *and play patience. I am glad when I don't work—I have worked too much* [Brewster 149]. Lawrence finished his Verga translations and wrote the Introduction [A39 and *Phoenix*].

17 SEPT.   *The translation is nearly done: it's a little book: then I shall do a longish foreword* [Secker 94].
*25 SEPT.   *Today I have finished my* Cavalleria Rusticana *translation: now I've only to do the introduction* [Moore 1004].
28 SEPT.   Lawrence sent the final text and the introduction to Curtis Brown.

OCTOBER 1927   At Irschenhausen until 5, then to Hotel Eden, Baden–Baden until 18, then back to the Villa Mirenda.

SUMMARY *I don't feel a bit like work: yet shall have to tackle a few things. Secker wants to do my collected poems: that means typing them out and arranging and doing: then he's bringing out a vol. of short stories in January: and then I ought to finish the Etruscan Essays, of which I've done just half. But I feel terribly indifferent to it all, whether it's done or not* [Moore 1012].

Lawrence returned to *The Finding of Moses* [A46], and began two stories: 'The Undying Man' [*Phoenix*] and 'A Dream of Life' (my title for the inaptly titled 'Autobiographical Fragment' of *Phoenix*).

*6 OCT.   To Koteliansky: *Had your letter and MS in Irschenhausen. I'll try and work the stories up, when I have an inspired moment, and let you see what I can make of them* [Zytaruk 322].

In February 1937 Koteliansky published in *The London Mercury* 'Two Jewish Stories' recorded by his mother in Yiddish. In his prefatory note he wrote: 'It must have been in 1926 or 1927, when I sent the two Jewish stories, in my translation, as given here, to D. H. Lawrence, saying, would he try either to render them into better English, or—which would be finer still—tell them in his own way. He replied at the time that he liked the stories very much; that he would try to remake them. . . . I heard no more from him about them. . . . "Maimonides and Aristotle" he did try to remake, although he left it unfinished. The fragment recently appeared under the title "The Undying Man" in the volume *Phoenix*.' See Zytaruk xxviii and the introduction to *The Princess and Other Stories* [Penguin, 1971], where the story is reprinted.

21 OCT.   *I might begin a painting of Adam and Eve pelting the Old Lord-God with apples, and driving him out of paradise—but I've got no canvas, and shall never go to Florence—and I don't care either. So there's David sitting on his thumbs* [Moore 1013].

26 OCT.   Lawrence told Norman Douglas that he was trying to do a sort of story to be published by Koteliansky in his proposed Intimate Series.

*28 OCT.   *I am already doing a story, and dabbing at my picture of five negresses—called* The Finding of Moses* [Lawrence 274]. Lawrence had begun this painting in June. It was not finished until April 1928.

31 OCT.   To Koteliansky: *If you want my MS by Christmas, I'll get it done—though it may be a bit long* [Moore 1015]. The story Lawrence began and never finished for Koteliansky must be 'A Dream of Life', where the narrator goes to sleep in October 1927, and wakes a thousand years later.

NOVEMBER 1927 At the Villa Mirenda.

SUMMARY *We sit here rather vaguely, and I still haven't been to Florence. . . I do bits of things—darn my underclothes and try to type out poems—old ones* [Moore 1020]. Lawrence wrote 'Rawdon's Roof' [A40 A63] and began work on his *Collected Poems* [A43]. He painted 'Throwing Back the Apple' [A46] and 'The Jaguar' [Levy] and returned to 'Fauns and Nymphs'.

*6 NOV.   *I am painting a picture, not very big, of a tiger who springs on a man: such a grinning tiger* [Lawrence 266].
*8 NOV.   *I am still a bit groggy and not very well pleased with myself: but painting pictures of large and ruddy nymphs and fauns, to keep me in countenance* [Moore 1017]. Lawrence had asked Earl Brewster to send him this painting: *Perhaps the sight of that coy nymph and grinning man—very orange, I remember them—might start me daubing a bit* [Moore].
11 NOV.   *I'm not really working—did a smallish picture of a jaguar jumping on a man—and a water-color of Adam and Eve pelting the Lord with apples to drive him out of the garden* [Irvine 2, 79]. *The Jaguar* is now at the University of Texas.
14 NOV.   *I am dabbing at poems, getting them ready for the* Collected Poems [Lawrence 253].
16 NOV.   *I am writing stories and am typing all my poems* [Moore 1021]. Lawrence was writing 'Rawdon's Roof', of which Nancy Pearn acknowledged the receipt 24 November. The Berkeley typescript has extensive interlinear revision, and pages of dialogue have been written on verso. But see 22 November 1928.
18 NOV.   *I am busy getting my poems in order, to go into one vol.—all the poems. My word, what ghosts come rising up! But I just tidy their clothes for them and refuse to be drawn* [Luhan 334–5].

DECEMBER 1927 At the Villa Mirenda.

SUMMARY   Lawrence began the third and final version of *Lady Chatterley's Lover* [A42], and possibly painted *Under the Mango Tree* [A46]. In an April letter to Aldous Huxley [Moore 1052] Lawrence refers to *The Mango Tree* as a painting already known to Huxley. Huxley's last opportunity to see it would have been his visit to the Villa Mirenda at Christmas 1927. Since the new year he had been in Switzerland.

3 DEC.   The beginning of the MS of *Lady Chatterley's Lover* bears this date.

18 DEC.   *I am rewriting the book for the third time, and am half way through again* [Centaur 31].

*18 DEC.   *I have spent yesterday and to-day doing a picture. Which I have just burnt—*[Brewster 155].

23 DEC.   To Koteliansky: *As for my novel, it's half done, but so improper, you wouldn't dare to touch it. It's the most improper novel ever written and as Jehovah you would probably find it sheer pornography. But it isn't. It's a declaration of the phallic reality* [Moore 1028].

JANUARY 1928   At Villa Mirenda until 19 or 20. At Les Diablerets (Chalet Beau Site), Vaud, Switzerland, 21.

SUMMARY   *I've been busy doing my poems—have at last got all the early poems together and complete. What a sweat! But I shall publish the others, 'Look!' and* Birds and Beasts *as they stand. Then I'll have to go through the novel, which I'm having typed in London. How glad I'll be when all this work is behind me, and I needn't give a damn any more. I'm sick to death of literature* [Lawrence 269].

Lawrence worked on the *Collected Poems*, the proofs of *The Woman Who Rode away* [A41], and the expurgating of *Lady Chatterley's Lover*. He wrote his Introduction to *The Mother* by Grazia Deledda [B25 and *Phoenix*].

5 JAN.   Lawrence sent his introduction to *The Mother* to Nancy Pearn.
*6 JAN.   *I've been rewriting my novel, for the third time. It's done, all but the last chapter. I think I shall re-christen it* Tenderness [Moore 1030].
8 JAN.   *I finished it today* [Moore 1032].
11 JAN.   To Secker: *Thanks for the poetry books. I've been typing out the early ones. . . . I've done a good bit of revising* [Secker 97].
17 JAN.   To Secker: *I was going over the poems, would you get the* New Poems *typed out for me, one carbon copy, so I can alter them a bit, and get this whole first half into order* [Secker 98]. The extent of Lawrence's alterations can be seen in Ferrier's *Variorum*, or, selectively, in *CP* appendix 3. Some of the poems were completely transformed.

The proofs of *The Woman Who Rode Away* arrived on this date. He found that the ending of 'The Border Line' was missing, both from the proofs and the MS. He was therefore obliged to write a new ending:
*27 JAN.   *I wrote a new ending, but it takes about 4½ pages* [Secker 99].

FEBRUARY 1928   At Chalet Beau Site, Les Diablerets, Switzerland.

SUMMARY   Lawrence finished the work on his *Collected Poems* and the expurgated version of *Lady Chatterley's Lover*.

3 FEB.   *I've been busy getting my poems together for a collected edition—rather a sweat—but now it's done, and the MS is ready to go off. Something else behind me* [Brewster 160].
Lawrence must have finished the proofs of *The Woman Who Rode*

Away by this time, since he told Secker on 10 February that he had sent them *a week ago.*

4 FEB.   *I'm going over my novel here—the typescript—and I'm going to try to expurgate and substitute sufficiently to produce a properish public version, for Alf Knopf, presumably, to publish* [Centaur 32]. Lawrence's labours were wasted, since both Knopf and Secker rejected even his expurgated version. They waited until 1932 to publish a much more expurgated version.

12 FEB.   To Dorothy Brett: *I'm working here on the typescript of my novel. Maria* [Huxley] *typed out the second half for me, and I was very grateful to her—am. But she makes far more mistakes than you do—oh, a simple chicken-pox of mistakes* [Moore 1039].

Nellie Morrison had typed the first five chapters before deciding that Lawrence was pandering to a pornographic taste. The rest of the first half was being typed by Catherine Carswell in London.

18 FEB.   Lawrence sent back the revised, that is second, proofs of *The Woman Who Rode Away* [Secker 101].

MARCH 1928   At Les Diablerets until 6. Then at the Villa Mirenda.

SUMMARY   Lawrence completed his expurgation of *Lady Chatterley's Lover,* corrected the proofs of his *Collected Poems,* and painted several pictures.

*2 MARCH   *At last I have got the complete typescript of* Lady Chatterley*—am going over the final chapters. . . . I find I simply don't know how much and how little to expurgate. So I'm not doing much* [Secker 103].

5 MARCH   To Secker: *I posted off the MS of the novel to Pollinger today—changed the title to:* John Thomas and Lady Jane: *which I hope you like, as it's much more suitable than the other. . . . Then the expurgations—I did a fair amount of blanking out and changing, then I sort of got colour-blind, and didn't know any more what was supposed to be proper and what not* [Moore 1041]. A few days later Lawrence wrote to McDonald: *I expurgated what I could—all the man's touching address to his penis, and things like that* [Moore 1042].

Lawrence felt the word 'penis' itself had to go, but hardly improved matters by substituting for it, in Tommy Dukes' speech at the end of chapter 4, successively 'tilter', jouster' and 'little Lancelot'. 'Fucking'

170

becomes, in the space of a page, 'making love', 'loving a woman up', 'love-practice', 'taking', 'sensation' and 'sensation-rousing'. 'Arse' becomes 'rear', 'tail', 'bottom' and 'behind'. One can see that Lawrence is thoroughly colour-blind when he changes: *An' if tha shits an' if tha pisses, I'm glad. I don't want a woman as couldna shit nor piss* into: *An' if tha comes an' goes, I'm glad. I don't want a woman as couldna come an' go.* He was obviously still colour-blind when he changed the title.

6 MARCH   *About* The Escaped Cock *. . . I had the idea I might add on to it perhaps another 5000 words. Of course I don't know if I could* [Lacy 67]. Lawrence wrote the second part in June.

8 MARCH   *I've been painting a water-colour: torch-dance by daylight!* [Huxley 706].

*9 MARCH   *Today I lunched with Orioli, and we took the MS of the novel to the printer: great moment* [Moore 1043]. The proofs of the *Collected Poems* also arrived [Secker 105].

15 MARCH   Lawrence tells Curtis Brown that if Spud Johnson does not publish *The Escaped Cock: I shall write a second half to it—the phallic second half I always intended to add to it* [Huxley 709].

*16 MARCH   *I sent back the proofs of the poems* [Moore 1048].

   I've done three more water-colours: not-bad, but I'd rather do oils: one can use one's elbow, and in water it's all dib-dab. . . . I've made my design of a phoenix rising from the nest in flames, for the cover [of *Lady Chatterley.*] [Huxley 715].

   Another letter to the Huxleys of 2 April enables us to identify these: *Maria can have any one of the water-colours: they are seven:* Adam Throwing the Apple, *and* The Mango Tree: *those you know. Then* The Torch Dance, Yawning. The Lizard, Under the Haystack, *and* Dandelions [Moore 1052–3]. The three must therefore be *Yawning, Lizard* and *Under the Haystack* [all A46].

27 MARCH   Lawrence had asked Earl Brewster for some photographs of people in various natural positions to help him with his paintings. He thanks him for the second batch and tells him he has painted from one of them a man pissing. This is *Dandelions* [Moore 1052].

APRIL 1928   At the Villa Mirenda.

SUMMARY   *I'm very busy with my novel—buying paper, hand-made—correcting proofs—making a phoenix from a nest in flames, like that* seal I gave Murry, for the cover stamp—getting cover-paper—etc. [Irvine 2, 82]. Lawrence wrote 'Chaos in Poetry' [C194 B33 and Phoenix], rewrote Sun [A35b], finished Fauns and Nymphs, and painted Rape of the Sabine Women and Family on a Verandah [both A46]. He probably also wrote 'The "Jeune Fille" Wants to Know' [C169 A53 and Phoenix 2].

*2 APRIL   I've corrected 41 pages of proofs, and it was almost Maria's typing over again. Dear Maria, all those little mistakes you made, and I followed like Wenceslas's page so patiently in your footsteps: now it's a Florentine printer. He writes dind't did'nt, dnid't, dind't, din'dt, didn't like a Bach fugue. . . . Now I'm doing a small thing in oil, called The Rape of the Sabine Women or A Study in Arses [Moore 1052]. Rape of the Sabine Women is at the La Fonda Hotel, Taos.

13 APRIL   I'm doing my Ravello Fauns up [Brewster 168]. See March 1927.

16 APRIL   I'm in the middle of the proofs—shall finish them this week [Huxley 723]. Lawrence was in fact unable to continue with the proofs, because the printer had only enough type to set up half the novel at a time, and could not print the first half until the paper arrived.

17 APRIL   To Harry Crosby: Send your complete book of poems, and I'll write a little introduction for it. . . . And I'll send you the MSS—'Man Who Loved Islands'—and 'Sun' [Moore 1057].

On 1 April Lawrence had written to Nancy Pearn: Have you got by any chance the manuscript of Sun in the office? An American asks me for it particularly, and offers $100. So there's a windfall, if it exists. If it doesn't, povero me! for I haven't got it, the MS [Huxley 717].

Nancy Pearn replied (13 April): 'Here is the list of recent manuscripts we have been holding for you, and how I regret that 'Sun' is one of those we previously returned! Are you sure you burnt them all; and tell me, would it be cheating to write out the story again in your own fair handwriting to sell to the eager Yank? If not, why not?' Lawrence apparently took her advice, but took the opportunity also to rewrite the story, more in the spirit of Lady Chatterley. In 1954 Frieda Lawrence obtained a statement of the copyright standing of all Lawrence's works. The entry for Sun reads: 'The original version was expanded and published by the Black Sun Press in Paris in October 1928.' Lawrence himself, although several times referring to this version as 'unexpurgated' also called it the final MS [Huxley 730].

25 APRIL   Am doing a Family in Garden—rather small—all nude, of course—ma in hammock, pa on his heels squatting—and two bambini

172

[Huxley 728]. *Family on a Verandah* is now in the possession of Mrs Betty Cottam.

26 APRIL   The introduction to *Chariot of the Sun* bears this date.

29 APRIL   Three more pages were added on this date. See Texas MS.

LATE   26 April Nancy Pearn had passed on to Lawrence a request from the editor of the *Evening News* for an article on the generation gap. 'When She Asks Why?' appeared there 8 May. A somewhat changed version 'The "Jeune Fille" Wants to Know' was included in *Assorted Articles*. The Texas holograph is slightly different from either, and is on paper torn from the 'John Galsworthy' and 'Man is a Hunter' notebook. Lawrence may therefore have rewritten something originally written a year or so earlier.

MAY 1928   At the Villa Mirenda.

SUMMARY   Lawrence wrote 'Mother and Daughter' [C184 A63], 'Laura Philippine' [C170 A53 and *Phoenix 2*], 'All There' [*Daily Chronicle* and *Phoenix*] and the introduction to his *Collected Poems* [A43 and *Phoenix CP*]. He revised his introduction to *Chariot of the Sun*. He continued with the proofs of *Lady Chatterley's Lover*.

1 MAY   The revised version of 'Chaos in Poetry' bears this date.

12 MAY   To Secker: *I have written out a longer note for the Poems, which I enclose. I wrote it longer than this, as an introduction or foreword, then thought you would perhaps have trouble getting it in, so cut it down to half. If this is still too long, you can cut it yourself to fit* [Secker 106]. The shorter version was used in A43, the longer in *Phoenix*. Both are in CP. Both are dated 12 May 1928.

13 MAY   Lawrence sent 'Laura Philippine' to Nancy Pearn. It is based on incidents which had taken place on 19–21 March 1927, when Lawrence stayed at Christine Hughes' flat in Rome.

21 MAY   Lawrence sent 'What Women Know' to Nancy Pearn. This appeared in *Assorted Articles* as 'All There'.

22 MAY   The printers at last began to set up the second half of *Lady Chatterley* and Lawrence was able to continue with the proofs. The printers knew no English, so the pure correcting necessary was considerable, but Lawrence also made a good many changes.

24 MAY   *I'm at the very last chapters now* [Centaur 33].

LATE MAY   'Mother and Daughter' must have been written this month, since by 4 June it was in Nancy Pearn's hands.

JUNE 1928 At Villa Mirenda until 10. The night of the 10 was spent in Turin, 11 in Chambery, 12 in Aix les Bains, 13 Grenoble and 14 St Nizier. From 15 at Grand Hotel, Chexbres-sur-Vevey, Switzerland.

SUMMARY Lawrence wrote the second half of *The Man Who Died* [A50c], 'Insouciance' [C171 A53], and 'Master in his Own House' [C174 A53]. He began 'The Blue Moccasins' [C183 A63], and probably painted before leaving the Villa Mirenda *Italian Landscape* [Levy], *Behind the Villa Mirenda* [Levy] and *Piero Pini Leading his Oxen to Work*.

4 JUNE Lawrence finished the proofs of *Lady Chatterley's Lover*.
*7 JUNE *Signed the last sheets for* Lady C. *today, so am free* [Zytaruk 343].
*21 JUNE *I worked over my Isis story a bit* [Lawrence 224].
27 JUNE Lawrence sent 'Insouciance' to Nancy Pearn.
28 JUNE Lawrence sent 'Men Must Rule' to Nancy Pearn. It appeared in *Vanity Fair*, November 1928, as 'Deserted Battlefields', and in the *Evening News*, 2 August 1928, and *Assorted Articles* as 'Master in his Own House'.
30 JUNE Lawrence told Laurence Pollinger that he had almost finished the second half of *The Escaped Cock*.

JULY 1928 At Grand Hotel, Chexbres-sur-Vevey until 6, then to the Hotel National, Gstaad until 9, then to Kesselmatte, Gsteig bei Gstaad, Bern, Switzerland.

SUMMARY *Of course there are no level walks—but I potter around among the trees, and they have made me a little table and bench where I sit and dibble away at a painting of men catching horses—just a little thing* [Moore 1062].

Lawrence finished *The Man Who Died* and 'Blue Moccasins'. He wrote the 'Autobiographical Sketch' [Nehls 3, 232–4 and *Phoenix 2*, 300–2], 'Matriarchy' [C177 A53], 'Ownership' [A 53], and his reviews of Robert Byron's *The Station*, Clough Williams-Ellis' *England and the Octopus*, Maurice Baring's *Comfortless Memory*, and W. S. Maugham's *Ashenden or the British Agent* [C172 and *Phoenix*]. He also did some paintings including, possibly, *Close-Up (Kiss)* [A46].

12 JULY Lawrence sent Nancy Pearn 'Matriarchy' and 'Ownership'.
17 JULY Lawrence sent Nancy Pearn his review for *Vogue*.
18 JULY Lawrence sent Miss Watson his autobiographical sketch.

20 JULY   *I haven't given Crosby Gaige the second half of* Escaped Cock, *though I've written it, and I think it's lovely. But somehow I don't want to let it go out of my hands. It lies here in MS—not typed yet* [Irvine 2, 88].

Sometimes Earl [Brewster] *comes and paints in the morning. I try to do just little things—small little panels—but I haven't got much art in me here* [Lacy 68].

To Dorothy Warren: *I am doing one or two small ones here, which I will send along later, all being well. I might even finish another biggish one, quite different* [Nehls 3, 231]. The largest painting subsequently sent to Dorothy Warren was *Close-Up (Kiss)*, which is only 15 in × 18 in. Dorothy Warren had this painting by 31 August when Frieda wrote to her: 'I want to keep the *Resurrection, Boccaccio,* and the *Kiss*' [Nehls 3, 240]. See August for other paintings which may have been begun in July.

26 JULY   Lawrence sent Nancy Pearn 'The Blue Moccasins' for *Eve* where it appeared on 22 November 1928. This was his last completed piece of fiction. On the Texas holograph MS. Lawrence has crossed out the last two pages and written between the lines a completely new ending, which extends for a further three pages. Tedlock summarises: 'In the struck-out ending Lina had returned the moccasins at Percy's urging so that the play might continue, and when Alice asked Percy what Lina, much older than he, meant to him, he answered that she was perfect and "really puts the final touch to life". In the new ending Lina does not yield the moccasins, and Lawrence changes from reconciliation to a final breach between husband and wife and a transferral of his allegiance to Alice' [Tedlock 70–1].

Achsah Brewster: 'We were sitting among the harebells when Lawrence opened his copy-book with green emerald corners, and began reading his story, 'The Blue Moccasins', which he had just finished. Before the ending he stopped and asked us how we would end it. We all agreed to the same dénouement. He replied that he also at first had closed the tale in like manner, but on further consideration he had felt forced to change it, whereupon he read the version as it stood' [Brewster 291].

AUGUST 1928   At Kesselmatte.

SUMMARY   Achsah Brewster: 'A rustic work-bench and a table had been made in the pine-grove for Lawrence, where he sat and wrote in view of the mountains, and near him the fragrant pines murmuring in the wind. The autumn crocuses swept over the hills. Yet for all that, as the days grew shorter he longed to go down into the world. The bleak green hills with their black trees patrolling them chilled the heart' [Brewster 291–2].

Lawrence wrote 'Dull London' [C175 A53] 'Cocksure Women and Hensure Men' [C181 A53], 'Hymns in a Man's Life' [C178 A53], and probably 'Women Are so Cocksure' [*Phoenix*]. He painted *Contadini* [A46] *The Milk-White Lady and the Coal-Black Smith* [University of Texas] and *Accident in a Mine* [A46].

*13 AUG. To Harry Crosby: *I'll give you a little painting I did of men catching sun-horses—quite tiny. . . . I enclose a drawing of the Sun, from a Maya design* [Huxley 747]. The Sun drawing was used as a frontispiece to the Black Sun Press *Sun*.

*15 AUG. To Earl Brewster: *I painted* Contadini *on the panel you gave me* [Moore 1075]. Philip Trotter: 'This fine painting disappeared with several others from a half-way house between our London home and the wartime sanctuary of Thomas Agnew & Son. It was, I believe, the only picture drawn from a living model' [Nehls 3, 715]. If that is so, Lawrence must have taken a sketch for this painting with him to Gsteig from the Mirenda.

20 AUG. Lawrence sent 'Dull London' to Nancy Pearn.

24 AUG. Lawrence sent 'Cocksure Women and Hensure Men' to Miss Pearn. Achsah Brewster: 'He read his last article, "Cocksure Women and Hensure Men", which particularly pleased Boshi Sen, who maintained every woman in India ought to read it. Lawrence shook his head—"But they won't publish it even though they have asked for it!"—which incredible as it seems, proved to be true' [Brewster 289]. The article was rejected by the *Evening News*.

29 AUG. The Brewsters left Gsteig on this date. Before their departure they saw two more Lawrence paintings: 'At that time he was painting small water-colours, among them *An Explosion in a Mine*—a group of naked men carrying the body of a wounded miner. As he showed it to us, he said: "You know the miners work in some mines naked". One afternoon we were singing "The Two Magicians"—

Oh, she looked out of the window,
    As white as any milk.
But he looked in the window
    As black as any silk.

That seemed to please Lawrence very much. "I believe I'll paint that milk-white lady with the black man gazing in through the window at her." Next time we climbed the hill he had painted her.' [Brewster 289].

30 AUG.   According to Achsah Brewster Lawrence wrote 'Hymns in a Man's Life' the day after their departure [Brewster 293]. Lawrence sent it to Nancy Pearn on 2 September.

SEPTEMBER 1928   At Kesselmatte until 18, then at Hotel Lowen, Lichtenthal, Baden-Baden.

SUMMARY   Lawrence wrote 'Red Trousers' [C176 A53], and painted 'North Sea' [A46] and a flower picture.

*2 SEPT.   *I've only painted one or two little things here—And now figures on the sand at the sea. There's something very dramatic about paint* [Moore 1085]. This was *North Sea*, subsequently given to Maria Huxley, and probably destroyed in the fire at the Huxley home.

*8 SEPT.   Lawrence sent Nancy Pearn the proofs of 'Things' for the *Fortnightly Review*, October 1928.

13 SEPT.   *I painted a flower picture . . . the Etruscan embroidery is done, save the background* [Brewster 179]. Lawrence sent 'Red Trousers' to Nancy Pearn. He returned the proofs of *Sun* to Harry Crosby before leaving Switzerland. Lawrence did at least two Etruscan embroideries. See June 1926.

OCTOBER 1928   At Le Lavandou until 15, then to La Vigie, Ile de Port-Cros, Var.

SUMMARY   Lawrence was ill at La Vigie, but managed to begin his translation of Il Lasca's *The Story of Doctor Manente* [A45] and to write 'Is England Still a Man's Country?' [C180].

20 OCT.   Lawrence wrote to his sister Emily that he was not working at all, just doing nothing.

*21 OCT.   *I have begun with the* Terza Cena *of Lasca* [Priest 456].

*27 OCT.   Wrote to Orioli that the Lasca story was half done.

30 OCT.   Lawrence received from Nancy Pearn the proofs of 'The Blue Mocassins' and a renewed request for 'Is England Still a Man's Country?'. He must have acted very quickly, for on November 5 he writes to ask Nancy Pearn if she has received them. These were presumably for *Eve*, 22 November 1928 [see Finney 3].

NOVEMBER 1928   At La Vigie, Ile de Port-Cros until 17, then at Hotel Beau-Rivage, Bandol, Var, France.

SUMMARY   Richard Aldington: 'It seems to me one up to Lawrence that he went tranquilly on with his writing although he was so ill, and was angry and bitter about the attacks on him in England. Every morning he sat up in bed, and produced a short story or one of the little essays of *Assorted Articles*. . . . He must also have been working secretly on *Pansies,* for two of them were inspired by books he read on the island. One was Aldous Huxley's *Point Counter Point* and the other a book on Attila' [Nehls 3, 254].

Lawrence finished his translation of Lasca, and began *Pansies* [A47].

The essays were 'Sex Versus Loveliness' [C179], 'Do Women Change?' [C185] and 'Enslaved by Civilization' [C191]. Lawrence may have begun *Pansies* immediately after 'Sex Appeal', a beginning of 'Sex Versus Loveliness' (which it follows in the MS notebook), but since he makes no mention of any poems until 22, and mentions them very frequently subsequently, it is more likely that he did not begin them until he had finished *Dr. Manente* in the middle of the month, which would also explain why Aldington heard nothing about them. Lawrence read *Point Counter Point* at the and of October, and received the reviews of *Lady Chatterley's Lover* on 30 October, but it does not follow that he wrote the poems which relate to these at once. He continues to discuss these topics in his letters for the next two months. Lawrence is not known to have written any fiction as late as this, except for the unfinished story which begins *'Henry', she said, 'I want to disappear for a year'* . . . [E159], a story which cannot have been written earlier than January 1929.

*1 NOV.   Lawrence wrote to Orioli that he had nearly done *Dr. Manente*.
5 NOV.   Lawrence sent Nancy Pearn 'Sex Appeal', published in the *Sunday Dispatch*, 25 November as 'Sex Locked Out', and in *Assorted Articles* as 'Sex Versus Loveliness'.
8 NOV.   Lawrence sent Nancy Pearn 'Do Women Change?', published as 'Women Don't Change' in the *Sunday Dispatch*, 28 August 1929, and in *Vanity Fair,* April 1929, in different versions. The former is in *Assorted Articles.*
*9 NOV.   Lawrence told Orioli that he will send the Lasca translation.
17 NOV.   Lawrence told Orioli that he has sent it.
22 NOV.   Lawrence told his sister Emily that he has done no work to speak of lately except a bit of verse. He told Pollinger that he has lengthened *Rawdon's Roof* by five pages as requested, and that the work took him a good hour.

23 NOV. According to Richard Aldington's description of MS B of *Last Poems*, which he called *More Pansies*, the inside cover of the notebook bears the date 23 November 1928. It does not. But the front free endpaper is now missing: presumably the inscription was there. The first nineteen poems in the notebook, which is headed *Pensées,* are early drafts of poems which went into *Pansies,* or in five cases seem to have been rejected. The rejected poems were published in Smailes. The order in the notebook is: (1) 'The Salt of the Earth' [*Pansies*]; (2) 'Amphibian' [Smailes]; (3) 'Salt Licks' [Smailes]; (4) 'Fresh Water' [*Pansies*]; (5) 'Widdershins' [Smailes]; (6) 'War' [*Pansies* as 'Peace and War' and Smailes]; (7) 'The Maleficent Triangle' [Smailes]; (8) 'Glory' [*Pansies*]; (9) 'Fight for Life' [*Pansies* as 'What Would You Fight For?']; (10) 'Woe is Over the World' [*Pansies* as 'Woe']; (11) 'Attila' [*Pansies*]; (12) 'Choice' [*Pansies*]; (13) 'To be Rich' [*Pansies* as 'Riches']; (14) 'To be Poor' [*Pansies* as 'Poverty']; (15) 'To be Noble' [*Pansies* as 'Noble']; (16) 'I am Well-off' [*Pansies* as 'Wealth']; (17) 'Intolerance' [*Pansies* as 'Tolerance']; (18) 'Compari' [*Pansies*]; and (19) 'Sick' [*Pansies*].

*24 NOV. Lawrence sends Nancy Pearn another article for the *Sunday Dispatch,* 'Enslaved by Civilization', which appeared in *Vanity Fair* in September 1929 as 'The Manufacture of Good Little Boys'. He also says that his next article will be on civilized savages he has seen, but I can think of no article which exactly answers this description.

DECEMBER 1928   At Hotel Beau-Rivage, Bandol.

SUMMARY   Rhys Davies: 'For all his fury and rages, he got immense fun out of writing *Pansies*. He would write them in bed in the mornings, cheerful and chirpy, the meek sea air blowing in from the enchanting little bay outside his window. . . . There was something perky and birdlike about him thus, and he was intensely happy and proud of the *Pansies;* he would read out the newest ones with delight, accentuating the wicked sharp little pecks in them. . . . But it was out of his painting he seemed to get the most joy, turning to it with relief and a sense of escape. . . . He was almost pathetic in his absorption in these paintings; he said that words bored him now' [Nehls 3, 274].

Lawrence finished *Pansies* and wrote the first version of the Foreword. He wrote 'Give Her a Pattern' [C187 A53], 'New Mexico' [C206 and *Phoenix*], and painted *Leda* [A 46] and *Renascence of Men* [A46].

9 DEC. Lawrence sends Nancy Pearn 'Oh These Women' which appeared in *Vanity Fair,* May 1929, as 'Woman in Man's Image', and in the

Daily Express, 19 June 1929, as 'The Real Trouble about Women' ['Give Her a Pattern' in *Assorted Articles*].

10 DEC.   *I am doing some little* Pensées—*sort of poems, but really thoughts—all in snatches: rather amusing* [Moore 1105].

15 DEC.   Lawrence tells Nancy Pearn that he doesn't mind if they use about fifteen hundred words of *that Autobiographical article*. This must refer to 'Myself Revealed', which appeared in the *Sunday Dispatch* on 17 February 1929.

To Maria Huxley: *I have been doing a book of* Pensées *which I call* pansies, *a sort of loose little poem form; Frieda says with joy: real doggerel.—But meant for* Pensées, *not poetry, especially not lyrical poetry. I think they'd amuse you, Maria. There's a little one to you, half catty—*

Thank you, dear Maria,
for helping with Lady C., *etc.*

but probably I shan't put it in [Moore 1106].

This is poem 155 of the 165 in the *Pansies* holograph [Tedlock 111]. It was printed in *Pansies* with the name changed from Maria to Clarinda.

19–22 DEC.   Rhys Davies reports that during his first stay with the Lawrences at Bandol, Lawrence was 'painting one or two pictures' [Nehls 3, 274]. These were probably *Leda* and *Renascence of Men*, which were shown to Brewster Ghiselin a fortnight later [Nehls 3, 289]. [See also Brewster 198.]

21 DEC.   Lawrence tells Koteliansky that he wants to write an introduction to the proposed edition of his paintings [Zytaruk 370]. Since this was completed by the time he next wrote to Koteliansky (11 January), it may have been begun in December. 'Introduction to Pictures' [*Phoenix*], which follows on from the Lasca translation in the same notebook, may well have been a false start at this.

*23 DEC.   Lawrence reported to Rhys Davies that he had really finished his pansies, except for the foreword, and got the MS in order. The first version of the foreword follows on from the poems in the same notebook, and is dated 'Christmas 1928'. It was published in the *Review of English Studies*, May 1970.

To Mabel Luhan; 19 Dec. *Yours about the article for the* Survey Graphic *came today. I'll have a shot at it when I can get a bit of time—people here now* [Luhan 338]. The 'people' were Stephenson, who left later that day, and Rhys Davies, who stayed until the evening of the 22nd. 'New Mexico' was sent to Nancy Pearn on Christmas Day.

JANUARY 1929   At Hotel Beau-Rivage, Bandol.

SUMMARY   Brewster Ghiselin: 'After lunch in the dining room and coffee on the terrace, we spent the hours until tea time in talk and in walking along the shore. Every evening after dinner, we gathered in Mrs Lawrence's bedroom, Lawrence usually sitting on the bed, Barbara Weekley or I beside him, and Mrs Lawrence in a chair by the window. Often Lawrence read briefly from the manuscript he had written during the day, and I frequently carried some of it off later to my room. In this way I read his "Introduction" to the *Paintings* as it came from his pen and some of the Pansies' [Nehls 3, 290].

Lawrence had Brewster Ghiselin and Barbara Weekley staying with him for the first half of January and the Huxleys for the last week, so had little time for work. He extended 'Do Women Change?', got the manuscript of *Pansies* off to Pollinger, wrote 'Introduction to These Paintings' [A46 and *Phoenix*], and painted *Venus in the Kitchen* [B56 Levy], *Electric Nudes* [A46], *Spring* [A46], *Summer Dawn* [A46] and, probably, *Dance Sketch* [A46]. The second version of the introduction to *Pansies,* used in the unexpurgated edition [A47c] and reprinted in *Phoenix* and CP, is dated January 1929. Immediately following it in the Berkeley notebook is the unfinished story beginning *'Henry,' she said, 'I want to disappear for a year'* [E159]. The only other work in the notebook, though beginning from the opposite end, is 'Nottingham and the Mining Countryside' [C202 and *Phoenix*]. Their presence in this notebook is the only clue to the dating of these pieces.

*5 JAN.   *Vanity Fair* had asked for 'Do Women Change?' to be extended by 650 words, and Lawrence agrees.

7 JAN.   MS of *Pansies* sent to Pollinger.

11 JAN.   *I have written the introduction—about 10,000 words—slain Clive Bell* [Zytaruk 372]. The introduction was revised in February.

Returns 'Myself Revealed' to Nancy Pearn [C182 = 'Autobiographical Sketch']. Tells her that he has been so busy doing the introduction that he has had no time to think of articles, but hopes to be clear in a day or two.

Brewster Ghiselin: 'Later, in his room, he showed me a black and white drawing he had been doing of a nude man and woman in a kind of complicated electric field' [Nehls 3, 295]. This drawing was reproduced at the end of the Mandrake *Paintings*. Rhys Davies apparently saw *Dance Sketch* at Bandol, since he refers to a goat [Nehls 3, 274]. But had *Dance Sketch* existed by 11 January,

181

Lawrence would surely have shown it to Ghiselin as the best illustration of what he told Ghiselin he was trying to do: 'He himself was trying to find some expression in paint for the relations of things, he told me, perhaps by means of the touching and mingling of colours flowing from different things: as the colour of the background, for example, approached any body it would diminish and take some of the colour and quality of that body' [Nehls 3, 295].

Lawrence wrote to Orioli that he had done the black and white frontispiece for Norman Douglas' *Venus in the Kitchen*.

14 JAN. Lawrence tells Orioli that he has done Venus again in grey and red. This version was used in the book. *I've nearly done that panel of which I made the sketch the night before you left—rather nice—and part done another, of bathers* [Moore 1121]. Ghiselin left on 15 January. *In November Lawrence wrote to him: And do you remember the drawing I was doing when you left? It became the painting* Spring [Nehls 3, 408].

24 JAN. Lawrence told Stephenson that he had done an oil panel of Bandol workmen in blue cotton trousers playing ball, and was doing another of two men going to bathe. This was *Summer Dawn*.

FEBRUARY 1929   At Hotel Beau-Rivage, Bandol.

SUMMARY Lawrence revised *Pansies*, finished *Spring* and *Summer Dawn*, and wrote 'A State of Funk' [A53] and the Foreword to *Bottom Dogs* [B26].

1 FEB. Wrote to Lahr that he is typing his poems again.

5 FEB. Returned the corrected typescript of 'Introduction to These Paintings' to Pollinger.

7 FEB. Wrote to Stephenson that he has finished *Spring* (having taken off the blue trousers formerly worn by his footballers) and *Summer Dawn*. *I have nearly retyped my* Pansies *and made them better* [Moore 1125].

*9 FEB. *The poems are almost finished typing* [Moore 1128].

9–12 FEB. Signed 531 sheets of *Rawdon's Roof* for Elkin Mathews.

*13 FEB. *I've typed them all out afresh—and revised many of course* [Moore 1130].

19 FEB. Returned corrected proofs of 'Mother and Daughter' [C184].

*23 FEB. Sent 'A State of Funk' to Nancy Pearn. Sent extended version of 'Do Women Change?' for the *Sunday Dispatch* [C185] with a different ending from that he had written for *Vanity Fair* two months earlier. This is the version used in *Assorted Articles*.

24 FEB.   Sent Nancy Pearn his Foreword to Dahlberg's *Bottom Dogs*.

MARCH 1929   At Hotel Beau-Rivage, Bandol, until 11; at Hotel de Versailles, Paris, until 18; at 3 rue du Bac, Suresnes (with the Aldous Huxleys) until 25; then back to the Hotel de Versailles.

SUMMARY   *All this jixing business has put me out of temper for writing* [Zytaruk 380].

I haven't been well in Paris. Sometimes one feels as if one were drifting out of life altogether—and not terribly sorry to go. These big cities take away my real will to live [Moore 1140].

Lawrence painted *Singing of Swans* [A46]; but after leaving Bandol he was too busy, too ill, or too miserable to do anything.

I MARCH   *I am correcting the Foreword to my paintings—proofs* [Zytaruk 380].

*4 MARCH   *Am doing a lovely one—water—of fighting men and singing swans* [Huxley 788].

APRIL 1929   At Hotel de Versailles, Paris until 7; 9–10 at Hotel de la Cité, Carcassonne; 11 probably at Perpignan; by 14 at Barcelona; 16 to Palma de Mallorca (Hotel Royal); by 22 at Hotel Principe Alfonso.

SUMMARY   Lawrence wrote *My Skirmish with Jolly Roger* [A42c A48a]; 'Making Pictures' [C188 A53], a new, shorter foreword for the Secker edition of *Pansies* [A47a and *Phoenix CP*], and *Pornography and Obscenity* [C190 and A49 *Phoenix*].

3 APRIL   *I have written a nice introduction telling them all* [the pirates] *what I think of them* [Moore 1139].

14 APRIL   *Also we must scrap that* introduction [Pansies] *and I will write another, briefer, and more to the point* [Secker 119]. The MS is dated April 1929. See the rest of this letter for Lawrence's attitude to Secker's proposed omissions and expurgations in *Pansies*.

*15 APRIL   Lawrence sends 'Making Pictures' to Nancy Pearn.

*29 APRIL   Lawrence sends *Pornography and Obscenity* to Nancy Pearn.

MAY 1929   At Hotel Principe Alfonso, Palma de Mallorca, Spain.

SUMMARY   *I agree this isn't a good place for work. I have tried to paint two pictures—and each time it's been a failure and made me all on edge. So I accept the decree of destiny, and shall make no further attempt to work at all while I am in Spain* [Moore 1152].

This is a wonderful place for doing nothing—the time passes rapidly in a long stretch of nothingness—broken by someone fetching us out in a motor, or somebody else in a donkey-cart. It is very good for my health, I believe. This letter is my most serious contribution to literature these six weeks [Huxley 804].

Lawrence wrote 'Pictures on the Walls' [C195 A53], and possibly wrote the first dozen poems of *More Pansies* [A62].

1 MAY   Sends Nancy Pearn 'Pictures on the Wall'.

20 MAY   Writes to J. M. Murry a letter corresponding closely to the poem 'Correspondence in After Years'.

21 MAY   Lawrence received the proofs of *Pansies* from Secker. Since four days later Lawrence speaks of having returned them 'a few days ago', he must have corrected them at once.

31 MAY   *Your letter this morning—as I was sitting in my pyjamas on bedroom floor painting a little picture which you would all thoroughly dislike* [Sagar 74].

JUNE 1929   At Hotel Principe Alfonso, Mallorca until 18; by 22 at Pensione Giuliani, Forte dei Marmi, Italy.

SUMMARY   Lawrence wrote at least sixty poems in *More Pansies* [A62], and made the drawing of himself which appeared as frontispiece to the definitive edition of *Pansies* [A47c].

7 JUNE   *I did a drawing of myself in sanguine that is really better* [than the attempts of a local artist], *though I don't know if you'll like it. . . . I'll see you have the drawing in a day or two, if I have to slave and do another myself. Alas, drawing my own face is unpleasant to me* [Moore 1161].

1–18 JUNE   'Andraixt—Pomegranate Flowers' begins: *It is June.*

12 JUNE   'Old Archangels' and 'Lucifer' correspond closely to a letter of this date to Else [Lawrence 286]. All the *More Pansies* poems from 'Andraixt' to 'A Spanish Wife' must have been written before 18 June. Those from 'The Painter's Wife' to 'Sea Bathers' were probably

184

written in the second half of the month, together with 'Modern Prayer' from *Nettles* [A52] which just preceeds the Forte dei Marmi poems in the MS.

JULY 1929 At Pensione Giuliani, Forte dei Marmi until 6; then at 6 Lungarno Corsini (with Orioli) until about 11; then at Hotel Porta Rossa, Florence, until 17; then at Hotel Löwen, Lichtenthal, Baden-Baden, until 23; then at Kurhaus Plattig, bei Buhl.

SUMMARY *I feel too bored and irritated by this last business to write anything serious against the Squirearchies and Noahsarkies. I can only let off a few* Pansies—Nettles, *rather—against them—and I do that—but I can't take them prosily* [Moore 1169].

Apart from some fifty or sixty poems from *More Pansies* and *Nettles*, Lawrence wrote only the introduction to *The Story of Dr Manente*.

10 JULY *Well now the police have raided my picture show in London, and carried off 13 pictures, and have them locked up, and want to burn them! Auto da fe!* [Mohr 533]. It is likely that Lawrence wrote '13 Pictures', 'Auto-da-fe', 'Give Me a Sponge', and 'Shows' at this time.

17 JULY Lawrence left Florence on this date. It was probably just before his departure that he wrote the introduction to *The Story of Dr Manente:* 'Orioli had a story that Lawrence wrote the whole of the introduction to his translation of *The Story of Doctor Manente* in the bookshop on the Lung'Arno. He was dissatisfied by the Introduction written by someone else, turned over the galleys, and produced his own, quite indifferent to the people coming in and out of the shop and all the resonant Italian voices' [Aldington 118].

20 JULY *Last night a long and lurid thunderstorm poured out endless white electricity* ... [Huxley 809]. This is probably the storm described in 'Storm in the Black Forest'. The previous poem in *More Pansies*, 'Trees in the Garden', is signed 'Lichtental', where Lawrence arrived 18.

*28 JULY Lawrence wrote to Orioli that he had started the second Cena of Lasca. Nothing of this survives.

29 JULY Lawrence returned to Orioli corrected proofs of *The Story of Dr Manente*.

AUGUST 1929 At Kurhaus Plattig, bei Buhl, until 4; then at Hotel Löwen, Lichtenthal, until 24; then at Kaffee Angermaier, Rottach-am-Tegernsee.

SUMMARY *At present I can do* nothing: *except write a few stinging* Pansies *which this time are* Nettles [Moore 1173].

All this persecution and insult, and most of all, the white-livered poltroonery of the so-called 'free' young people in England puts me off work. Why should one produce things, in such a dirty world! [Brewster 208].

Lawrence wrote 'The Risen Lord', 'Men and Women', and probably completed *Nettles* [A52] and all but the last half-dozen poems in *More Pansies*. He also did the *Escaped Cock* watercolours.

*2 AUG. 'The Risen Lord' sent to Nancy Pearn. Published in *Everyman*, 3 October 1929 [C192] and in *Assorted Articles*.

5 AUG. 'Men and Women' sent to Nancy Pearn. Published in the *Star Review*, November 1929 [C193] and in *Assorted Articles* as 'Men Must Work and Women as Well'.

7 AUG. Lawrence returned to Orioli a further batch of Lasca proofs.

*8 AUG. *The proofs* [The Escaped Cock] *came at lunch-time—I have already done head-piece and little tail-piece for Part I. Shall have a go at the others tomorrow and forward to you as quickly as possible* [Moore 1180].

10 AUG. Lawrence returned to Orioli the last of the Lasca proofs.

12 AUG. To Orioli: *Now if you send me the proofs with the lines numbered, I will do the notes and it is finished* [Moore 1177].

I have done the four small bits of decoration for the Cock, and have nearly finished the frontispiece [Lacy 79].

15 AUG. *Here are the decors for the Cock, and the corrected proofs go off by the same mail* [Lacy 80].

19 AUG. Lawrence sent Orioli the Lasca notes and proofs *once more* revised.

23 AUG. Lawrence sent Lahr several poems, apparently just written: 'Puss Puss', 'London Mercury', 'My Little Critics', 'Never had a Daddy', 'Editorial Office', and 'The Great Newspaper Editor to his Subordinate'.

*24 AUG. *I got the paper this morning with the Earp cackle. It aroused me to a squib, which I enclose* [Moore 1181]. Thomas Earp had reviewed Lawrence's exhibition in *The New Statesman*. See 'I heard a little chicken chirp' [CP 680].

24 AUG.   To Rhys Davies: *Your idea of the lily-white policeman of London fainting with shock at the sight of one of my nudes would make an A1 squib* [Moore 1186]. See 'Gross, Coarse, Hideous' [CP 680].

SEPTEMBER 1929   At Kaffee Angermaier, Rottach-am-Tegernsee, until 18; then, after a few days in Munich, at Hotel Beau-Rivage, Bandol by 23.

SUMMARY   Frieda Lawrence: 'We left the heat of Florence for the Tegernsee to be near Max Mohr. . . . My sister Else came to see him, and Alfred Weber. When he was alone with Alfred Weber, he said to him: "Do you see those leaves falling from the apple tree? When the leaves want to fall you must let them fall." Max Mohr had brought some doctors from Munich, but medicine did not help Lawrence. . . . I remember some autumn nights when the end seemed to have come. I listened for his breath through the open door, all night long, an owl hooting ominously from the walnut tree outside. In the dim dawn an enormous bunch of gentians I had put on the floor by his bed seemed the only living thing in the room. But he recovered and slowly Max Mohr and I travelled with him south again to Bandol' [Lawrence 213].

I feel much better in the strong light of this sea. But still the thought of the Great British Public puts me off work entirely—either painting or writing [Moore 1203].

At Rottach Lawrence wrote the final poems in the *More Pansies* MS, including the first drafts of 'Bavarian Gentians' and 'The Ship of Death'. [For the genesis of 'Bavarian Gentians' see Sagar 4.] 'Nottingham and the Mining Countryside' [C202 and *Phoenix*] begins: *I was born nearly forty-four years ago* [*Phoenix* 133]. It cannot, therefore, have been written later than early September. But since it is in the same MS as the Introduction to *Pansies* dated January 1929, it may have been written earlier.

8 SEPT.   Lawrence sent Pollinger a lengthened version of *Pornography and Obscenity* for Faber and Faber [A49].
13 SEPT.   Sent Orioli the proofs of the Lasca notes [Moore 1194]. *The Story of Dr Manente* was published in November 1929 (Lawrence received his copies on 9 November), and not in March as stated by both McDonald and Roberts [A45].

OCTOBER 1929   At Villa Beau-Soleil, Bandol.

SUMMARY   *I still love the Mediterranean, it still seems young as Odysseus, in the morning. . . . When the morning comes, and the sea runs silvery and the distant islands are delicate and clear, then I feel again, only man is vile* [Moore 1205].

Lawrence wrote one or two articles, probably 'We Need One Another' [C198 and *Phoenix*] and 'Nobody Loves Me' [C203 and *Phoenix*]; extended *My skirmish with Jolly Roger* into *À Propos of Lady Chatterley's Lover* [A48b and *Phoenix* 2]; wrote the first fifty or so poems in the *Last Poems* MS; and did the preparatory reading for *Apocalypse* [A57].

4 OCT.   Sent Nancy Pearn the proofs of 'Men and Women'.

5 OCT.   *Now the sea is blue again, and the terrace full of light, so I'll get up—having written a newspaper article—and it's nearly noon* [Priest 485]. This was probably 'We Need One Another', the first of the three articles Lawrence sent to Nancy Pearn on 4 November.

*10 OCT.   *Was writing a few poems: then the essays* [Huxley 833]. In his previous letter to Maria Huxley, 29 September, Lawrence had said: *I want to write essays on various trees, olive, vine, evergreen oak, stone-pine, of the Mediterranean, and should like a bit of technical* Encyclopaedia Britannica *sort of information* [Huxley 832]. Maria Huxley had sent him some notes; but no such essays seem to have been written.

17 OCT.   Lawrence tells Pollinger that *À Propos of Lady Chatterley's Lover* is nearly done.

*27 OCT.   An unpublished letter of this date to Max Mohr describes a stormy sea in terms very similar to the poem 'Mana of the Sea'. Lawrence also uses the term 'Mana' in a letter of 29 to Frederick Carter; it must have cropped up in his reading at that time.

NOVEMBER 1929   At Villa Beau-Soleil, Bandol.

SUMMARY   *In fact, I don't really do anything, writing or painting or anything else—unusual for me, but I suppose it's a mood. My health is better, but not very good—and I simply don't want to do anything on earth, even read* [Lawrence-Ada 204].

Lawrence wrote his review of Rozanov's *Fallen Leaves* [C196 and *Phoenix*], the mystical notes to *Birds, Beasts and Flowers* [A27c *Phoenix*], and probably the last sixteen or so poems in *Last Poems* [A62], and 'The Real Thing' [C201 and *Phoenix*].

1 NOV.   Sends Pollinger the proofs of *Pornography and Obscenity*.

2 NOV.   Lawrence presumably wrote 'All Souls' Day' and the poems immediately following it on this date.

4 NOV.   Lawrence sent Nancy Pearn three articles for *Vanity Fair:* 'We Need One Another' and 'Nobody Loves Me' (see October), and 'The Real Thing'.

7 NOV.   Sends Nancy Pearn his review of *Fallen Leaves* by V. V. Rozanov.

*12 NOV.   Lawrence sent his Notes for the Cresset Press edition of *Birds, Beasts and Flowers* to his illustrator, Blair Hughes-Stanton.

DECEMBER 1929   At Villa Beau-Soleil, Bandol.

SUMMARY   Lawrence prepared *Nettles* [A52] for publication, and began writing *Apocalypse* [A57]. He also probably wrote the two prose-poems 'The Elephants of Dionysos' [*Phoenix*] and 'Fire' [*SP*]. 'Fire' is also published in Smailes, but incorrectly, as verse.

*9 DEC.   *I am getting the* Nettles *ready* [Moore 1220].

13 DEC.   Lawrence sent *Nettles* to Pollinger.

15 DEC.   *I have roughly finished my introduction* [Moore 1222]. This was intended to be an introduction to Frederick Carter's *The Revelation of St. John the Divine* (see January), but developed instead into *Apocalypse*. A manuscript [Tedlock 212–14] containing notes for *Apocalypse* also contains 'The Elephants of Dionysos' and 'Fire'.

Lawrence had central heating at the Beau Soleil, and much appreciated the open fire at the Brewsters' house. According to the Brewsters, 'Fire' was written at this time [Brewster 306]. The Brewsters did not move into their new house at Bandol until late December.

JANUARY 1930   At Villa Beau Soleil, Bandol

SUMMARY   *The doctor came from England, and said I must lie in bed for two months, and do no work, and see no people only rest. So I do that. On sunny days I lie out of doors in the garden on a higestuhl—otherwise I am in bed. And I get weary in my soul* [Mohr 540].

Lawrence wrote his Introduction to Frederick Carter's *The Revelation of St. John the Divine* [C204 and *Phoenix*]. Carter's book did not appear until 1932, as *Dragon of the Apocalypse,* and without Lawrence's introduction. Also his Introduction to Koteliansky's translation of Dostoevsky's *The Grand Inquisitor* [B28 and *Phoenix*].

6 JAN.   To Frederick Carter: *I meant to write before—but I waited, getting bothered by my Introduction. It became so long and somehow unsuitable to go in front of your essays. So at last I laid it aside, and have written you now a proper introduction, about 5000 words, I think, which is really quite good and to the point* [Moore 1228].

15 JAN.   To Koteliansky: *Just a word to say I have the* Inquisitor *and will try to do a nice little introduction—though I shall never be able to squash myself down to a thousand words* [Zytaruk 396].

*25 JAN.   *Pollinger took the* Introd. *back with him—about 4000 words I suppose* [Zytaruk 397].

FEBRUARY–MARCH 1930   At Villa Beau Soleil until 6, then to Ad Astra Sanatorium, Vence, until 1 March, then to Villa Robermond, Vence, where Lawrence died on 2 March.

SUMMARY   At Ad Astra Lawrence wrote only his review of Eric Gill's *Art Nonsense and Other Essays* [C212 and *Phoenix*]. Frieda Lawrence: 'Lawrence wrote this unfinished review a few days before he died. The book interested him, and he agreed with much in it. Then he got tired of writing and I persuaded him not to go on. It is the last thing he wrote' [Powell 65].

A CHECKLIST OF
THE MANUSCRIPTS OF D. H. LAWRENCE

Section E of Warren Roberts' *A Bibliography of D. H. Lawrence*
revised and extended by Lindeth Vasey

ACKNOWLEDGEMENTS

I would like to thank Dr David Farmer and Dr Carole Ferrier for allowing me the use of their dissertations on the D. H. Lawrence manuscript collection at the University of Texas and Lawrence poetry manuscripts and for providing insight into the relationship between differing versions.

Thanks are also due to all the librarians and private collectors who responded to my requests for information about their Lawrence holdings. Mr. George Lazarus was especially gracious about checking his extensive collection to resolve several perplexing problems. The staff of the Humanities Research Center, University of Texas, deserves special commendation for bearing with my numerous queries and prowlings in the stacks in the continuing search for yet another bit of Lawrentiana.

I am very pleased to have this opportunity to acknowledge a special debt to Dr Warren Roberts, not only for permission to update the manuscript section of *A Bibliography of D. H. Lawrence,* published by Rupert Hart-Davis, but more personally for his gracious support and encouragement throughout my Lawrence career.

NOTES ON USING THIS LIST

This list includes all known Lawrence manuscripts. Entries are in alphabetical order by title. The original number sequence used by Roberts has been retained with new entries added using decimals. Manuscripts known to have existed because of a published reference are included even when they are currently unlocated or have been destroyed.

All manuscripts of one work are described under the last title used by Lawrence. Within each entry, the manuscripts are listed chronologically, if precedence has been established: however, no attempt is made to order the poetry entries. The number of pages and corrections of typescripts and proofs by Lawrence are given when known. Entries may also include such information as: fragmentary or incomplete manuscript, duplicate pages, manuscript written in another hand, enclosure in a letter and references to published descriptions.

191

Checklist

Bucknell University	PLeB
Columbia University	NNC
Cornell University	NIC
Dartmouth College	NhD
Various dealers	Dealer
Duke University	NcD
Harvard University	MH
William Heinemann, Ltd.	Heinemann
Henry E. Huntington Library and Art Gallery	CSmH
Indiana University	InU
Iowa State Education Association	IaE
George Lazarus	Lazarus
Mills College	COMC
New York Public Library	NN
Newberry Library	ICN
Northwestern University	IEN
Nottingham County Record Office	NCRecord
Nottinghamshire County Libraries	NCL
Pierpont Morgan Library	NNPM
Princeton University	NjP
Privately owned	Private
Royal Literary Fund	RLF
Southern Illinois University	ICSo
Stanford University	CSt
State University of New York at Buffalo	NBuU
University of California at Berkeley	CU
University of California at Los Angeles	CLU
University of Chicago	ICU
University of Cincinnati	OCU
University of Illinois	IU
University of Liverpool	ULiv
University of New Mexico	NmU
University of Nottingham	N
University of Salford	USal
University of Texas at Austin	TxU
University of Toronto	CaOTU
University of Tulsa	OkTU
University of Virginia	ViU
Yale University	CtY

E1   **À la Manière de D. H. Lawrence**
       Holograph manuscript, 1 p.   Njp

E1.5   **À Propos of Lady Chatterley's Lover**
       a Holograph manuscript, 13 pp.   ICSo
           MS titled: *Introd. to Lady C.*
           Published as *My Skirmish with Jolly Roger*
       b Corrected carbon typescript, 8 pp.   NmU
           MS titled: *Intro. to French ed. Lady Chatterley*
       c Holograph manuscript, 42 pp.   TxU
           MS titled: *Continuation of Jolly Roger article*
           Powell 9

E1.7   **A woman of about thirty-five, beautiful, a little over-
       wrought . . .**
       Holograph manuscript, 4 pp.   CtY
       Outline for a joint novel with Catherine Carswell

E2   **Aaron's Rod**
       a Corrected original and carbon typescript, 479 pp.   TxU
       b Carbon typescript, 31 pp.   NNC
           Chapter XIII only (pp. 171–202)

E2.1   **Aaron's Rod, Foreword to**
       Holograph manuscript, 1 p.   Unlocated
       With letter of 15 August 1921 to Thomas Seltzer
       American Art Association catalogue (29–30 January
       1936)
       item No. 378

E2.2   **Aaron's Rod, Introduction to**
       Holograph manuscript   Unlocated
       With letter of 22 October 1921 to Thomas Seltzer

E3   **Accumulated Mail**
       a Holograph manuscript, 10 pp.   InU
       b Corrected carbon typescript, 8 pp.   NmU
       c Typescript, 8 pp.   TxU
       d Carbon typescript, 12 pp.   CU

E3.3   **Adolf**
       a Typescript, 10 pp.   TxU
       b Typescript and carbon copy, 12 pp., 12 pp.   TxU
       c Typescript, 7 pp.   CtY

E3.6   **After All Saints' Day**
       Holograph manuscript, 1 p.   TxU
       In Frieda Lawrence's hand

E8   **Ah, Muriel!**
Holograph manuscript, 1 p.   TxU

E9.5   **All Souls' Day**
Holograph manuscript, 1 p.   TxU
In Frieda Lawrence's hand

E10   **All There**
a Holograph manuscript, 4 pp.   CU
     Tedlock p. 211, Powell 84A
b Typescript, 4 pp.
                              CU

E11   **All Things Are Possible**
a Holograph manuscript, 157 pp.   Lazarus
     Includes *Foreword*, 4 pp.
b Corrected page proofs   Unlocated
     First 16 pp. are present in two states
     Parke-Bernet Galleries catalogue (19 February 1963)
     item No. 130

E12   **Almond Blossom**
a Typescript, 5 pp.   CU
b Proof   Unlocated
     With letter of 26 January 1922 to Curtis Brown

E12.7   **Altercation**
Holograph manuscript, 1 p.   ICSo

E13   **Altitude (An unfinished play)**
a Holograph manuscript, 28 pp.   CU
     Tedlock pp. 121–3, Powell 68
b Carbon typescript, 26 pp.   CU
c Carbon typescript, 26 pp.   TxU
d Typescript, 14 pp.   TxU
     Revisions in Spud Johnson's hand
e Carbon typescript, 14 pp.   CU

E14   **American Eagle, The**
a Holograph manuscript, 1 p.   IaE
     Incomplete, begins: The new, full-fledged Republic . . .
b Holograph manuscript, 2 pp.   Unlocated
     Scriptorium catalogue (1976)

E14.3   **Americans, Review of**
Corrected typescript, 9 pp.   CtY
MS titled: *Model Americans*

E14.5   **Amores**
a Holograph manuscript or typescript   Destroyed:
                                     Duckworth fire

b Carbon typescript, 100 pp.	TxU
c Author's copy with holograph corrections, 138 pp.	Lazarus

E16 **And what do I care . . .**
  a Holograph manuscript, 3 pp. CU
  Powell 63 C
  b Typescript, 3 pp. NmU

E17 **Apocalypse**
  a Holograph manuscript, 102 pp. TxU
  Five fragments in a notebook, pp. 11–53, 23–58[57],
  27–32, 43–56, 13–4
  Tedlock pp. 146–8, Powell 110B
  b Holograph manuscript, 11 pp. TxU
  A fragment, pp. 33, 34, 34–42
  MS titled: *Apocalypsis II: DHL*
  Tedlock p. 149, Powell 110B
  c Holograph manuscript, 160 pp. TxU
  Tedlock pp. 143–4, Powell 110A
  d Corrected carbon typescript, 121 pp. TxU
  Tedlock pp. 144–5, Powell 110C
  e Galley proofs Dealer
  f Proof sheets, 155 pp. Lazarus
  g Proof copy Dealer
  Orioli, 1931
  h Proof copy Dealer
  Orioli, 1931

E18 **Apocalypse, Outline for**
  a Holograph manuscript, 7 pp. CU
  p. 2 is missing
  Tedlock pp. 148–9, Powell 84A
  b Holograph manuscript, 1 p. TxU
  p. 2 only in *Apocalypse* fragments notebook
  Tedlock p. 148

E19 **Apostrophe of a Buddhist Monk**
  Holograph manuscript, 1 p. TxU

E22 **Are you pining to be superior? . . .**
  Holograph manuscript, 1 p. CSt
  Powell 61

E23 **Aristocracy**
  a Holograph manuscript, 16 pp. CU
  Tedlock p. 140, Powell 84A
  b Corrected carbon typescript, 12 pp. CU

Tedlock p. 141
c Carbon typescript, 18 pp.   CU
d Carbon typescript, 18 pp.   NmU
e Carbon typescript, 18 pp.   TxU

E23.1 Aristocracy, German translation
Holograph manuscript, 7 pp.   TxU
Incomplete
MS titled: *Aristokratie*
In Frieda Lawrence's hand

E24 Art and Morality
a Holograph manuscript, 1 p.   Lazarus
An early version of the first paragraph only
Tedlock p. 164
b Holograph manuscript, 9 pp.   TxU
An early version
Tedlock pp. 165–6, Powell 116
c Typescript, 8 pp.   CU
d Typescript and carbon copy, 8 pp., 8 pp.   TxU
e Holograph manuscript, 10 pp.   TxU
A later version
Tedlock pp. 165–6, Powell 116
f Corrected carbon typescript, 11 pp.   CU
Tedlock p. 166
g Typescript, 10 pp.   CU
h Typescript, 8 pp.   TxU
i Carbon typescript, 10 pp.   TxU

E24.3 Art and the Individual
a Holograph manuscript, 7 pp.   Private
b Holograph manuscript, 3 pp.   Private
Comments for expansion of essay

E24.5 Art Nonsense and Other Essays, Review of
a Holograph manuscript, 7 pp.   Unlocated
Tedlock p. 263, Powell 105
b Carbon typescript, 8 pp.   TxU

E24.7 As for Me, I'm a Patriot
Holograph manuscript, 1 p.   TxU

E26 Ass, The
Holograph manuscript, 2 pp.   IaE

E27 Assorted Articles
Corrected and uncorrected original and carbon type-

196

scripts, 112 pp.   TxU
Tedlock pp. 217–9, 221–3, 225–6, 228–33, 235–8,
Powell 84B
  Men Must Work and Women As Well, 18 pp.
  Enslaved by Civilization, 8 pp.
  The Risen Lord, 12 pp.
  The State of Funk, 9 pp.
  Red Trousers, 5 pp.
  Dull London, 4 pp.
  Insouciance, 5 pp.
  Give Her a Pattern, 7 pp.
  Do Women Change?, 8 pp.
  Ownership, 5 pp.
  Master in His Own House, 5 pp.
  Matriarchy, 7 pp.
  Cocksure Women and Hensure Men, 5 pp.
  On Human Destiny, 8 pp.
  On Being a Man, 7 pp.

E29   **August Holidays**
      Holograph manuscript, 3 pp.   TxU

E30   **Autobiographical Fragment**
      a Holograph manuscript, 42 pp.   CU
        MS untitled, begins: Nothing depresses me more . . .
        MS titled by Powell: *Newthorpe in 2927*
        Titled by Sagar: *A Dream of Life*
        Tedlock pp. 64–5, Powell 50
      b Carbon typescript, 34 pp.   CU

E31   **Autobiographical Piece**
      Holograph manuscript, 20 pp.   OCU
      Published in *Phoenix II* with title [Return to Bestwood].

E31.3 **Autobiographical Sketch**
      Holograph manuscript, 4 pp.   TxU
      Published in Nehls and *Phoenix II*
      p. 300
      With letter of 18 July 1928 to Jean Watson

E31.5 **Autumn at Taos**
      Corrected typescript, 1 p.   TxU

E33   **Baby Asleep After Pain, A**
      Holograph manuscript, 2 pp.   TxU
      Tedlock pp. 77–9, Powell 52

E34.5 **Baby Running Barefoot**
Holograph manuscript, 2 pp.   TxU
Tedlock pp. 77–9, Powell 52

E36 **Bad Side of Books, The**
a Holograph manuscript, 4 pp.   TxU
MS titled: *Introduction to Bibliography*
Tedlock p. 243, Powell 90
b Corrected typescript, 5 pp.   TxU
MS titled: *Introduction to Bibliography*
c Carbon typescript, 5 pp.   OkTU
Untitled

E38 **Ballad of Another Ophelia**
a Holograph manuscript   Private
MS on verso of *A Fragment of Stained Glass*
b Holograph manuscript, 1 p.   ICU

E39 **Bare Fig-Trees**
Typescript, 3 pp.   CU

E40 **Bathing Resort**
Holograph manuscript, 1 p.   TxU
Incomplete

E40.5 **Bay**
a Holograph manuscript   Unlocated
With letter of 11 December 1916 to Lady Cynthia
Asquith
b Holograph manuscript   Unlocated
With letter of 11 December 1916 to J. B. Pinker
c Holograph manuscript, 1 p.   Lazarus
Dedication page
d Printer's pulls, 23 pp.   Lazarus
Includes one extra sheet printed on one side only
e Sheet proofs, 5 pp.   TxU
Unfolded gatherings, complete
f Corrected rough proofs, 16 pp.   OCU
pp. 9–24
g Corrected rough proofs, 28 pp.   ICSo
pp. 9–24, 32–43
h Corrected page proofs, 8 pp.   TxU
pp. 25–32
i Proof pages, 23 pp.   Lazarus

E41 **Be Men—be individual men . . .**
a Holograph manuscript, 2 pp.   TxU

   b Holograph manuscript, 2 pp.   Lazarus
      MS untitled, begins: to all men who are men: Be men, be
      individual men . . .
      With letter of 28 December 1928 to Charles Wilson

E43   **Bells**
      Typescript and Carbon copy, 1 p., 1 p.   TxU

E45   **Beyond the Rockies**
   a Holograph manuscript, 2 pp.   TxU
      Tedlock p. 101, Powell 118
   b Typescript and carbon copy, 2 pp., 2 pp.   TxU
   c Carbon typescript, 2 pp.   CU

E47   **Birds, Beasts and Flowers**
   a Holograph manuscript, 22 pp.   CU
      Tedlock pp. 87–101, Powell 56
         Tropic
         Peace
         Southern Night
         Sicilian Cyclamens
         Hibiscus and Salvia Flowers
         Purple Anemones
         The Ass
         Eagle in New Mexico
         The American Eagle
   b Typescript   Unlocated
      12 poems sent to Harriet Monroe by Robert Mountsier,
      his letter of 6 September 1922 to Monroe, her letter of 16
      September 1922 to Mountsier, including:
         Turkey Cock
         The Evening Land
         St. Matthew
         9 unidentified
   c Holograph manuscript and typescript, 128 pp.   Lazarus
      Lacking *Tortoises* poems, *The American Eagle; Almond
      Blossom* supplied from printed source
   d Corrected typescript, 125 pp.   NIC
      Printer's copy for American edition
   e Corrected carbon typescript, 124 pp.   CaOTU
      Lacking title page and *The American Eagle; Tortoises*
      poems supplied from printed source
   f Corrected galley proofs, 95 pp.   IaE
   g Proofs, 207 pp.   TxU
      Secker, 1923

	h Author's copy with holograph corrections Secker, 1923	TxU
E47.1	**Birds, Beasts and Flowers, French translation**	
	a Carbon typescript, 99 pp.	TxU
	b Typescript, 11 pp.	CU

        Grenade (Pomegranate)
        Nefles et Sorbes (Medlars and Sorb-Apples)
        Tropique (Tropic)
        Le Colibri (Humming-Bird)
        Nuit du Sud (Southern Night)
        Fleur d'Amandier (Almond Blossom)
        Anemones Pourpes (Purple Anemones)

These two typescripts make a complete copy, including *Tortoises* poems

E47.2	**Birds, Beasts and Flowers, Section Introductions**	
	Holograph manuscript, 3 pp.	TxU

With letter of 12 November [1929] to Blair Hughes-Stanton

E49	**Bits**	
	a Holograph manuscript, 6 pp.	ICU

        The Last Minute
        Vicar's Son
        Drill in the Heat
        Mother's Son in Salonika
        Casualty
        Maiden's Prayer
        Man Hauling a Wagon
        Sighs
        Daughter of the Great Man
        The Child and the Soldier
        Pietà
        The Grey Nurse
        Litany of Grey Nurses
        Message to a Perfidious Soldier
        Dust in the East
        The Girl in Cairo
        The Jewess and the V.C.
        Zeppelin Nights
        Munitions
        Land-Worker
        Mourning
        Mesopotamia

Tales (The Gazelle Calf)
Foreign Sunset
Prisoner at Work in a Turkish Garden
Response From the Harem
Swing Song of a Girl and a Soldier
Prisoners at Work in the Rain
The Well in Africa
Neither Moth nor Rust

b Corrected carbon typescript, 34 pp.   Lazarus

Farewell and Adieu (The Last Minute)
Star Sentinel: A young woman muses on her betrothed,
    who is in Mesopotamia (Mother's Son in Salonika)
Near the Mark: A timid girl sighs her unconfessed love for
    the man in Flanders (Sighs)
Man Hauling a Waggon
The Well of Kilossa: A thirsty soldier in East Africa praises
    the well at which he drank (The Well in Africa)
Straying Thoughts: A girl goes to the cathedral church, to
    pray for her beloved (Maiden's Prayer)
Twofold: A young lady hears that her lover is wounded
    (Casualty)
Fragile Jewels: A child speaks to his brother, who is a
    soldier (The Child and the Soldier)
Benediction: An old father kisses his son, who is a soldier
    (Vicar's Son)
Supplication: A young lieutenant who joined the Roman
    Catholic Church whilst at Oxford, prays on the battle-
    field (Pietà)
The Grey Nurse
The Saint: Litany of Grey Nurses (Litany of Grey Nurses)
The Wind, the Rascal: A girl, sitting alone at night, starts at
    the sound of the wind (The Wind, the Rascal)
Rose, Look Out Upon Me: A soldier catches sight of a
    young lady at her window in Salonika
Unrelenting: Message from a pious mistress to a soldier
    (Message to a Perfidious Soldier)
Dust: Drought in the Near East (Dust in the East)
A Powerful Ally: A young lady speaks to the colonel of her
    lover's regiment (The Girl in Cairo)
The Daughter of the Great Man: A wounded captain is
    entertained by a young lady (Daughter of the Great
    Man)
Drill on Salisbury Plain in Summer Time (Drill in the Heat)

An Elixir: A woman of the East encourages her young man,
  who is home on leave (The Jewess and the V.C.)
Night-Fall in the Suburbs (Zeppelin Nights)
Munitions Factory (Munitions)
Forlorn: A maiden weeps for her dead husband (Land-
  Worker)
Needless Worry: A poor girl thinks of the dead (Mourning)
The Gazelle Calf: A blind soldier tells his children about
  Arabia (The Gazelle Calf)
Foreign Sunset: Coloured labourers behind the fighting-line
  complain that they are done up (Foreign Sunset)
Too Late: A Straggler in Mesopotamia finds himself lost
  (Mesopotamia)
Antiphony: A British sailor, prisoner of war, works in a
  garden in Turkey (Prisoner at Work in a Turkish Gar-
  den)
Swing Song: A girl in a swing, and a soldier swinging her
  (Swing Song of a Girl and a Soldier)
Prisoners at Work in the Rain
Neither Moth Nor Rust
MS titled: *All of Us*

E49.5   **Black Swans, Preface to**
Holograph manuscript, 4 pp.   TxU
Tedlock pp. 243–4, Powell 118

E49.6   **Blessed Are the Powerful**
Holograph manuscript, 12 pp.   Unlocated
MS titled: *Power*
Harry Levinson (Beverley Hills) catalogue (5 June 1951)
item No. 31

E50   **Blue Moccasins**
a Holograph manuscript, 7 pp.   TxU
  An early version, incomplete
  Tedlock p. 71, Powell 48B
b Holograph manuscript, 32 pp.   TxU
  Tedlock pp. 69–71, Powell 48A
c Carbon typescript, 27 pp.   CU

E52   **Books**
a Holograph manuscript, 8 pp.   Cu
  Tedlock pp. 160–1, Powell 84A
b Carbon typescript, 7 pp.   CU
c Carbon typescript, 7 pp.   NmU
d Carbon typescript, 7 pp.   TxU

E53   **Border Line, The**
       a Holograph manuscript, 15 pp.   Lazarus
          An early version
          Powell 36B
       b Holograph manuscript, 25 pp.   Lazarus
          Another early version, follows printed version up to
          p. 17 and then entirely different
          Powell 36A

E54   **Bottom Dogs, Introduction to**
       a Holograph manuscript, 8 pp.   CU
          Tedlock pp. 249–50, Powell 93
       b Carbon typescript, 11 pp.   CU
       c Carbon typescript, 11 pp.   NmU
          MS titled: *Introduction to Edward Dahlberg's novel*
       d Carbon typescript, 11 pp.   TxU
          MS also titled: *Introduction to Edward Dahlberg's
          novel, for Putnams*

E55   **Boy in the Bush, The**
       a Holograph manuscript, 580 pp.   CU
          Chapters 1–25 (lacking Chapter 26)
       b Holograph manuscript, 10 pp.   IaE
          Chapter 26 only
       c Holograph notes, 1 p.   Unlocated
          List of Characters
          Tedlock p. 134
       d Holograph notes, 2 pp.   IaE
          Alterations requested by Mollie Skinner for publication
       e Corrected original and carbon typescript, 543 pp.   TxU
       f Corrected typescript, 543 pp.   NNC
       g Secker, 1924 edition marked by Mollie Skinner   TxU

E57.5 **Britisher Has a Word with an Editor, A**
       Holograph manuscript, 1 p.   TxU
       MS titled: *A Britisher Has a Word with Harriett Monroe*

E59.3 **[Burns Novel]**
       Holograph manuscript, 13 pp.   TxU
       Two fragments, pp. 1–12, 1

E59.5 **But the Captains brow was sad . . .**
       Holograph manuscript, 1 p.   N
       With letter of 2 September 1908 to Louie Burrows

E60.5 **Captain's Doll, The**
       a Holograph manuscript, 77 pp.   Dealer

Tedlock pp. 49–50, Powell 12

b Corrected typescript, 85 pp.   PLeB

E61   **Casualty**
Holograph manuscript, 1 p.   N
MS titled: *Two-fold*

E62   **Cavalleria Rusticana and Other Stories**
Holograph manuscript, 60 pp.   CU
Tedlock pp. 272–3, Powell 108
Cavalleria Rusticana, 10 pp.
The She-Wolf, 7 pp.
Fantasticalities, 10 pp.
Jeli the Shepherd, 33 pp.

E63   **Cavalleria Rusticana and Other Stories, Translator's Preface**
a Holograph manuscript, 11 pp.   CU
Tedlock pp. 273–4, Powell 108
b Corrected typescript, 28 pp.   Unlocated
Argus Book Shop catalogue No. 827 (1943) item No. 26
c Corrected carbon typescript, 23 pp.   TxU
Includes title page and table of contents

E63.3   **Certain Americans and an Englishman**
Typescript, 13 pp.   TxU

E64   **Change of Life**
Holograph manuscript, 8 pp.   Unlocated
Powell 63F

E65   **Chaos in Poetry**
a Holograph manuscript, 9 pp.   TxU
MS titled: *Introduction to Chariot of the Sun*
b Corrected typescript, 10 pp.   TxU
Tedlock pp. 247–9, Powell 92
c Carbon typescript, 14 pp.   TxU

E66   **Chapel Among the Mountains, A**
a Holograph manuscript, 16 pp.   CtY
Tedlock p. 117, Powell 28
b Typescript, partly carbon, 15 pp.   CU
Tedlock p. 178

E67   **Cherry Robbers**
a Holograph manuscript, 1 p.   ULiv
With letter of 20 January 1909 to Blanche Jennings

	b Holograph manuscript, 1 p.	Private
	MS titled: *Throstles in the Cherry Tree*	
E68.2	**Christening, The**	
	Holograph manuscript, 9 pp.	TxU
	Powell 33	
E68.5	**Climbing Down Pisgah**	
	a Holograph manuscript, 6 pp.	TxU
	Tedlock pp. 161–2, Powell 118	
	b Corrected typescript and corrected carbon copy, 7 pp.,	TxU
	7 pp.	
E68.7	**Clouds**	
	Holograph manuscript, 12 pp.	CtY
E 70	**Cocksure Women and Hensure Men**	
	Holograph manuscript, 3 pp.	CU
	Tedlock pp. 223–4, Powell 84A	
E72	**Collected Poems Volume I**	
	Corrected original and carbon typescript, 193 pp.	TxU
	Tedlock pp. 102–3, Powell 57	
E73	**Collected Poems, Foreword to**	
	a Holograph manuscript, 8 pp.	CLU
	Powell 58	
	b Carbon typescript, 7 pp.	TxU
E73.1	**Collected Poems, Note to**	
	Holograph manuscript, 4 pp.	IaE
E74	**Collier's Friday Night, A**	
	a Holograph manuscript, 134 pp.	TxU
	b Carbon typescript, 95 pp.	CU
E76	**Corasmin and the Parrots**	
	a Holograph manuscript, 8 pp.	TxU
	MS titled: *Mornings in Mexico. Friday Morning*	
	Tedlock pp. 186–7, Powell 76	
	b Corrected carbon typescript, 9 pp.	TxU
	MS titled: *Mornings in Mexico. Corasmin and the Parrots*	
	Tedlock pp. 187–8, Powell 76	
E80	**Crown, The**	
	a Holograph manuscript, 48 pp.	TxU
	Chapters IV–VI	

b Typescript, 35 pp.	TxU
Chapters I–III	
c Carbon typescript, 11 pp.	CU
Chapter II	
d Carbon typescript, 6 pp.	NmU
Chapter III, incomplete, pp. 6–11 only	

E81   **Crown, Note to The**

a Holograph manuscript, 2 pp.   TxU
MS titled: *Note to the Crown*
Tedlock pp. 244–5

b Corrected typescript, 2 pp.   CU
Tedlock p. 245

E81.5   **Crucifix Across the Mountains, The**

a Holograph manuscript, 6 pp.   TxU
Tedlock pp. 179–80, Powell 70

b Carbon typescript, 8 pp.   TxU
MSS titled: *Christs in the Tirol*

E83.5   **Dance of the Sprouting Corn, The**

Holograph manuscript, 6 pp.   Private
Tedlock pp. 182–3, Powell 73

E84   **Daughter-in-Law, The**

a Holograph manuscript, 63 pp.   NN
b Typescript, 105 pp.   TxU
c Carbon typescript, 106 pp.   CU
d Typescript prompt copy, 164 pp.   USal
MS titled: *My Son's My Son*
Adapted by Walter Greenwood for his production at
Playhouse Theatre, London, 1936

E86   **Daughters of the Vicar**

a Holograph manuscript, 23 pp.   Lazarus
An early version, incomplete, pp. 23, 34–49, 49–54 (also
numbered: 57, 58–77, 77A, 78)
Untitled
p. 23 (57) may be from an untraced version or an early
page of this version

b Holograph manuscript, 45 pp.   Lazarus
A complete second draft, heavily revised and substantial
passages crossed out
Close to *Time and Tide* version of *Two Marriages*
MS titled: *Two Marriages*

c Two carbon typescripts, 44 pp., 44 pp.   CU

206

Revision of second version, incomplete
Equivalent to first IX and a half sections of *The Prussian Officer and Other Stories*
Published in *Time and Tide* as *Two Marriages*
MS titled: *Two Marriages*

  d Holograph manuscript and corrected typescript, 58 pp.   Lazarus
MS: 1–22, 23A [23], 23B [24], TS: 19–23 [25–29],
MS: 24 (also numbered: 29) [30], TS: 25 (30) [31],
MS: 26 (31) [32], TS: 29–52 (32–50, 50A, 51–4)
[33–56],
MS: 53–4 (55–6) [57–8]
A complete third version
The 30 pp. of heavily corrected typescript are from an
earlier version
Unpublished in this version

E87   **David (play)**
  a Holograph manuscript, 191 pp.   Lazarus
pp. 1–70, 80–94, 94B, 95–121, 121B, 122–48, 150–5,
155B, 156–7, 170, 157–71, 170–3, 173B, 174–8, 178B,
180–6, 172–4, 174B, 175–8
Two versions of last two scenes, many pages crossed out
Tedlock pp. 123–4, Powell 69A
  b Typescript, 118 pp.   TxU
  c Corrected page proofs, 123 pp.   TxU
  d Author's proof copy with holograph corrections   Unlocated
Melvin Rare Book Catalogue (1949) item No. 32

E87.1   **David (play), German translation**
  a Holograph manuscript, 254 pp.   CU
Translated by Lawrence and Frieda Lawrence
  b Corrected typescript, 104 pp.   CU
MS titled: *David, ein Schauspiel*
Tedlock pp. 124–5, Powell 69B

E87.2   **David, Music for (play)**
  a Holograph manuscript, 4 pp.   NhD
Lyrics and notes
With letter of 16 October 1926 to Robert Atkins
  b Holograph manuscript, 6 pp.   TxU
Tedlock p. 20

E88   **David (essay)**
  a Corrected carbon typescript, 7 pp.   CU
Tedlock pp. 180–1, Powell 82
  b Cabon typescript, 8 pp.   TxU

E90.5   **Delilah and Mr Bircumshaw**
    a Holograph manuscript, 11 pp.   CU
       An early version, incomplete, pp. 9–19 only
       MS untitled, begins: Then 'Come into the kitchen,' said
       Mrs Bircumshaw . . .
       Tedlock p. 41, Powell 51D
    b Typescript, 13 pp.   TxU

E91   **Democracy**
    a Corrected carbon typescript, 29 pp.   CU
       Tedlock pp. 132–3, Powell 112
    b Carbon typescript, 36 pp.   NmU
    c Carbon typescript, 36 pp.   TxU

E93   **Diary**
    Holograph manuscript, 13 pp.   CU
    In Notebook with *Birds, Beasts and Flowers*
    Tedlock pp. 87–101, Powell 56

E95   **Discipline**
    a Holograph manuscript, 1 p.   TxU
       A three-stanza fragment
       Tedlock pp. 79–81
    b Holograph manuscript, 3 pp.   TxU
       Tedlock pp. 77–9, Powell 52

E96   **Do Women Change?**
    a Holograph manuscript, 4 pp.   TxU
       Tedlock p. 232, Powell 84A
    b Corrected typescript, 7 pp.   CSt

E97   **Doe at Evening, A**
    Typescript, 1 p.   ICU

E98.5   **Dolour of Autumn**
    Holograph manuscript, 2 pp.   MH
    MS titled: *Dolor of Autumn*

E100   **Dostoevsky**
    a Holograph manuscript, 8 pp.   NN
    b Typescript, 4 pp.   TxU

E101   **Dragon of the Apocalypse, Introduction to**
    a Holograph manuscript, 21 pp.   CU
       Tedlock pp. 141–3, Powell 95
    b Carbon typescript, 24 pp.   CU
    c Carbon typescript, 20 pp.   CU
    d Carbon typescript, 13 pp.   CU

E104   **Dreams Old and Nascent**
Holograph manuscript, 5 pp.   TxU
Dreams Old and Nascent: Old, incomplete
Tedlock pp. 77–9, Powell 52

E 106   **Duc de Lauzun, The**
a Holograph manuscript, 8 pp.   CU
First version
Tedlock pp. 245–7, Powell 89
b Carbon typescript, 8 pp.   TxU
c Two carbon typescripts, 8 pp., 8 pp.   CU
d Holograph manuscript, 9 pp.   CU
Second version
Title *The Duc de Lauzun* struck out, begins: There is
something depressing about French eighteenth-century
literature . . .
Published as *The Good Man*
Tedlock pp. 245–7, Powell 89
e Carbon typescript, 9 pp.   CU
f Carbon typescript, 9 pp.   TxU

E107   **Dull London**
a Holograph manuscript, 4 pp.   TxU
Tedlock p. 222, Powell 84A
b Carbon typescript, 4 pp.   CU
MSS titled: *Why I Don't Like Living in London*

E107.5   **Dusk-flower, look hither . . .**
Holograph manuscript, 1 p.   N
With letter of 15 December 1910 to Louie Burrows

E109   **Eagle in New Mexico**
a Holograph manuscript, 5 pp.   TxU
b Holograph manuscript, 3 pp.   CSmH
Powell 63A
c Corrected typescript, 3 pp.   TxU

E112   **Education of the People**
a Holograph manuscript, 116 pp.   TxU
Tedlock pp. 131–2, Powell 111
b Two carbon typescripts, 143 pp., 143 pp.   CU
c Carbon typescript, 142 pp.   TxU
Lacking p. 141

E113   **Elephants of Dionysus, The**
a Holograph manuscript, 1 p.   CU
Tedlock pp. 212–13, Powell 84A

	b Two carbon typescripts, 2 pp., 2 pp.	CU
	c Carbon typescript, 2 pp.	TxU
E113.2	**Eloi, Eloi Lama Sabachthani?**	
	a Holograph manuscript, 3 pp.	PLeB
	An early version, incomplete	
	b Holograph manuscript, 3 pp.	ICU
	Extracts of another early version, incomplete	
	In Harriet Monroe's hand	
	MS titled: *Passages from Ecce Homo*	
	c Holograph manuscript, 4 pp.	NNPM
E113.3	**Elysium**	
	Holograph manuscript, 1 p.	TxU
	In *Women in Love* notebook	
	MS titled: *The Blind*	
E114.5	**England, My England**	
	Corrected galley proofs, 5 pp.	NCL
E115	**Enslaved by Civilization**	
	Holograph manuscript, 4 pp.	TxU
	Tedlock pp. 234–5, Powell 84A	
E115.7	**Erinnyes**	
	Holograph manuscript, 4 pp.	MH
E116	**Escaped Cock, The**	
	Part I	
	a Holograph manuscript, 22 pp.	IaE
	An early version	
	b Corrected original and carbon typescript, 25 pp.	OkTU
	pp. 1–14, 14a [15], 15–24 [16–25]	
	Tedlock pp. 65–6, Powell 19A	
	c Corrected typescript, 23 pp.	TxU
	A later version	
	d Corrected typescript, 32 pp.	TxU
	Final version	
	e Corrected carbon typescript, 32 pp.	TxU
	Part II	
	f Holograph manuscript, 32 pp.	Lazarus
	An early version, incomplete	
	Tedlock pp. 66–9, Powell 19B	
	g Two typescripts, 10 pp., 10 pp.	CU
	Copies of early version of Part II, incomplete	
	h Holograph manuscript, 49 pp.	IaE
	i Corrected typescript, 39 pp.	TxU

Parts I and II
j Corrected carbon typescript, 52 pp.   NmU
  Corrections in another hand (Frieda Lawrence?)
k Corrected page proofs, 102 pp.   CLU
  Black Sun Press, 1929
l Corrected page proofs, 94 pp.   TxU
  Black Sun Press, 1929

E117   **Etruscan Places**
a Holograph manuscript, 192 pp.   TxU
  MS titled: *Sketches of Etruscan Places*
b Corrected typescript, 160 pp.   TxU
  Tedlock pp. 195–7, Powell 83A
c Corrected carbon typescript, 56 pp.   TxU
  MS titled: *Sketches of Etruscan Places*
  The Painted Tombs of Tarquinia II and *Vulci* only
d Corrected original and carbon typescript, 56 pp.   TxU
  MS titled: *Sketches of Etruscan Places*
  The Painted Tombs of Tarquinia II and *Vulci* only
e Corrected carbon and original typescript, 84 pp.   OkTU
  Tarquinia, The Painted Tombs of Tarquinia and *Vol-
  terra* only
f Page proofs, 200 pp.   OkTU
  Secker, 1932

E118   **Etruscan Places, Notes for**
Holograph manuscript, 1 p.   CU
Tedlock pp. 62–3

E118.5 **Etruscan Places, Photographs for**
47 photographs of places and relics with Lawrence's titles
and notes on 44   CU
Tedlock p. 197, Powell 83B

E124   **Fallen Leaves, Review of**
a Holograph manuscript, 8 pp.   TxU
  Tedlock p. 262, Powell 104
b Carbon typescript, 7 pp.   CU
c Carbon typescript, 8 pp.   CU
d Carbon typescript, 6 pp.   NmU
  Incomplete
e Carbon typescript, 8 pp.   TxU

E125   **Fantasia of the Unconscious**
a Corrected typescript and holograph manuscript, 126 pp.   Private
b Corrected typescript and holograph manuscript, 138 pp.   TxU

211

    c Corrected carbon typescript, 10 pp.   NmU
    From Chapter VIII
    MS titled: *Education and Sex*
    d Carbon typescript, 7 pp.   NmU
    From Chapter XI
    MS titled: *On Love and Marriage*

E126   **Fantasia of the Unconscious, Foreword to**
    a Holograph manuscript, 16 pp.   TxU
    b Corrected typescript, 19 pp.   TxU
    MSS titled: *Foreword. An answer to Some Critics*

E130   **Fight for Barbara, The**
    a Holograph manuscript, 56 pp.   TxU
    Tedlock pp. 119–21, Powell 67
    b Three typescripts, 92 pp., 92 pp., 92 pp.   CU
    c Carbon typescript, 92 pp.   TxU
    d Holograph manuscript, 4 pp.   TxU
    A fragment in Frieda Lawrence's hand
    e Carbon typescript, 1 p.   TxU
    A fragment, beginning of Act IV

E130.5   **Figs**
    Holograph manuscript, 2 pp.   IaE
    MS titled: *Fig*

E131   **Fire**
    Holograph manuscript, 1 p.   Unlocated
    Powell 63D

E132   **Fire: did you ever warm your hands . . .**
    Holograph manuscript, 2 pp.   CU
    MS titled by Powell: *Invocation to Fire*
    Tedlock pp. 213–4, Powell 84A

E133.5   **Firelight and Nightfall**
    Holograph manuscript   NN
    First and second stanzas only
    MS titled: *Grief*
    With letter of 17 December 1913 to Edward Marsh

E134   **Fireworks**
    Holograph manuscript, 8 pp.   TxU
    Tedlock pp. 192–3, Powell 80

E134.2   **Flapper**
    Holograph manuscript, 1 p.   TxU

MS titled: *Song*
With letter of 23 December 1909 to Grace Crawford

E134.7   **[Flat-foot's Song]**
Holograph manuscript, 1 p.   TxU
Included in *Him With His Tail in His Mouth (essay)* and
later published separately as a poem

E135   **Flowery Tuscany**
a Typescript, partly carbon, 33 pp.   CU
b Carbon typescript, 8 pp.   CU
    Part IV only

E135.5   **Fly in the Ointment, The**
a Holograph manuscript, 8 pp.   Private
b Corrected typescript, 8 p.   TxU
c Typescript, 6 pp.   TxU

E136   **Flying Fish, The (An unfinished story)**
a Holograph manuscript, 40 pp.   Unlocated
    Tedlock pp. 55–6, Powell 17
b Corrected carbon typescript, 34 pp.   TxU
c Carbon typescript, 34 pp.   CU

E139   **Fox, The**
a Holograph manuscript, 22 pp.   Lazarus
    An early version
b Corrected galley sheets, 8 pp.   Private
    For *Hutchinson's Story Magazine*
c Holograph manuscript and corrected carbon typescript,
    68 pp.   TxU
    Includes 30 pp. of typescript
    Powell 11

E140   **Fragment of Stained Glass, A**
a Holograph manuscript, 6 pp.   Private
    An early version, incomplete
    MS titled: *Legend* and *Legend: Ruby-Glass*
    MS on verso: *Ballad of Another Ophelia*
b Holograph manuscript, 8 pp.   TxU
    Another early version
    MS titled: *Legend*
    Tedlock pp. 31–2, Powell 20
c Holograph manuscript, 26 pp.   N
d Carbon typescript, 10 pp.   CU
e Carbon typescript, 10 pp.   NmU

E140.5 **[Fragments]**
. . . that where . . .
Holograph manuscript, 1 p. N
MS untitled

E142 **Frost Flowers**
Typescript, 2 pp. ICU

E143.3 **Gentleman from San Francisco, The**
Corrected typescript, 32 pp. TxU
Corrections in Leonard Woolf's hand

E143.7 **Germans and Latins**
a Holograph manuscript, 10 pp. Unlocated
MS titled: *Summer in Tuscany,* or, *Germans and Latins*
Powell 81
b Carbon typescript, 8 pp. TxU
c Typescript and two carbon copies, 10 pp., 10 pp., 10 pp. TxU
Another version
Published as *Germans and English* in *Phoenix II*

E144 **Getting On**
Holograph manuscript, 8 pp. OCU
Early version of
[Return to Bestwood] in *Phoenix 2*

E145 **Gifts of Fortune, Review of**
a Holograph manuscript, 8 pp. TxU
Tedlock pp. 256–7, Powell 98
b Carbon typescript, 7 pp. TxU

145.5 **Gipsy**
a Holograph manuscript, 1 p. N
MS titled: *Self-contempt*
With letter of 6 December 1910 to Louis Burrows
b Holograph manuscript, 1 p. TxU

E147 **Give Her a Pattern**
a Holograph manuscript, 6 pp. CU
Tedlock pp. 225–6, Powell 84A
b Carbon typescript, 7 pp. CU
c Carbon typescript, 7 pp. TxU
MSS titled: *Oh These Women!*

E148 **Glad Ghosts**
a Holograph manuscript, 9 pp. Lazarus
An early version, incomplete
Powell 39B

    b Holograph manuscript, 78 pp.   Lazarus
      Incorrectly paginated
      Powell 39A
    c Corrected typescript, 48 pp.   CtY
      Lacking 1 p.
    d Advance proof copy, 84 pp.   Private
      Ernest Benn, 1926

E150.7   **Goose Fair**
    a Holograph manuscript, 12 pp.   N
    b Holograph manuscript, 13 pp.   Unlocated
      Powell 21

E151   **Grand Inquisitor, Introduction to The**
    a Holograph manuscript, 14 pp.   CU
      Tedlock pp. 250–1, Powell 94
    b Typescript, 13 pp.   CU
    c Two carbon typescripts, 14 pp., 14 pp.   TxU

E152   **Green**
    Typescript, 1 p.   CtY

E152.5   **Grey Evening**
    Holograph manuscript   NN
    Third stanza only
    MS titled: *Grief*
    With letter of 17 December 1913 to Edward Marsh

E154.7   **'Gross, Coarse, Hideous'**
    Holograph manuscript, 1 p.   CSt
    With letter of Saturday [14 September 1929] to Charles
    Lahr

E155   **Guards**
    a Holograph manuscript, 1 p.   CSt
      MS titled: *Guards! A Review in Hyde Park,* 1913
      MS subtitled: *The Crowd Watches, Evolutions of Sol-*
      diers
    b Holograph manuscript, 2 pp.   TxU
      MS titled: *Guards A Review in Hyde Park, before the*
      War
      MS subtitled: *The Crowd Watches, Evolutions of Sol-*
      diers, Potency of Men

E157   **Hay-Hut Among the Mountains, A**
    Carbon typescript, 13 pp.   CU
    Includes an erased ending, pp. 62–3

Tedlock pp. 178–9

E158	**Heat, Review of**	
	a Holograph manuscript, 8 pp.	CU
	Tedlock p. 256, Powell 97	
	b Carbon typescript, 6 pp.	CU
	Incomplete	
E159	**'Henry,' she said, 'I want to disappear for a year.'** . . .	
	Holograph manuscript, 5 pp.	CU
E159.5	**Her Turn**	
	Holograph manuscript, 10 pp.	Unlocated
	Powell 26	
E161	**Him With His Tail in His Mouth** (essay)	
	a Holograph manuscript, 10 pp.	TxU
	Tedlock p. 139	
	b Corrected carbon typescript, 11 pp.	CU
	Tedlock pp. 139–40	
	Includes poems later published separately as *Him With His Tail in His Mouth* and [*Flat-foot's Song*]	
E161.1	**Him With His Tail in His Mouth** (poem)	
	Holograph manuscript, 1 p.	TxU
	Included in *Him with His Tail in His Mouth (essay)* and later published separately as a poem	
E164	**Hopi Snake Dance, The**	
	a Holograph manuscript, 18 pp.	TxU
	Tedlock pp. 184–6, Powell 72	
	b Corrected carbon typescript, 19 pp.	CU
	Tedlock p. 186	
E164.9	**Hymn to Nothingness**	
	Holograph manuscript, 3 pp.	TxU
E165	**Hymns in a Man's Life**	
	Holograph manuscript, 6 pp.	N
E167	**If you are a woman, and if ever you can pray** . . .	
	Holograph manuscript, 9 pp.	CU
	Tedlock pp. 73–4, Powell 51F	
E170	**In a Boat**	
	Holograph manuscript	MH
	MS titled: *Tired of the Boat*	

E170.3 **In Love**
    a Holograph manuscript, 20 pp.   TxU
       MS titled: *More Modern Love*
       Tedlock pp. 63–4, Powell 41
    b Typescript, 17 pp.   CtY
       MS titled: *Modern Love*

E170.8 **Indians and an Englishman**
    a Corrected typescript, 12 pp.   CtY
    b Carbon typescript, 14 pp.   TxU

E171 **Indians and Entertainment**
    a Holograph manuscript, 13 pp.   CU
       Tedlock p. 183, Powell 74
    b Carbon typescript, 18 pp.   CU
    c Carbon typescript, 18 pp.   TxU

E172 **[Individual Consciousness v. the Social Consciousness, The]**
    a Holograph manuscript, 6 pp.   TxU
       MS untitled, begins: The more one reads of modern novels . . .
       Tedlock pp. 170–1, Powell 84A
    b Carbon typescript, 6 pp.   CU
    c Carbon typescript, 6 pp.   TxU

E174 **Insouciance**
    Holograph manuscript, 4 pp.   TxU
    Tedlock pp. 220–1, Powell 84A

E177 **Is England Still a Man's Country?**
    a Holograph manuscript, 6 pp.   TxU
       Tedlock p. 226, Powell 84A
    b Two corrected carbon typescripts, 4 pp., 4 pp.   CU
       Tedlock p. 227, Powell 84B

E177.3 **Island Pharisees, Review of**
    Holograph manuscript, 2 pp.   Unlocated
    Argus Book Shop catalogue No. 827 (1943) item No. 34

E177.4 **It depends! And that is always the disconcerting answer! . . .**
    Holograph manuscript, 1 p.   Lazarus
    Tedlock pp. 163–4

E179 **'Jeune Fille' wants to Know, The**
    a Holograph manuscript, 4 pp.   TxU

Tedlock p. 220, Powell 84A
b Holograph manuscript, 1 p.   Lazarus
A fragment, the final paragraph is written on a scrap torn
from the foot of the last galley sheet for *Assorted Articles*

E181 **Jimmy and the Desperate Woman**
a Holograph manuscript, 31 pp.   Lazarus
Powell 37A
b Corrected typescript, 25 pp.   Lazarus
Powell 37B

E181.3 **John Galsworthy**
a Holograph notes, 1 p.   TxU
MS untitled, begins: 'The moon at her curve's summit
floated at peace . . .'
Tedlock pp. 169–70
b Holograph manuscript, 16 pp.   TxU
MS titled: *A Scrutiny of the Work of John Galsworthy*
Tedlock pp. 171–2, Powell 87

E181.9 **Just Back from the Snake Dance**
a Holograph manuscript, 2 pp.   CtY
b Typescript, 4 pp.   IEN

E182 **Kangaroo**
a Holograph manuscript, 572 pp.   TxU
Chapters I–XVII (lacking Chapter XVIII)
Tedlock pp. 16–18, Powell 6
b Holograph manuscript, 20 pp.   Private
Chapter XVIII only
c Corrected typescript, 331 pp.   NN
An early version, incomplete
d Corrected carbon typescript, 313 pp.   NN
Carbon of above, incomplete
e Corrected carbon typescript, 569 pp.   NN
Printer's copy

E185 **Labour Battalion**
Corrected galley proof, 1 p.   TxU

E186 **Lady Chatterley's Lover**
a Holograph manuscript, 398 pp.   TxU
First version
Tedlock pp. 20–1
b Holograph manuscript, 580 pp.   TxU
Second version
Tedlock pp. 23–4

    c Holograph manuscript, 728 pp.   TxU
       Third version
       MS titled: *My Lady's Keeper*
       Tedlock pp. 24–7

    d Holograph manuscript, 6 pp.   ICSo
       MS titled: *The Grange Farm*
       An early form of concluding letter, third version

    e Corrected typescript, 3 pp.   TxU
       A fragment, conclusion of Chapter IX (i.e., XII) of the
       third version

    f Corrected original and carbon typescript, 423 pp.   TxU
       Third version
       MS titled: *John Thomas and Lady Jane*
       Powell 8

    g Corrected proof of title page, 1 p.   Unlocated
       Argus Book Shop catalogue No. 827 (1943) item No. 40f

E187   **Ladybird, The**
       Holograph manuscript, 108 pp.   NN
       pp. [1]–15, 15–22 [16–23], [23] [24], 22–96 [25–99],
       95–103 [100–8]

E189   **Last Hours**
       Corrected typescript, 1 p.   CtY

E190   **Last Laugh, The**
    a Holograph manuscript, 24 pp.   Lazarus
       Powell 38A

    b Corrected typescript, 21 pp.   Lazarus
       Powell 38B

E192   **Last Poems**
    a Holograph manuscript, 195 pp.   TxU
       In two notebooks
       Powell 64

    b Typescript and page proofs, 192 pp.   TxU
       Incomplete

E193.5 **Late at Night Along the Home Road**
       Holograph manuscript, 2 pp.   MH

E193.7 **Late in Life**
       Corrected proof copy, 1 p.   Private

E194   **Laura Philippine**
    a Holograph manuscript   Unlocated
       Bumpus case No. 5

	b Corrected typescript, 7 pp.	CU
E194.1	**Laura Philippine, French translation** Carbon typescript, 7 pp. Corrections in an unknown hand	CU
E196.4	**Lessford's Rabbits** *a* Holograph manuscript *b* Typescript *Phoenix II* p. 630	Heinemann Unlocated
E196.5	**Lesson on a Tortoise, A** *a* Holograph manuscript *b* Typescript *Phoenix II* p. 630	Heinemann Unlocated
E196.6	**Let the flood rise and cover me . . .** Holograph manuscript, 1 p.	TxU
E197	**Letter from Germany** *a* Holograph manuscript, 6 pp. Tedlock pp. 181–2, Powell 78 *b* Two carbon typescripts, 7 pp., 7 pp.	TxU CU
E200	**Life** *a* Corrected typescript, 5 pp. Tedlock p. 203 *b* Carbon typescript, 7 pp.	CU CU
E203.5	**Little Moonshine with Lemon, A** *a* Holograph manuscript, 6 pp. Powell 75 *b* Typescript and two carbon copies, 5 pp., 5 pp., 5 pp. MS titled: 'Ye Gods, He Doth Bestride the Narrow World Like a Colosses—!' *c* Carbon typescript, 4 pp. MS titled: 'Ye Gods, He Doth Bestride the Narrow World Like a Collosus—!'	Unlocated TxU TxU
E204	**Little Novels of Sicily** Holograph manuscript, 181 pp. Tedlock pp. 270–2, Powell 107	TxU
E204.5	**Little Town at Evening, The** Holograph manuscript, 1 p.	IaE
E205.8	**'Look! We Have Come Through!'** *a* Holograph manuscript	Unlocated

220

With letter of 18 February 1917 to Catherine Carswell
  b Corrected proofs, 163 pp.   Lazarus
  c Author's copy with holograph corrections, 168 pp.   TxU
    Chatto and Windus, 1917, for *Collected Poems*, 1928
    Includes corrected and uncorrected carbon typescripts of
      Bie Hennef, 1 p.
      Everlasting Flowers (Everlasting Flowers:
        For a Dead Mother), 2 pp.
      Coming Awake, 1 pp.
      Song of a Man Who is Loved, 1 p.

E206   **Looking Down on the City**
      Corrected typescript, 5 pp.   CLU

E209   **Lost Girl, The**
    a Holograph manuscript, 450 pp.   TxU
    b Holograph manuscript, 20 pp.   ICSo
      An early version, incomplete
      MS untitled, begins: My mother made a failure of her
      life. . . .
      Tedlock pp. 44–6, Powell 51A
    c Corrected page proofs, 122 pp.   Unlocated
      City Book Auction catalogue No. 247 (18 September
      1943) item No. 175

E210   **Love (essay)**
    a Corrected typescript, 7 pp.   CU
      Tedlock p. 202
    b Carbon typescript, 10 pp.   CU

E211   **Love Among the Haystacks**
      Carbon typescript, 60 pp.   CU
      Tedlock pp. 42–3

E213   **Love Poems**
    a Holograph manuscript, 37 pp.   TxU
      Kisses in the Train
      Cruelty and Love (Love on the Farm)
      Lilies in the Fire
      Coldness in Love
      Reminder
      Bei Hennef
      Lightning
      Song-Day in Autumn
      A Pang of Reminiscence
      A White Blossom

> *Red Moon-Rise*
> *Return*
> *The Appeal*
> *Repulsed*
> *Dream-Confused*
> *Corot*
> *Morning Work*
> *Transformations*
> *Renascence*
> *Dog-Tired*

b Holograph manuscript, 8 pp.   N

> *Wedding Morn*, 3 pp.
> *Cherry Robbers*, 1 p.
> *End of Another Home-Holiday (End of Another Home Holiday)*, 3 pp.
> *Aware*, 1 p.

Both were originally one manuscript; *Lightning* supplied from a printed source

Tedlock pp. 82–5, Powell 53

c Holograph manuscript   Unlocated

> *Michael-Angelo*
> *Violets*
> *Whether or Not*
> *A Collier's Wife (The Collier's Wife)*
> *The Drained Cup*
> *The Schoolmaster*

E214   **Love Poems and Others**

a Corrected page proofs, 72 pp.   TxU

Powell 54

b Author's copy with holograph corrections   NBuU

Duckworth, 1913

E214.3   **Love Song, A**

Holograph manuscript   N

A four-line fragment

E215   **. . . Love Was Once a Little Boy**

a Holograph manuscript, 17 pp.   TxU

b Corrected carbon typescript, 21 pp.   CU

Tedlock pp. 208–9

E216   **Lovely Lady, The** (story)

a Holograph manuscript, 32 pp.   Lazarus

b Corrected typescript, 42 pp.   CtY

Original version

c Carbon typescript, 20 pp.   CU
  Condensed version for *The Black Cap*
d Carbon typescript, 2 pp.   NmU
  Incomplete, pp. 19–20 only

E216.5 **Lovely Lady, The (book)**
Proof copy, 208 pp.   TxU
Spacing between lines was adjusted and the number of
  pages increased before publication
Secker, 1933

E221 **Making Love to Music**
a Holograph manuscript, 13 pp.   CtY
  Tedlock p. 210, Powell 84A
b Two carbon typescripts,.11 pp., 11 pp.   CU
c Carbon typescript, 11 pp.   TxU

E222 **Making Pictures**
a Holograph manuscript, 6 pp.   TxU
  Tedlock pp. 233–4, Powell 114
b Corrected carbon typescript, 9 pp.   TxU
  Tedlock p. 234, Powell 114

E225 **Man in the Street, The**
Typescript and carbon copy, 1 p., 1 p.   Unlocated
Tedlock p. 114, Powell 62

E226 **Man Is a Hunter**
a Holograph manuscript, 4 pp.   TxU
  Tedlock pp. 191–2
b Carbon typescript, 3 pp.   NmU
c Carbon typescript, 5 pp.   TxU

E226.5 **Man is essentially a soul . . .**
Holograph manuscript, 4 pp.   TxU
A philosophical fragment
Tedlock p. 138, Powell 118

E227 **Man Who Died, A**
Holograph manuscript, 2 pp.   N
MS untitled, begins: Ah stern, cold man . . .

E227.3 **Man Who Loved Islands, The**
a Holograph manuscript, 44 pp.   PLeB
b Corrected typescript, 30 pp.   CtY

E227.4 **Man Who Was Through with the World, The (unfinished
story)**

a	Holograph manuscript, 10 pp. Tedlock pp. 62–3, Powell 51E	CU
b	Typescript, 7 pp.	TxU
c	Carbon typescript, 7 pp. MSS untitled	CU

E227.7 **Market Day**
Holograph manuscript, 9 pp.   TxU
MS titled: *Mornings in Mexico. Saturday Morning*
Tedlock pp. 186–7, Powell 76

E229 **Married Man, The**

a	Holograph manuscript, 67 pp. Tedlock pp. 118–19, Powell 66	CU
b	Typescript, 84 pp.	CU
c	Typescript, 84 pp.	TxU
d	Two typescripts, 62 pp., 62 pp.	CU
e	Typescript, mostly carbon, 63 pp. Incomplete, all MSS lacking pp. 1–5	OkTU

E229.5 **Martyr à la Mode**
Holograph manuscript, 2 pp.
MS untitled, begins: Ah Life, God, Law, whatever name
you have . . .

E230 **Master in His Own House**
Holograph manuscript, 4 pp.   TxU
MS titled: *Men Must Rule*
Tedlock pp. 220–1, Powell 84A

E230.9 **Mastro-Don Gesualdo**

a	Holograph manuscript, 582 pp. Tedlock pp. 267–9, Powell 106	TxU
b	Typescript, 401 pp.	TxU
c	Corrected galley proofs, 128 pp.	TxU

E231 **Mastro-Don Gesualdo, Introductions to**

a	Holograph manuscript, 6 pp. First version, unpublished MS titled: *Introductory Note* Tedlock p. 269, Powell 106	TxU
b	Corrected typescript, 4 pp.	TxU
c	Holograph manuscript, 6 pp.	TxU

Second version, published as *Biographical Note* in
Mastro-Don Gesualdo (A28a)
MS titled: *Introductory Note*
Includes also principal characters, bibliography

    d Two carbon typescripts, 5 pp., 5 pp.   TxU
       MS titled: *Introductory Note*
    e Holograph manuscript, 17 pp.   TxU
       Third version, published in *Phoenix*
       MS titled: *Introduction to Mastro don Gesualdo—Translation from Verga* (written in unknown hand)
       Tedlock pp. 269–70, Powell 106
    f Carbon typescript, 15 pp.   CU
       Third version
       Untitled, begins: It seems curious that modern Italian literature . . .
    g Corrected typescript, 10 pp.   Unlocated
       Argus Book catalogue No. 827 (1943) item No. 25

E232   **Matriarchy**
      Holograph manuscript, 6 pp.   TxU
      Tedlock p. 101, Powell 84A

E233   **Mediterranean in January**
    a Holograph manuscript, 2 pp.   TxU
       Tedlock p. 101, Powell 118
    b Carbon typescript, 3 pp.   CU
    c Carbon typescript, 3 pp.   TxU

E233.5   **Meeting Among the Mountains**
      Carbon typescript, 2 pp.   TxU

E234.5   **Men in New Mexico**
    a Corrected typescript, 2 pp.   TxU
    b Typescript, 2 pp.   TxU

E235   **Men Must Work and Women as Well**
    a Holograph manuscript, 12 pp.   TxU
       Tedlock p. 237, Powell 84A
    b Carbon typescript, 18 pp.   CU
       MSS titled: *Men and Women*

E236   **Mercury**
    a Holograph manuscript, 9 pp.   CU
       Tedlock pp. 193–4, Powell 79
    b Carbon typescript, 8 pp.   CU
    c Carbon typescript, 8 pp.   TxU

E237   **Merry-Go-Round, The**
    a Holograph manuscript, 152 pp.   CU
       Tedlock p. 117, Powell 65
    b Typescript, 146 pp.   CU

c Carbon typescript, 146 pp.		TxU
d Two typescripts, 110 pp., 110 pp.		CU
e Carbon typescript, 110 pp.		OkTU
2 pp. are original typescript		

E240   **Mr Noon**

a Holograph manuscript, 450 pp.		TxU
b Corrected typescript, 407 pp.		TxU
c Corrected carbon typescript, 143 pp.		TxU
Tedlock pp. 48–9, Powell 13		
d Carbon typescript, 156 pp.		CU

E240.7   **Modern Lover, A**

Holograph manuscript, 56 pp.		NN

E244   **Morality and the Novel**

a Holograph manuscript, 9 pp.		TxU
First version		
Tedlock pp. 166–7, Powell 85D		
b Typescript and carbon copy, 8 pp., 8 pp.		TxU
c Carbon typescript, 8 pp.		CU
d Holograph manuscript, 10 pp.		TxU
Second version		
Tedlock pp. 166–7, Powell 85D		
e Carbon typescript, 10 pp.		CU
Tedlock p. 168		
f Carbon typescript, 9 pp.		CU
g Carbon typescript, 9 pp.		TxU
h Typescript, 7 pp.		TxU

E246   **Morning Work**

Holograph manuscript, 1 p.		TxU

E246.2   **Mornings in Mexico**

Page proofs		Unlocated
Union Square Book Shop catalogue (30 September 1930)		
item No. 68		

E246.8   **Mortal Coil, The**

Typescript, 8 pp.		TxU
Incomplete		

E248   **Mother, Introduction to The**

a Holograph manuscript, 7 pp.		CU
Tedlock p. 249, Powell 91		
b Carbon typescript, 6 pp.		CU
c Carbon typescript, 6 pp.		TxU

E249   **Mother and Daughter**
       a Holograph manuscript, 44 pp.   TxU
          Tedlock pp. 72–3, Powell 46
       b Carbon typescript, 34 pp.   CU
       c Corrected galley proofs, 8 pp.   TxU

E255   **Movements in European History**
       a Holograph manuscripts, 134 pp.   Lazarus
          Incomplete, Chapters 1–8 and 6 pp. of Chapter 9
          MS titled: *Landmarks in European History*
       b Author's copy with holograph corrections   IaE
          Milford, 1921

E256   **Movements in European History, Epilogue to**
       Carbon typescript, 24 pp.   CLU

E258   **Mozo, The**
       a Holograph manuscript, 13 pp.   TxU
          MS titled: *Mornings in Mexico. Monday Morning*
          Tedlock pp. 186–7, Powell 76
       b Corrected carbon typescript, 14 pp.   TxU
          MS titled: *Mornings in Mexico. The Mozo*
          Tedlock p. 188, Powell 76

E260   **Mushrooms**
       Holograph manuscript, 1 p.   OCU
       An unfinished autobiographical sketch.

E264.7 **Near the Mark**
       Holograph manuscript, 1 p.   N
       With letter of 6 December 1910 to Louie Burrows

E266   **Nettles**
       a Holograph manuscript, 6 pp.   TxU
          A Rose is not a Cabbage, 1 p.
          The Man in the Street
          Britannia's baby, 1 p.
          Change of Government, 1 p.
          The British Workman and the Government, 1 p.
          Clydesider
          Flapper Vote, 1 p.
          Neptune's little affair with Freedom, 1 p.
       b Holograph manuscript, 5 pp.   Lazarus
          Puss-Puss!, 1 p.
          London Mercury
          My Little Critics

Never had a Daddy (Emasculation), 1 p.
Editorial Office, 3 pp.
The Great Newspaper Editor and His Subordinate
    (The Great Newspaper Editor to His Subordinate)
With letter of 23 August [1929] to Charles Lahr
c Carbon typescript, 18 pp.   CU
    A Rose is not a Cabbage
    Britannia's Baby
    Change of Government
    The British Workman and the Government
    Cyldesider
    Flapper vote
    Neptune's little affair with freedom
    My Native Land
    The British Boy
    13000 People
    Innocent England
    Give me a sponge
    Puss-Puss!
    London Mercury
    My little critics
    Daddy-Do-Nothing
    Question
    Editorial Office
    British Sincerity
    The Great Newspaper Editor to his subordinate
    Modern Prayer
    Cry of the masses
    What have they done to you—?
    The People
    The factory cities
    Leaves of grass, flowers of grass
    Magnificent democracy

E268 **New Eve and Old Adam**
    a Holograph manuscript, 14 pp.   OkTU
     Powell 27
    b Two carbon typescripts, 38 pp., 38 pp. CU

E269 **New Mexico**
    a Holograph manuscript, 8 pp.   Unlocated
     Tedlock pp. 194–5, Powell 71
    b Typescript, 12 pp.   TxU
    c Carbon typescript, 12 pp.   CU

E269.5   **New Poems**

     a Holograph manuscript, 47 pp.   TxU

       From a College Window, 1 p.

       Flapper, 1 p.

       In the Street (Birdcage Walk), 1 p.

       Letter from Town: The Almond Tree (Letter from Town: The Almond-Tree), 1 p.

       Flat Suburbs S. W., in the Morning (Flat Suburbs, S. W., in the Morning), 1 p.

       Thief in the Night, 1 p.

       Letter from Town: On a Grey Evening in March (Letter from Town: On a Grey Morning in March) 1 p.

       Suburbs on a Hazy Day, 1 p.

       Hyde Park at Night—Clerks (Hyde Park at Night, Before the War: Clerks), 1 p.

       Gipsy, 1 p.

       Two-Fold (Twofold), 1 p.

       Under the Oak, 1 p.

       Sigh No More, 1 p.

       Suburbs on the Hills in the Evening (Parliament Hill in the Evening), 1 p.

       Piccadilly Circus at Night—Street Walkers (Piccadilly Circus at Night: Street-Walkers), 1 p.

       Tarantella, 1 p.

       In Church, 1 p.

       Piano, 1 p.

       Embankment at Night—Charity (Embankment at Night, Before the War: Charity), 1 p.

       Phantasmagoria (Late at Night), 1 p.

       Next Morning, 1 p.

       Palimpsest of Twilight (Twilight), 1 p.

       Embankment at Night—Outcasts (Embankment at Night, Before the War: Outcasts), 4 pp.

       Winter in the Boulevard, 1 p.

       School on the Outskirts, 1 p.

       Sickness, 1 p.

       Everlasting Flowers (Everlasting Flowers: For a Dead Mother), 2 pp.

       The North Country, 1 p.

       Bitterness of Death (A Man Who Died), 3 pp.

       Late in Life, 1 p.

       Reading a Letter, 1 p.

       Apprehension (Noise of Battle), 1 p.

Twenty Years Ago, 1 p.
Heimweh (At the Front), 1 p.
Débâcle (Reality of Peace, 1916), 1 p.
Narcissus, 1 p.
Spring Sunshine (Autumn Sunshine), 1 p.
On That Day, 1 p.
Includes title page, dedication and table of Contents,
3 pp.
b Proofs   Unlocated
With letter of 23 September 1918 to Amy Lowell

E269.6   **New Poems, Preface to**
a Holograph manuscript, 3 pp.   TxU
b Holograph manuscript, 3 pp.   Private
With letter of 29 August 1919 to Thomas Moult

E271   **Nigger Heaven, Flight, Manhattan Transfer and In Our
           Time, Review of**
a Holograph manuscript, 10 pp.   CLU
MS titled: *Four Reviews: Nigger Heaven, Flight, Man-
hattan Transfer, In Our Time*
Powell 99
b Carbon typescript, 11 pp.   CU
MS titled: *Review of Books*
c Carbon typescript, 11 pp.   TxU
MS titled: *Review of Books*

E272   **Nightingale, The**
a Holograph manuscript, 8 pp.   CtY
b Corrected typescript, 5 pp.   CU
c Typescript, 7 pp.   TxU
d Typescript and carbon copy, 8 pp., 8 pp.   TxU
e Holograph manuscript, 8 pp.   Lazarus
Incomplete
Published in *'Not I, But the Wind . . .'*
In Frieda Lawrence's hand

E272.5   **No News**
Corrected proof, 1 p.   Lazarus

E273   **Noah's Flood**
a Holograph manuscript, 11 pp.   TxU
A longer early version
Tedlock pp. 125–6, Powell 118
b Holograph manuscript, 10 pp.   CU
A later version

Tedlock pp. 127–8, Powell 84
c Carbon typescript, 8 pp.   CU
d Carbon typescript, 8 pp.   NmU
e Carbon typescript, 8 pp.   TxU

E274   **Nobody Loves Me**
a Holograph manuscript, 12 pp.   CtY
Notebook cover titled: *Three Essays for Vanity Fair*
Powell 117
b Carbon typescript, 12 pp.   TxU
c Typescript, 13 pp.   TxU
d Carbon typescript, 13 pp.   CU

E275   **None of That!**
Typescript, 33 pp.   CU

E276   **Nostalgia**
Holograph manuscript, 1 p.   Private

E277   **Notes concerning 'The Hand of Man'**
Holograph manuscript, 2 pp.   TxU
Written to Earl H. Brewster

E279   **Nottingham and the Mining Countryside**
a Holograph manuscript, 9 pp.   CU
b Carbon typescript, 13 pp.   CU
c Carbon typescript, 14 pp.   NmU

E280   **Novel, The**
a Holograph manuscript, 13 pp.   TxU
A shorter early version
MS titled: *The Modern Novel*
Tedlock p. 162, Powell 85B
b Corrected typescript, 7 pp.   TxU
Tedlock p. 163
c Holograph manuscript and corrected typescript, 12 pp.   CtY
pp. 1–5 typescript, pp. 6–12 holograph manuscript

E281   **Novel and the Feelings, The**
a Holograph manuscript, 12 pp.   TxU
Tedlock p. 169, Powell 85C
b Typescript, 9 pp.   TxU
c Two carbon typescripts, 9 pp., 9 pp.   CU

E281.7   **Now It's Happened**
Holograph manuscript, 2 pp.   TxU
MS untitled, begins: One cannot now help thinking . . .

231

E282   **O! Americans**
Holograph manuscript, 8 pp.   COMC
Powell 64E

E283   **Obsequial Ode**
a Holograph manuscript, 1 p.   ICN
   MS titled: *Obsequial Chant*
b Holograph manuscript, 2 pp.   Private
c Corrected typescript, 2 pp.   Lazarus
d Typescript, 1 p.   TxU

E284   **Odour of Chrysanthemums**
a Holograph manuscript, 6 pp.   TxU
   A fragment from an early version
   Tedlock pp. 33–7, Powell 22
b Holograph manuscript, 39 pp.   TxU
   A later version
   In Louie Burrow's hand
   Tedlock pp. 33–7, Powell 22
c Corrected proof sheets, 35 pp.   N
   Includes 8 pp. of holograph corrections
   For *English Review*

E286   **Old Adam, The**
Holograph manuscript, 27 pp.   Lazarus
Powell 23

E287   **Old Orchard, The**
Holograph manuscript, 2 pp.   OCU

E288.5   **On Being in Love**
Holograph notes, 1 p.   Unlocated
Tedlock pp. 203–4

E289   **On Being Religious**
a Holograph manuscript, 2 pp.   Unlocated
   A fragment
   MS untitled, begins: There is no real battle between me
   and Christianity . . .
   Tedlock pp. 134–6, Powell 84A
b Corrected typescript, 7 pp.   NmU
c Carbon typescript, 7 pp.   TxU
d Carbon typescript, 11 pp.   CU

E290   **On Coming Home**
a Holograph manuscript, 11 pp.   TxU
b Corrected typescript, 11 pp.   CU

Tedlock pp. 296–8
c Typescript, 8 pp.   TxU
A shorter and possibly earlier version

E292.5   **On Taking the Next Step**
Holograph manuscript, 3 pp.   Unlocated
Tedlock pp. 205–6, Powell 84

E294.5   **On the Lago di Garda**
a Holograph manuscript, 26 pp.   TxU
    The Spinner and the Monks, 8 pp.
    *The Lemon Garden of the Signor di P. (The Lemon
        Gardens),* 10 pp.
    The Theatre, 8 pp.
MS titled: *By the Lago di Garda*
MS titled in other hand: *Italian Studies*
b Corrected typescript, 2 pp.   NCRecord
A fragment, pp. 15–16 of *The Lemon Gardens*

E295   **On the March**
Corrected typescript, 2 pp.   CtY

E296   **Once**
a Holograph manuscript, 13 pp.   TxU
b Carbon typescript, 14 pp.   CU
    Tedlock pp. 43–4

E297   **Origins of Prohibition, Review of The**
a Holograph manuscript, 7 pp.   TxU
    Tedlock p. 255, Powell 96
b Carbon typescript, 5 pp.   CU
c Carbon typescript, 5 pp.   TxU

E298   **Overtone, The**
a Holograph manuscript, 12 pp.   TxU
b Corrected carbon typescript, 21 pp.   NmU

E299   **Ownership**
a Holograph manuscript, 4 pp.   CU
    Tedlock p. 227, Powell 84A
b Carbon typescript, 5 pp.   CU

E300   **Paintings, Introduction to these**
a Holograph manuscript, 37 pp.   TxU
    Powell 113
b Typescript and carbon copy, 58 pp., 58 pp.   CU
c Carbon typescript, 58 pp.   CLU

d Carbon typescript, 58 pp.	TxU
e Carbon typescript, 58 pp.	NNC

MSS titled: *Introduction to Painting*

E300.5 **Pan in America**

a Holograph manuscript, 7 pp. TxU
An early version
Tedlock pp. 136–7

b Holograph manuscript, 12 pp. NcD

c Carbon typescript, 18 pp. TxU

E302 **Pansies**

a Holograph manuscript, 10 pp. Unlocated
Powell 60
> *Finding Your Level*
> *Altercation*
> *What is Man Without an Income?*
> *Climbing Up*
> *Canvassing for the Election*
> *A Rise in the World*

b Holograph manuscript, 2 pp. TxU
> *Morality (Man's Image)*, 1 p.
> *Roses*
> *The Gazelle Calf*
> *The Mosquito (The Mosquito Knows)*, 1 p.
> *Self Pity (Self-Pity)*
> *Seaweed (Sea-Weed)*

MS titled: *Pensées for Achsah [Brewster] from D. H. L.*

c Holograph manuscript notes, 1 p. TxU
A list of 9 titles and first lines
Tedlock p. 71

d Holograph manuscript, 99 pp. TxU
An early version
Includes a list of titles of poems
Tedlock pp. 104–12, Powell 59

e Corrected typescript, 102 pp. Lazarus
An early version
Includes introduction and table of contents

f Galley proofs, 98 pp. Unlocated
Union Square Book Shop catalogue (30 September 1930)
item No. 67

E302.5 **Pansies, Foreword to**

Holograph manuscript, 2 pp. TxU
With letter of 27 April 1929 to Laurence Pollinger

E303   **Pansies, Introduction to**
        a Holograph manuscript, 2 pp.   CU
        b Holograph manuscript, 3 pp.   TxU
           Another version
           Tedlock p. 103, Powell 59

E305   **Peace**
        Holograph manuscript, 1 p.   ViU
        MS titled: *Slopes of Etna*
        With letter of 1 December 1920 to Professors John C.
           Metcalf and Wilson

E306   **Pedro De Valdivia, Review of**
        Corrected typescript, 7 pp.   CU
        Tedlock p. 257

E307   **Peep Show, Review of**
        a Holograph manuscript, 6 pp.   CU
           An early version, incomplete, pp. 3–8 only
           MS titled on first page in other hand: *Review of Puppet
           Show*
           Tedlock pp. 258–9, Powell 101
        b Two carbon typescripts, 5 pp., 5 pp.   TxU
           MS titled: *Review of Puppet Show*
        c Holograph manuscript, 10 pp.   CU

E308.8 **Physician, The**
        Holograph manuscript, 1 p.   N
        With letter of 15 December 1910 to Louie Burrows

E310   **Pictures, Introduction to**
        a Holograph manuscript, 17 pp.   TxU
           Tedlock pp. 172–3, Powell 109
        b Carbon typescript, 13 pp.   CU

E311   **Pictures on the Walls**
        a Holograph manuscript, 9 pp.   Unlocated
           MS titled: *Pictures on the Wall*
           Tedlock p. 238, Powell 115
        b Carbon typescript, 14 pp.   TxU
           Tedlock pp. 238–9, Powell 115

E313   **Plumed Serpent, The**
        a Holograph manuscript, 594 pp.   TxU
           First version
           MS titled: *Quetzalcoatl*
        b Corrected typescript, 360 pp.   MH

    c Holograph manuscript, 806 pp.   TxU
      Second version
      MS titled: *Quetzalcoatl*
    d Corrected original and carbon typescript, 743 pp.   TxU
      Powell 7
    e Corrected typescript, 18 pp.   CLU
      Chapter VI only
    f Corrected typescript, 5 pp.   CU
      Chapter VII, incomplete
      Tedlock pp. 18–20
    g Corrected carbon typescript, 24 pp.   CU
      Chapters VI and VII, latter is incomplete
      Tedlock pp. 18–20
    h Two sets of galley proofs, 156 pp, 160 pp.   TxU
      One set lacks sheet No. 156; the other has three duplicate sheets

E314   **Poems**
    Holograph manuscript, 4 pp.   CLU
    Tedlock pp. 112–14, Powell 62
      Bells, 1 p.
      The Triumph of the Machine, 1 p.
      Father Neptune's Little Affair with Freedom, 1 p.
      (Neptune's Little Affair with Freedom)
      The Man in the Street, 1 p.

E314.1   **Poems**
    Holograph manuscript   Unlocated
    Three poems sent to Austin Harrison, his letter of 6 April 1911 to Lawrence
      Sorrow
      A Husband Dead (A Man Who Died)
      1 unidentified

E314.2   **Poems**
    Holograph manuscript or typescript   Unlocated
    Four poems with letter of 27 February 1914 to Harold Monro
      Ballad of Another Ophelia
      3 unidentified

E314.3   **Poems**
    Typescript   Unlocated
    Two batches of poems sent to Amy Lowell, her letter of 15 February 1916 to Lawrence, including:

At the Window
Brooding Grief
In Trouble and Shame
Perfidy (Turned Down)

E314.4 **Poems**
Holograph manuscript   Unlocated
Three poems with letter of 7 March 1921 to J. C. Squire,
see also letter of 4 April 1921 to Curtis Brown and *Diary*
entry for 7 March 1921
Hibiscus and Salvia Flowers
Purple Anemones
Pomegranate

E314.5 **Poems**
Typescript   Unlocated
Three poems sent to Robert Mountsier, letter of 4 April
1921 to Curtis Brown
Hibiscus and Salvia Flowers
Purple Anemones
The Ass

E314.6 **Poems**
Holograph manuscript or typescript   Unlocated
Two poems sent to Austin Harrison, letter of 10 February
1923 to Curtis Brown
Elephant
1 unidentified

E315 **Poems**
a Two carbon typescripts, 30 pp., 30 pp.   CU
Restlessness, 1 p.
Traitors, oh, liars . . ., 1 p.
Softly, then, softly . . ., 2 pp.
Fire, 2 pp.
And what do I care . . ., 3 pp.
Change of Life, 9 pp.
O! Americans, 9 pp.
The Man in the Street, 1 p.
Rainbow, 2 pp.
b Carbon typescript, 30 pp.   TxU
A copy of each poem as above, except: *Fire* (two
different copies), *Change of Life* (two copies)

E316 **Poems**
Typescript, 7 pp.   CU

Tedlock pp. 85–6
The Mowers (A Youth Mowing), 1 p.
Green, 1 p.
Fireflies in the Corn, 1 p.
A Woman and Her Dead Husband (A Man Who Died),
   1 p.
Illicit (On the Balcony), 1 p.
Birthday (On That Day), 1 p.

E317   **Poems**
Holograph manuscript, 84 p.   N
A Nottingham University College Notebook, also contain-
ing Latin notes. Includes three torn pages and two inside
covers.
The Crow (In Church, At the Front, The North Country)
Honeymoon (second draft, Excursion Train)
Sorrow (second draft)
Last Words to Muriel (Last Words to Miriam)
Campions
Guelder Roses
From a College Window
Study
The Last Hours of a holiday (Last Hours)
The Fall of Day
Evening of a Week-day (Twilight)
Eastwood—Evening (The Little Town at Evening)
The Piano (Piano)
Lightning
Married in June
[Untitled], *Into a deep pond, an old sheep dip, . . .*
   (The Wild Common)
The Worm Turns
On the Road (On the March)
The Death of the Baron
Song (Flapper)
Love Comes Late (Late in Life)
A Tarantella (Tarantella)
Song (Song: Wind Among the Cherries)
[Untitled fragment, page torn], *An . . .*
Cherry Robbers
In a Boat
Dim Recollections (Narcissus)
Renaissance (Renascence)
A Failure

A Winter's Tale
A Decision
Dog-tired (Dog-Tired)
A Train at Night
Violets for the Dead (Violets)
Baby Songs Ten Months Old (Ten Months Old)
Trailing Clouds
Triolet (Birdcage Walk)
Coming Home From School   Rondeau Redoublé (Rondeau of a Conscientious Objector)
Eve
After School
School (A Snowy Day in School)
A Snowy Day at School
Letter from Town The Almond Tree (Letter from Town: The Almond-Tree)
Letter from Town The City (Letter from Town; On a Grey Morning in March)
[Untitled fragment, page torn], *Letters f . . .*
Discipline
A Still Afternoon in School (first draft, *Dreams Old and Nascent*)
A Still Afternoon in School (second draft, *Dreams Old and Nascent*)
Reading in the Evening (Reading a Letter)

MOVEMENTS   1. *A Baby Running Barefoot (Baby Running Barefoot)*
2. *A Baby Asleep After Pain*
3. *The Body Awake (Virgin Youth)*
4. *A Man at Play on the River*
5. *The Review of the Scots Guards (Guards)*

Restlessness
A Passing Bell (A Passing-Bell)
Lost (Turned Down)
After the Theatre (Embankment at Night, Before the War: Outcasts)
Brotherhood (first draft, *Embankment at Night, Before the War: Charity*)
The End of Another Home-holiday (first draft, *End of Another Home Holiday*)
End of Another Home-holiday (second draft, *End of Another Home Holiday*)

Brotherhood (second draft, *Embankment at Night,
Before the War: Charity*)
THE SONGLESS 1. *Today* (*Hyde Park at Night,
Before the War: Clerks*)
2. *Tomorrow* (*Piccadilly Circus at
Night: Street-Walkers*)
[Untitled], *When on the autumn roses* . . . (*Song-Day in
Autumn*)
Amour (Autumn Sunshine)
At the Window
Weeknight Service
Fooled (Rebuked)
Dream (first draft, *Dream-Confused*)
Dream (second draft, *Dream-Confused*)
Bereavement (two drafts)
Loss
Brooding
Grief
Sorrow (first draft)
Honeymoon (first draft, *Excursion Train*)

E318   **Poems**
Holograph manuscript, 9 pp.   CSt
The Mowers (A Youth Mowing)
Green
*All of Roses (River Roses, Gloire de Dijon, Roses on the
Breakfast Table, All of Roses: IV*)
Fireflies in the Corn
A Woman and Her Dead Husband (A Man Who Died)
The Wind, the Rascal
Illicit (On the Balcony)
Birthday (On That Day)
The Mother of Sons (Monologue of a Mother)

E319   **Poems**
Holograph manuscript, 4 pp.   ICU
Tommies in the Train, 1 p.
After the Opera, 1 p.
War-Baby
Bread Upon the Waters, 1 p.
Nostalgia, 1 p.

E319.1   **Poems**
a Holograph manuscript, 3 pp.   NBuU
True love at last!, 1 p.

 Lucifer
 Sphinx, 1 p.
 Intimates
 Image-making love (Image-Making Love), 1 p.
 Ultimate Reality
b Corrected carbon typescript, 5 pp.   NBuU
 Mournful young man, 1 p.
 There is no way out
 Money-madness
 My naughty book, 1 p.
 The little wowser, 1 p.
 The young and their moral guardians
 Volcanic Venus, 1 p.
 What does she want?
 Wonderful spiritual women
 Poor bit of a wench!
 Demon justice, 1 p.
With a letter of 10 August 1929 to Hilda Doolittle

E319.2   **Poems**
   Holograph manuscript, 11 pp.   NN
   The Chief Mystery, 3 pp.
   At the Cearne, 2 pp.
   Pear-Blossom, 2 pp.
   Assuming the Burden, 2 pp.
   She Was a Good Little Wife, 1 p.
   [Untitled], *Other women have reared in me . . . ,* 1 p.

E319.3   **Poems**
   Holograph manuscript, 4 pp.   N
   Elixir (The Jewess and the V. C.), 1 p.
   Good Night, 1 p.
   Sympathy
   Love Message (Message to a Perfidious Soldier), 1 p.
   The Witch: 1
   The Witch: II, 1 p.

E319.4   **Poems**
   Holograph manuscript, 3 pp.   Lazarus
   For God's Sake (Let Us Be Men), 1 p.
   O! Start a revolution! (O! Start a revolution)
   It's either you fight or you die
   My naughty book, 1 p.
   An old acquaintance (The Little Wowser), 1 p.
   Character in a novel (I Am in a Novel)

With letter of 28 December 1928 to Charles Wilson

E319.5   **Poems**
Holograph manuscript, 2 pp.   N
   At Midnight (Mother's Son in Salonika), 1 p.
   Beloved (Land-Worker)
   The Prophet in the Rose Garden (The Grey Nurse)
   Moth and Rust (Neither Moth nor Rust), 1 p.
   Irreverent Thoughts (Maiden's Prayer)

E319.6   **Poems**
Galley proofs, 3 pp.   CtY
   To Let Go or to Hold On—?
   Things Men Have Made
   Whatever Man Makes—
   Work
   What Would You Fight For?
   Attila
   Sea-Weed
   Lizard
   Censors
   November by the Sea
MS titled: *Ten Poems*

E319.7   **Poems**
Typescript, 5 pp.   NN
   All of Roses (River Roses, Gloire de Dijon, Roses on the
      Breakfast Table, All of Roses: IV)
   Green
   Illicit (On the Balcony)
   The Wind, the Rascal

E320   **Poems**
Holograph manuscript, 3 pp.   ICU
   Town (Town in 1917)
   Going Back
   Winter-Lull

E320.1   **Poems**
Holograph manuscript notebook   Private
A Nottingham University College Notebook
   Discipline (two drafts, Discipline; Prophet)
   A Still Afternoon   Dreams Old and Nascent (Dreams
      Old and Nascent)
   BABY MOVEMENTS 1. Running Barefoot (Baby
                              Running Barefoot)

2. *'Trailing Clouds' (A Baby
Asleep After Pain)*

Restlessness
A Beloved (Love on the Farm)
The Punisher
An Epistle from Thelma
An Epistle from Arthur (Disagreeable Advice)
Epilogue from Thelma (Forecast)
Sickness
A Day in November (Next Morning)
A LIFE HISTORY IN HARMONIES AND DIS-
CORDS
  First Harmony
  Discord
  Second Harmony
  Discord
  Third Harmony (Twenty Years Ago)
  Discord (Discord in Childhood)
  Fourth Harmony
  Baiser (A Kiss)
  Discord
  Last Harmony
Kiss (A Kiss)
The Street-Lamps (People, Street Lamps)
The Complaint of the Soul of a Worker
Monologue of a Mother
SCHOOL   1. Morning   *The Waste Lands (Ruination)*
                      The Street
                      Scripture (The Schoolmaster)
                *Afternoon (Last Lesson of the After-
                      noon)*
Malade (in prose)
A Love-Passage   A Rift in the Lute (A Love-Passage)
[Title crossed out: *Spring in the City*] *(Bombardment)*
Infidelity (Ah, Muriel!)
Scent of Irises
Sigh No More
Late at Night Along the Home Road
New Wine (Late at Night)
Ophelia (first draft, *Ballad of Another Ophelia*)
Liaison (first draft, *The Yew-Tree on the Downs*)
Liaison (second draft, *The Yew-Tree on the Downs*)
Dolor of Autumn (Dolour of Autumn)

E320.1

Unwitting *(Reality of Peace, 1916)*
[Fragment], *Nocturne (Repulsed)*
Nocturne (Repulsed)
The Appeal (Under the Oak, The Appeal)
Reproach (Release)
Nils Lykke Dead (A Man Who Died)
Submergence
Reminder
A Wise Man (Tease)
A Plaintive Confession (Coldness in Love, Aloof in Gaiety)
To Lettice, My Sister (Brother and Sister)
Anxiety (Endless Anxiety)
Patience (Suspense)
[Fragment], *(Winter in the Boulevard)*
Winter (Winter in the Boulevard)
Another Ophelia (second draft, *Ballad of Another Ophelia*)
To My Mother—Dead (The End)
The Dead Mother (The Bride)
My Love, My Mother (The Virgin Mother)
TRANSFORMATIONS   1. *Evening (Parliament Hill in the Evening)*
2. *Morning (Flat Suburbs, S. W., in the Morning)*
3. *Men in the Morning (Morning Work)*
4. *The Inanimate that Changes Not in Shape*
Oh stiffly shapen houses that change not . . . (Suburbs on a Hazy Day)
The Town (Transformations: I. The Town)
The Earth (Transformations: II. The Earth)
5. *The Changeful Animate Men: Whose Shape is Multiform (Transformations: III. Men)*
6. *Corot*
7. *Raphael (Michael Angelo)*
Blue (first draft, *The Shadow of Death, Blueness*)
Blue (second draft, *The Shadow of Death, Blueness*)

244

II. *Red Passion and Death (Red)*
Silence (first draft, *Silence, Listening*)
Silence (second draft, *Silence, Listening*)
The Inheritance (with interlined, *Noise of Battle*)
A Drama
Mating (Come Spring, Come Sorrow)
Meeting (After Many Days)
Return
Separated
Troth With the Dead (Troth With the Dead, The Enkin-
dled Spring, At a Loose
End)

A Love-Song (A Love Song)
Her Birthday (On That Day)
Hands (The Hands of the Betrothed)
Drunk
[Untitled], *Do not hold me Siegmund . . . (A Love-*
Passage)

E320.2 **Poems**
Holograph manuscript, 66 pp.   Private
A notebook also containing *Accounts at Porthcothan*
Includes three trial dedications and an untitled joking
poem, *Two, there are two words only . . .*
The numbering given for some of the poems is that of the
notebook
Apprehension (Noise of Battle)
Suburb in the Morning (Flat Suburbs, SW., in the
Morning)
Suburb in the Evening (Parliament Hill in the Evening)
Premonition (first draft, *Under the Oak*)
Suburbs on the Hills (Suburbs on a Hazy Day)
Winter in the Boulevard
Under the Oak (second draft)
The Interim (Reality of Peace, 1916)
Voice of a Woman (A Man Who Died)
Reading a Letter
Sigh No More
Ruination
Bombardment
Hyde Park, Years Ago. A Review of the Scots Guards
(Guards)
Twenty Years Ago
Groping (Sickness)

Next Morning (two drafts)
On that Day (On That Day)
From the Italian Lakes (Everlasting Flowers: For a Dead Mother)
Phantasmagoria (Late at Night)
From a College Window
Palimpsest of Twilight (first draft, *Twilight*)
The Piano (second draft, *Piano*)
In Church
Engulphed (At the Front)
Indoors and Out (Twofold)
Tarantella
Late in Life
Flapper
In the Park (Birdcage Walk)
Sentimental Correspondence 1. The Almond Tree (Letter from Town: The Almond Tree)
Letter to the North (Letter from Town: On a Grey Morning in March)
The North Countrie (The North Country)
The School on the Waste Lands (School on the Outskirts)
Neckar (Narcissus)
LONDON NIGHT *Year 1910* (first draft, *Embankment at Night, Before the War: Outcasts*)
LONDON NIGHT *Year 1910: Charing Cross Railway Bridge* (second draft, *Embankment at Night, Before the War: Outcasts*)
LONDON NIGHTS *Year 1910 Clerks in the Parks (Hyde Park at Night, Before the War: Clerks)*
LONDON NIGHTS *Embankment 1910 (Embankment at Night, Before the War: Charity)*
LONDON NIGHTS *Piccadilly Circus (Piccadilly Circus at Night: Street-Walkers)*
Spring-Fire (Autumn Sunshine)
 1 *Martyr (Martyr à la Mode)*
 2 *In Trouble and Shame*
 3 *Brooding Grief*
 4 *Lotus Hurt by the Cold (Lotus and Frost)*
 5 *Mystery* (two drafts)
 6 *Last Words to Miriam*
 7 *Study*
   Evening of a Week-day (second draft, *Twilight*)

[Fragment], *Eastwood (The Little Town at Evening)*
8 *Piano* (first draft)
[Fragment], *Married in June*
9 *In a Boat*
10 *A Winter's Tale*
11 *A Baby Asleep After Pain*
12 *Perfidy (Turned Down)*
 Amour (Autumn Sunshine)
 The End
 The Bride
15 *The Virgin Mother*
 Silence (first draft, *Silence, Listening*)
16 *The Inheritance*
17 *Troth with the Dead*
18 *The World after her Death (The Enkindled Spring)*
19 *Bitterness (At a Loose End)*
20 *Silence* (second draft, *Silence*)
21 *Listening*
22 *Sorrow*
23 *Brother and Sister*
24 *Anxiety (Endless Anxiety)*
25 *Patience (Suspense)*
26 *Passing Bell (A Passing-Bell)*
27 *Discipline*
28 *Dreams Old and Nascent: Old*
29 *Dreams Old and Nascent: Nascent*
30 *A Baby Running Barefoot (Baby Running Barefoot)*
31 *Virgin Youth*
32 *Restlessness*
33 *The Punisher*
34 *Irony (Disagreeable Advice)*
35 *Epilogue (Forecast)*
36 *Discord in Childhood*
37 *Monologue of a Mother*
38 *Malade* (in prose)
39 *Liaison (The Yew-Tree on the Downs)*
40 *Dolor of Autumn (Dolour of Autumn)*
41 *Reproach (Release)*
 [Fragment], *Blue (The Shadow of Death)*
 [Fragments, three untitled] *(Autumn Sunshine)*

E320.3 **Poems**
Holograph manuscript, 25 pp. CU
The numbering given is that of the manuscript pages

Tedlock pp, 81–2, Powell 55
1–7 *Restlessness*
  9 *Violets for the Dead (Violets)*
13 *Song (Flapper)*
15 *Song Wind Among the Cherries*
17 *Cherry-stealers (Cherry Robbers)*
19 *A Letter from Town The Almond Tree (Letter from Town: The Almond-Tree)*
21 *Lost (Turned Down)*
25 [Fragment], *A Bell (A Passing-Bell)*
27 *The End of Another Home-Holiday* (two drafts and a fragment, *End of Another Home Holiday*) [Fragment, untitled] *(Embankment at Night, Before the War: Charity)*
35 [Fragment, untitled] *(Restlessness)*
38 [Fragment], *Lost (Turned Down)*
39 [Fragment, untitled] *(Letter from Town: The Almond-Tree)*
42 [Fragment, untitled] *(Flapper)* [Fragment, untitled] *(Cherry Robbers)*
44 [Second fragment, untitled] *(Restlessness)*
48–50 [Second fragment, untitled] *(End of Another Home Holiday)*

E320.4   **Poems**
Holograph manuscript, 95 pp.   N
Ah with his blessing bright on thy mouth and thy brow . . . (Michael Angelo), 1 p.
Moon New-Risen, 1 p.
Erotic, 1 p.
Separated, 1 p.
Aloof in Gaiety, 1 p.
A Love-Passage, 2 pp.
A Drama, 9 pp.
Red, 2 pp.
Fooled! (Rebuked), 1 p.
Infidelity (Ah, Muriel!), 1 p.
Teasing (Tease), 2 pp.
In a Boat, 2 pp.
Weeknight Service, 2 pp.
A STILL AFTERNOON IN SCHOOL 1. *The Old Dream . . .* 2. *The Nascent (Dreams Old and Nascent),* 5 pp.
BABY-MOVEMENTS 1. *Running Barefoot (Baby Run-*

ning Barefoot), 2 pp.
Another Ophelia (Ballad of Another Ophelia), 3 pp.
BABY-MOVEMENTS 2. *Trailing Clouds (A Baby Asleep After Pain*, written with *Baby Running Barefoot)*
At the Window, 1 pp.
Intoxicated (Drunk), 4 pp.
Beneath the Yew Tree (The Yew-Tree on the Downs), 3 pp.
Her Hands (The Hands of the Betrothed), 3 pp.
Mating (Come Spring, Come Sorrow), 3 pp.
A Love Song in Actuality (A Love Song), 1 p.
Snap-Dragon, 6 pp.
A Bell (A Passing-Bell), 2 pp.
Blue (Blueness, The Shadow of Death), 4 pp.
An Address to the Sea (The Sea, Moonrise), 3 pp.
Street-Lamps (People, Street Lamps), 2 pp.
Song (Flapper), 1 p.
SONGS OF WORK PEOPLE AT NIGHT
  1. *Tired (Hyde Park at Night, Before the War: Clerks)*, 1 p.
  2. *Tired But Dissatisfied (Piccadilly Circus at Night: Street-Walkers)*, 1 p.
And Jude the Obscure and his Beloved (Passing Visit to Helen), 2 pp.
Tarantella, 2 pp.
Brotherhood (Embankment at Night, Before the War: Charity), 1 p.
Nils Lykke Dead (A Man Who Died), 3 pp.
White (Two Wives), 9 pp.

E320.5 **Poems**
Typescript, 11 pp.
  Drunk, 3 pp.
  In a Boat, 1 p.
  Tease, 1 p.
  Mystery, 1 p.
  Study, 1 p.
  Submergence, 1 p.
  Last Words to Miriam, 1 p.
  A Winter's Tale, 1 p.
  Lotus Hurt by the Cold (Lotus and Frost), 1 p.

E320.6 **Poems**
Holograph manuscript, 17 pp.

> Song of a Man Who is Loved, 1 p.
> Afterwards (Grey Evening, Firelight and Nightfall)
> Don Juan, 1 p.
> Storm in Rose-Time (Love Storm), 2 pp.
> Purity (Paradise Re-Entered), 2 pp.
> Mystery, 1 p.
> Illicit (On the Balcony), 1 p.
> A Kiss, 1 p.
> The Wind, the Rascal, 1 p.
> The Inheritance (The Inheritance, Noise of Battle), 1 p.
> Ballad of a Wayward Woman (Ballad of a Wilful
>   Woman), 5 pp.

E320.8   . . . polite to one another—through the glass partitions . . .
Holograph manuscript, 5 pp.   Unlocated
A fragment
Tedlock pp. 204–5, Powell 84A

E320.9   **Pomegranate**
Typescript, 1 p.   CtY

E322   **Pornography and Obscenity**
a Holograph manuscript, 32 pp.   TxU
   Powell 10
b Typescript, 38 pp.   CU
   Tedlock pp. 173–4
c Carbon typescript, 19 pp.   CU

E322.2   **Prelude, A**
Typescript, 13 pp.   TxU
MS titled: *An Enjoyable Christmas. A Prelude*

E322.5   **Prestige**
Holograph manuscript, 1 p.   ICSo
A fragment

E322.7   **Primrose Path, The**
a Holograph manuscript, 21 pp.   N
b Corrected typescript, 21 pp.   TxU
c Corrected typescript and carbon copy, 25 pp., 25 pp.   TxU

E322.8   **Princess, The**
Holograph manuscript, 51 pp.   TxU
Tedlock pp. 54–5, Powell 16

E326   **Proper Study, The**
a Holograph manuscript, 10 pp.   TxU

	b Carbon typescript, 6 pp.	TxU
	c Carbon typescript, 6 pp.	OkTU
	d Three carbon typescripts, 9 pp., 9 pp., 9 pp.	CU
	e Carbon typescript, 9 pp.	TxU

E326.2 **Prophet**
Holograph manuscript   TxU
Tedlock pp. 77–9, Powell 52

E326.5 **Prussian Officer, The**
Holograph manuscript, 16 pp.   TxU
MS titled: *Honour and Arms*
Tedlock pp. 46–8, Powell 30

E326.6 **Prussian Officer and Other Stories, The**
Corrected page proofs, 310 pp.   NCL

E326.7 **Psychoanalysis and the Unconscious**
a Corrected typescript, 29 pp.   Unlocated
Chicago Book and Art Auctions catalogue (27–28 October 1931) item No. 286
b Author's copy with holograph corrections   TxU
Seltzer, 1921

E326.8 **Punisher, The**
Holograph manuscript, 2 pp.   MH

E328 **Purple Anemones**
Holograph manuscript, 2 pp.   IaE

E330 **Rabbit Snared in the Night**
Typescript, 2 pp.   ICU

E330.5 **Rachel Annand Taylor**
Holograph manuscript, 8 pp.   Private

E331 **Rainbow, The (novel)**
a Holograph manuscript and corrected typescript, 811 pp.   TxU
Tedlock pp. 12–16, Powell 4
b Corrected typescript and holograph manuscript, 732 pp.   TxU

E332 **Rainbow (poem)**
a Holograph manuscript, 1 p.   TxU
Untitled poem on verso, begins: There's no immortal heaven . . .
b Typescript, 2 pp.   Unlocated
Powell 63B

E334   **Rawdon's Roof**
    a Holograph manuscript, 21 pp.   Lazarus
      Version published in *The Lovely Lady*
      Powell 44A
    b Corrected typescript, 20 pp.   Lazarus
      pp. 1–11 follow Elkin Mathews, 1928; pp. 12–20 devi-
      ate from both published versions
      Powell 44B
    c Corrected typescript, 21 pp.   CU

E335   **Reach over, then, reach over across the chasm . . .**
    Holograph manuscript, 1 p.   CSt
    Powell 61

E337   **Real Thing, The**
    a Holograph manuscript, 10 pp.   CtY
      Notebook cover titled: *Three Essays for Vanity Fair*
      Powell 117
    b Carbon typescript, 12 pp.   CU
    c Carbon typescript, 12 pp.   TxU

E338   **Reality of Peace**
    a Typescript, 30 pp.   CU
      Tedlock pp. 201–2
    b Carbon typescript, 45 pp.   CU
    c Carbon typescript, 45 pp.   TxU

E340   **Red Trousers**
    Holograph manuscript, 4 pp.   Private
    Tedlock p. 229, Powell 84A

E340.3   **Red Wolf, The**
    Corrected typescript, 3 pp.   TxU

E340.4   **Reflections on the Death of a Porcupine**
    Corrected carbon typescript, 20 pp.   TxU
    Tedlock pp. 209–10

E340.5   **Reflections on the Death of a Porcupine, German transla-
    tion**
    Holograph manuscript, 15 pp.   TxU
    Incomplete
    In Frieda Lawrence's hand
    MS titled: *Betrachtungen über den Tod eines
    Stachelschweins von D. H. Lawrence*

E340.6   **Reflections on the Death of a Porcupine and Other Essays**
    Corrected typescript, 151 pp.   OkTU

Includes title page and table of contents

E342 **Renascence**
Holograph manuscript, 1 p. ULiv
MS titled: *Renaissance*
With letter of 20 January 1909 to Blanche Jennings

E346 **Resurrection (poem)**
a Holograph manuscript, 4 pp. MH
b Holograph manuscript, 4 pp. ICU
c Holograph manuscript, 5 pp. TxU
d Holograph manuscript, 1 p. TxU
A six-line fragment
With letter of 28 November 1915 to Lady Cynthia Asquith
e Typescript, 3 pp. ICU
f Proof, 1 p. ICU
A six-line fragment

E346.1 **Resurrection (essay)**
a Holograph manuscript, 4 pp. TxU
Tedlock p. 137, Powell 118
b Typescript and carbon copy, 4 pp., 4 pp. CU
Tedlock pp. 137–8
c Carbon typescript, 5 pp. TxU
d Carbon typescript, 5 pp. CU
e Carbon typescript, 5 pp. NmU

E346.5 **Resurrection of the Flesh**
Holograph manuscript, 2 pp. Unlocated
Argus Book Shop catalogue No. 827 (1943) item No. 29

E349.5 **Rex**
a Holograph manuscript, 7 pp. CtY
With letter of 30 May [1920] to Richard Aldington
b Carbon typescript, 11 pp. Private

E350 **Risen Lord, The**
a Holograph manuscript, 6 pp. CU
Tedlock pp. 235–6, Powell 84A
b Carbon typescript, 12 pp. CU

E351 **Rocking-Horse Winner, The**
a Holograph manuscript, 30 pp. Lazarus
Powell 45
b Carbon typescript, 24 pp. CU

E351.3	**Rondeau of a Conscientious Objector**	
	a Holograph manuscript, 1 p.	Private
	b Corrected typescript, 1 p.	CtY

| E352.3 | **Ruination** | |
| | Holograph manuscript, 1 p. | CtY |

E352.5	**St. John**	
	Typescript, 3 pp.	CtY
	MS also titled: *The Apostolic Beasts*	

E352.53	**St. Luke**	
	Typescript, 3 pp.	CtY
	MS also titled: *The Apostolic Beasts*	

E352.55	**St. Mark**	
	Typescript, 3 pp.	CtY
	MS also titled: *The Apostolic Beasts*	

E352.6	**St. Mawr**	
	a Holograph manuscript, 41 pp.	Destroyed: Huxley fire
	An early version, incomplete, pp. 17–58 only Powell 14A	
	b Holograph manuscript, 129 pp.	Destroyed: Huxley fire
	Powell 14A	
	c Corrected typescript, 183 pp.	Lazarus
	pp. 1–178 and 38A, 125A, 128A, 138A and 19 & 20 (one page) Powell 14B	

E352.7	**Samson and Delilah**	
	Holograph manuscript, 34 pp.	TxU
	Incomplete by several paragraphs MS titled: *The Prodigal Husband*	

| E352.9 | **Scent of Irises** | |
| | Holograph manuscript, 3 pp. | MH |

E355	**Sea and Sardinia**	
	a Corrected typescript, 307 pp.	TxU
	MS titled: *Diary of a Trip to Sardinia* Powell 77	
	b Corrected typescript, 305 pp.	NNC
	c Corrected carbon typescript, 305 pp.	CtY
	d Typescript, 32 pp.	CtY

As Far as Palermo, 14 pp.
Cagliari, 18 pp.

E356.5 **Second Best**
Holograph manuscript, 14 pp.   N

E356.7 **Second Supper, Introduction to**
Holograph manuscript, 2 pp.   Unlocated
Argus Book Shop catalogue No. 827 (1943) item No. 40e

E357 **See Mexico After, by Luis Q.**
a Holograph manuscript, 8 pp.   Private
Lawrence has apparently rewritten this essay on Quintanilla's typescript which was titled *Mexico, Why Not?*
b Holograph manuscript, 1 p.   CU
A twenty-line fragment
Tedlock p. 189
c Holograph manuscript, 8 pp.   TxU
Tedlock pp. 189–90, Powell 118
d Typescript, 7 pp.   Private
e Corrected, mostly carbon, typescript, 7 pp.   CU
Tedlock pp. 190–1
f Two carbon typescripts, 10 pp., 10 pp.   CU
g Carbon typescript, 10 pp.   TxU

E359.1 **Sex Versus Loveliness**
a Holograph manuscript, 10 pp.   TxU
MS titled: *Sex Appeal*
Tedlock pp. 231–2, Powell 84A
b Holograph manuscript, 1 p.   TxU
A two-line fragment
Tedlock p. 231

E359.3 **Shades**
a Holograph manuscript, 1 p.   ICN
MS titled: *Pentecostal*
b Corrected typescript, 1 p.   Lazarus

E359.4 **Shades of Spring, The**
a Corrected typescript, 27 pp.   NN
MS titled: *The Soiled Rose*
b Corrected page proofs   NCL
MS titled: *The Dead Rose*

E359.5 **Shadow in the Rose Garden, The**
a Holograph manuscript, 7 pp.   TxU
Tedlock pp. 32–3, Powell 29

         b Two carbon typescripts, 6 pp., 6 pp.   CU
           MSS titled: *The Vicar's Garden*

E360.5   **Ship of Death, The**
          Corrected typescript   Unlocated
          Argus Book Shop catalogue No. 827 (1943) item No. 37

E361.3   **Sick Collier, A**
         a Holograph manuscript, 11 pp.   Lazarus
           Powell 34
         b Corrected galley proofs, 2 pp.   Private
           For *New Statesman*

E362.6   **Smile**
          Holograph manuscript, 9 pp.   Unlocated
          Powell 43

E362.7   **Snake**
          Typescript, 2 pp.   CtY

E365   **Snowy Day in School, A**
          Holograph manuscript, 1 p.   TxU
          Two fragments

E365.5   **So vivid a vision, everything so visually poignant . . .**
          Holograph manuscript, 8 pp.   TxU
          Published as a letter of 1 December 1915 to Lady Ottoline
          Morrell in *Letters*

E366   **Social Basis of Consciousness, Review of The**
         a Holograph manuscript, 12 pp.   TxU
           Tedlock pp. 259–60, Powell 102
         b Carbon typescript, 11 pp.   CU

E367   **Softly, then, softly . . .**
         a Holograph manuscript   Unlocated
           Powell 61
          b Typescript, 2 pp.   NmU

E368   **Solitaria and The Apocalypse of Our Times, Review of**
         a Holograph manuscript, 10 pp.   TxU
           Tedlock p. 259, Powell 100
          b Carbon typescript, 8 pp.   CU
         c Carbon typescript, 8 pp.   TxU

E371   **Song of a Man Who is Loved**
          Holograph manuscript   Unlocated
          Argus Book Shop catalogue No. 827 (1943) item No. 30

E371.5   **Song of Death**
         Holograph manuscript, 1 p.   TxU
         In Frieda Lawrence's hand

E373   **Sons and Lovers**
         a Holograph manuscript, 58 pp.   CU
            An early draft, incomplete
         b Holograph manuscript, 22 pp.   Unlocated
            A fragment, pp. 203–26
            Known as *The Miriam Papers*
         c Holograph manuscript, 17 pp.   TxU
            Five fragments
            In Jessie Chamber's hand
               *On Saturday afternoon Agatha and Miriam were
                  upstairs dressing . . .,* 3 pp.
               Easter Monday, 4 pp.
               [*Flower sequence*] *Miriam had discontinued the
                  habit of going each Thursday evening . . .,* 2 pp.
               *Again, the first time that Miriam saw Paul to
                  perceive him . . .,* 4 pp.
               Chapter IX, 4 pp.
         d Holograph manuscript, 271 pp.   TxU
            An early draft, incomplete
            MS titled: *Paul Morel*
            Powell 3
         e Holograph manuscript, 530 pp.   CU
            Final version used by printers
         f Corrected page proofs, 423 pp.   TxU
            Duckworth, 1913
            Two extra sets of pp. 337–52

E373.1   **Sons and Lovers, Foreword to**
         Holograph manuscript, 7 pp.   TxU

E376.4   **Spirits Summoned West**
         Corrected typescript, 3 pp.   TxU

E377   **State of Funk, The**
         a Holograph manuscript, 6 pp.   TxU
            Tedlock p. 228, Powell 84A
         b Carbon typescript, 4 pp.   CU
         c Carbon typescript, 1 p.   NmU
            Incomplete, p. 6 only

E377.5   **Station: Athos, Treasures and Men, The; England and the Octopus; Comfortless Memory; and Ashenden, or The British Agent; Review of**
    a Holograph manuscript, 4 pp.   TxU
      An early version
      MS titled: *Review for Vogue*
      Tedlock pp. 261–2, Powell 103B
    b Holograph manuscript, 1 p.   TxU
      An eight-line fragment
      Tedlock pp. 260–1
    c Holograph manuscript, 8 pp.   TxU
      MS titled: *Review for Vogue*
      Tedlock pp. 261–2, Powell 103A

E379.9   **Story of Doctor Manente, The**
    a Holograph manuscript, 1 p.   TxU
      Introductory synopsis
      MS titled: *Third Supper*
    b Holograph manuscript, 69 pp.   TxU
      MS titled: *Tenth Story and Last*
      Tedlock pp. 274–5, Powell 109
    c Holograph notes, 2 pp.   Lazarus
      Not used in published version
    d Holograph manuscript, 9 pp.   Lazarus
      Notes to the text
    e Corrected galley proofs, 30 pp.   Lazarus

E380   **Story of Doctor Manente, Foreword to The**
    a Holograph manuscript, 7 pp.   Lazarus
    b Corrected galley sheets, 8 pp.   CLU
      Orioli, 1929

E380.1   **Story of Doctor Manente, Prospectus for The**
    Holograph manuscript, 4 pp.   Lazarus
    Leaflet to promote this work and Lungarno series

E381   **Strike Pay**
    Holograph manuscript, 15 pp.   Lazarus
    Powell 25

E382   **Studies in Classic American Literature**
    a Holograph manuscript, 7 pp.   NNPM
      Whitman
    b Typescript, 9 pp.   OkTU
      Incomplete, begins: Whitman the great poet, has meant so much to me. . . .

Whitman

c Holograph notes, 9 pp.   PLeB
  Early notes for *Nathaniel Hawthorne and 'The Scarlet
  Letter'*
  MS titled: *A Study of Sin*

d Holograph manuscript and corrected typescript, 28 pp.   TxU
  MS titled: *Studies in Classic American Literature (VII)
  by D. H. Lawrence. Nathaniel Hawthorne.*
  Nathaniel Hawthorne and 'The Scarlet Letter'
  Tedlock pp. 153–6, Powell 88A

e Corrected typescript, 12 pp.   TxU
  MS titled: *The Scarlet Letter*
  Hawthorne's 'Blithedale Romance'
  Tedlock pp. 157–8, Powell 88B

f Corrected typescript, 19 pp.   TxU
  Herman Melville's 'Moby Dick'
  Tedlock pp. 159–60, Powell 88D

g Corrected typescript, 23 pp.   NmU
  MS titled: *Studies in Classic American Literature (XII).*
  Herman Melville's 'Moby Dick'
  Herman Melville's 'Moby Dick'

h Corrected typescript, 13 pp.   TxU
  MS titled: *Studies in Classic American Literature (XI)*
  Herman Melville's 'Typee' and 'Omoo'
  Herman Melville's 'Typee' and 'Omoo'
  Tedlock p. 159, Powell 88C

i Corrected typescript, 23 pp.   Unlocated
  American Art Association catalogue (29–30 January
  1936)
  item No. 379
      Foreword
      The Spirit of Place
      Benjamin Franklin

E384   **Study of Thomas Hardy**

a Typescript, partly carbon, 186 pp.   CU
  MS titled: *Le Gai Savaire*
  Powell 86

b Carbon typescript, 215 pp.   TxU

c Typescript, 244 pp.   TxU

d Carbon typescript, 244 pp.   TxU

E384.8   **Suggestions for Stories—never carried out! D. H. L.**
  Holograph notes, 2 pp.   TxU
  Tedlock pp. 56–8, Powell 118

E385   **Sun**
    a Holograph manuscript, 44 pp.   TxU
    b Corrected typescript, 21 pp.   Lazarus
      Altered version
    c Corrected typescript, 21 pp.   TxU
      Altered version
      Tedlock pp. 58–9, Powell 40

E385.5   **Surgery for the Novel—Or a Bomb**
    a Holograph manuscript, 11 pp.   NNC
    b Corrected typescript, 6 pp.   NNC
    c Carbon typescript, 6 pp.   OkTU
      MSS titled: *The Future of the Novel*

E388   **Taos**
    a Carbon typescript, 4 pp.   CU
      Tedlock p. 181
    b Carbon typescript, 6 pp.   CU

E389.4   **Tease**
    a Holograph manuscript, 1 p.   N
      A two-stanza fragment
      With letter of 29 March 1911 to Louie Burrows
    b Typescript, 2 pp.   Lazarus
      MS titled: *Teasing*

E389.6   **Ten Months Old**
    Holograph manuscript, 1 p.   ULiv
    With letter of 20 January 1909 to Blanche Jennings

E390   **That Women Know Best**
    Holograph manuscript, 5 pp.   CU

E392   **There is a small cottage off the Addiscombe Road about a mile from East Croydon station.... (An unfinished story)**
    a Holograph manuscript, 48 pp.   CU
      Tedlock pp. 37–9, Powell 51C
    b Typescript, and carbon copy, 29 pp., 29 pp.   TxU
    d Two carbon typescripts, 29 pp., 29 pp.   CU
    d Typescript, 22 pp.   TxU

E394.5   **There was a gay bird named Christine ...**
    Holograph manuscript, 1 p.   TxU

E395.5   **There was a young man in the corridor ...**
    Holograph manuscript   Unlocated

260

Poem on title page of *The Rainbow* (Methuen, 1915)
Myers & Co. Autumn Catalogue of Modern Books . . . No.
297 (1933) item No. 31

E396 **There were, three years back, two schools in the mining
village of High Park . . . (An unfinished story)**
Holograph manuscript, 7 pp.   CU
Tedlock pp. 40–1, Powell 51B

E396.3 **There's no immortal heaven . . .**
Holograph manuscript, 1 p.   TxU
Poem on verso: *Rainbow*

E396.7 **Thimble, The**
a Holograph manuscript, 244 pp.   CSt
b Typescript, 14 pp.   TxU

E397 **Things**
a Holograph manuscript, 19 pp.   TxU
Tedlock p. 72, Powell 47
b Carbon typescript, 16 pp.   CU
c Typescript and two carbon copies, 19 pp., 19 pp., 19 pp. TxU
d Corrected proof sheets, 8 pp.   NmU

E398 **Thinking About Oneself**
a Holograph manuscript, 4 pp.   TxU
Tedlock p. 211, Powell 84A
b Carbon typescript, 4 pp.   CU
c Two carbon typescripts, 4 pp., 4 pp.   CU
Another typing
d Carbon typescript, 4 pp.   TxU

E400 **Tommies in the Train**
Corrected typescript, 2 pp.   CtY

E401.5 **Tortoises**
Corrected page proofs, 30 pp.   NjP
Text pages without half titles, duplicates for pp. 23–4

E401.6 **Touch and Go**
Holograph manuscript   Unlocated
Frieda Lawrence wrote to Willie Hopkin on 9 November
1936 that she will give him the MS if she can get it from a
woman who says Lawrence gave it to her

E404.5 **Train, with your smoke flag waving . . .**
Holograph manuscript, 1 p.   N
A fragment

E405 **Traitors, oh, liars . . .**
Holograph manuscript, 1 p.   CSt
Powell 61

E407 **Trespasser, The**
 a Holograph manuscript, 182 pp.   CU
  Fragments of an early version, pp. 13–207
  Tedlock pp. 11–12, Powell 2B
 b Holograph manuscript, 485 pp.   CU
  Tedlock pp. 7–11, Powell 2A
 c Page proofs, 292 pp.   NCL
  Duckworth, 1912

E409 **Triumph of the Machine, The**
Carbon typescript, 1 p.   TxU

E409.5 **Tropic**
Holograph manuscript, 1 p.   ViU
With letter of 1 December 1920 to Professors John C.
Metcalf and Wilson

E411 **Turning Back**
 a Holograph manuscript, 4 pp.   TxU
 b Holograph manuscript, 2 pp.   TxU
  Part III only
  With letter of 2 November 1915 to Lady Cynthia
  Asquith
 c Typescript and carbon copy, 3 pp., 3 pp. TxU
 d Typescript, 5 pp.   TxU

E411.7 **Twilight in Italy**
Corrected page proofs, 128 pp.   TxU

E412 **Two Blue Birds**
 a Holograph manuscript, 30 pp.   CLU
  Tedlock p. 61, Powell 42
 b Typescript, 26 pp.   CtY

E415 **Undying Man, The (An unfinished folk-tale)**
 a Holograph manuscript, 8 pp.   Unlocated
  Powell 49
 b Typescript and carbon copy, 6 pp., 6 pp. TxU
 c Carbon typescript, 6 pp.   TxU
  Another typing
 d Two carbon typescripts, 6 pp., 6 pp. CU

E416 **Verism, naturalism, realism—these names seem big with
meaning. . . .**

Holograph manuscript copy, 4 pp.   TxU
An introduction to the novels and tales of Giovanni Verga
Written in another hand

E420   **Virgin and the Gipsy, The**
        a Holograph manuscript, 160 pp.   TxU
          Tedlock pp. 59–60, Powell 18
        b Galley proofs, 98 pp.   TxU

E421.7 **Walk to Huayapa**
        a Holograph manuscript, 14 pp.   TxU
          MS titled: *Mornings in Mexico. Sunday Morning*
          Tedlock pp. 186–7, Powell 76
        b Corrected typescript, 16 pp.   IU
          MS titled in another hand: *Sunday Stroll*

E422.5 **Was feeling for a new rhythm— . . .**
        Holograph manuscript, 1 p.   TxU
        A fifteen-line fragment

E422.7 **We Need One Another**
        Holograph manuscript, 11 pp.   CtY
        Notebook cover titled: *Three Essays for Vanity Fair*
        Powell 117

E424   **Weeknight Service**
        Holograph manuscript, 2 pp.   MH

E426.5 **What Is Man Without an Income?**
        Holograph manuscript, 1 p.   ICSo

E428   **Which Class I Belong To**
        Holograph manuscript, 10 pp.   OCU

E430   **White Peacock, The**
        a Holograph manuscript, 58 pp.   CU
          Two fragments of an early version
          Tedlock pp. 3–6, Powell 1A
        b Holograph manuscript, 1 p.   TxU
          A fragment, left half of one page
        c Holograph manuscript, 1 p.   Private
          A fragment, left half of one page
        d Holograph manuscript, 802 pp.   Lazarus
          645 pp. are in Lawrence's hand; 157 pp. are in the hands
          of Agnes Holt, Agnes Mason and Helen Corke
        e Corrected galley sheets, 123 pp.   CLU
          Lacking No. 59
          Tedlock pp. 6–7, Powell 1B

263

	f Review copy	Unlocated
	Notes by Edward Garnett	
	Elkin Mathews catalogue (December 1930) item No. 494	

E430.3 **White Stocking, The**
Holograph manuscript, 18 pp.   Private
MS also titled: *Amusing*

E432 **Why the Novel Matters**
a Holograph manuscript, 14 pp.   TxU
    Tedlock p. 168, Powell 85A
b Typescript, 10 pp.   TxU
c Carbon typescript, 10 pp.   CU
d Carbon typescript, 10 pp.   CU
    Another typing

E432.6 **Wilful Woman, The (An unfinished story)**
Holograph manuscript, 7 pp.   CU
MS untitled, begins: November of the year 1916. A woman
    travelling from New York to the South West . . .
MS titled by Powell: *Journey to the Southwest*
Titled by Sagar: *The Wilful Woman*
Tedlock pp. 50–2, Powell 108

E432.7 **Wilful Woman, The Notes for**
Holograph manuscript, 1 p.   CU
Notes for a novel about Mabel Dodge Luhan
Tedlock pp. 52–3

E433 **Wind, the Rascal, The**
a Holograph manuscript   N
    With letter of 15 December 1910 to Louie Burrows
b Holograph manuscript, 1 p.   TxU
c Holograph manuscript, 1 p.   Private

E436 **Winter's Tale, A**
Holograph manuscript, 1 p.   ULiv
With letter of 20 January 1909 to Blanche Jennings

E437 **Wintry Peacock**
a Holograph manuscript, 16 pp.   Lazarus
b Corrected typescript, 26 pp.   Unlocated
    Powell 35
c Corrected proof sheets, 4 pp.   TxU
    Metropolitan sheets revised for *The New Decameron III*
    MS also titled: *The Poet's Tale*

E438	**Witch à la Mode, The**	
	a Holograph manuscript, 36 pp.	PLeB
	MS titled: *Intimacy*	
	Powell 24A	
	b Holograph manuscript, 29 pp.	PLeB
	MS titled: *The White Woman*	
	Powell 24B	
	c Corrected typescript, 26 pp.	PLeB
	Powell 24C	
	d Carbon typescript, 27 pp.	CU
E439.5	**Woman Who Rode Away, The**	
	a Holograph manuscript, 45 pp.	Unlocated
	Tedlock pp. 53–4, Powell 15	
	b Corrected typescript, 48 pp.	CtY
E440	**Women Are So Cocksure**	
	a Holograph manuscript, 4 pp.	CU
	Tedlock p. 212, Powell 84A	
	b Holograph manuscript, 7 pp.	TxU
	Fair copy in Frieda Lawrence's hand	
	c Carbon typescript, 4 pp.	TxU
	d Two carbon typescripts, 4 pp., 4 pp.	CU
E440.5	**Women aren't fools, but men are . . .**	
	Holograph manuscript, 1 p.	TxU
	A seventy-word fragment	
E441	**Women in Love**	
	a Holograph manuscript, 14 pp.	TxU
	Two fragments, pp. 291–6, 373–80	
	b Holograph manuscript, 55 pp.	TxU
	Chapter I Prologue and *Chapter II The Wedding* only	
	c Holograph manuscript, 436 pp.	TxU
	In ten exercise books	
	Chapters XXIII-XXXI only	
	d Corrected original and carbon typescript, 665 pp.	TxU
	e Corrected, mostly carbon, typescript, 666 pp.	CaOTU
	f Corrected typescript, 766 pp.	TxU
	g Corrected proof copy, 508 pp.	TxU
	Secker trade edition, 1921	
	Powell 5	
E442	**Women in Love, Foreword to**	
	a Holograph manuscript, 1 p.	Missing from CSt

b Page proofs, 4 pp.   CSt
c Final proofs, 4 pp.   CSt

E445.5   **Yew-Tree on the Downs, The**
            Holograph manuscript, 2 pp.   MH
            MS titled: *Affaire d'Amour*

E446.5   **Young Soldier with Bloody Spurs, The**
            Holograph manuscript, 4 pp.   NN

APPENDIX   LOCATION OF LAWRENCE'S MAJOR PAINTINGS

SAKI KARAVAS COLLECTION: LA FONDA HOTEL, TAOS, NEW MEXICO

Oils Flight Back into Paradise	39 in × 58 in
A Holy Family	26 in × 30 in
Fight with an Amazon	39 in × 29 in
Fauns and Nymphs	38 in × 32 in
Dance-Sketch	15 in × 17 in
Summer Dawn	12 in × 19 in
Rape of the Sabine Women	12 in × 16 in
Red Willow Trees	26 in × 40 in
Close-Up (Kiss)	15 in × 18 in
The Lawrence Ranch (by Brett, Lawrence and Frieda)	47 in × 23 in

ICONOGRAPHY DEPARTMENT, ACADEMIC CENTRE, UNIVERSITY OF TEXAS, AUSTIN

Oils Resurrection	38 in × 38 in
Boccaccio Story	28 in × 47 in
Jaguar Leaping at a Man	28½ in × 14½ in
Behind the Villa Mirenda	19½ in × 16 in

Water colour   The Milk-White Lady and the Coal-Black Smith

UNIVERSITY OF TULSA

Oil Men Bathing	19½ in × 17 in

MARSHALL FLAUM

Water colour Fire-Dance	9 in × 12 in

MRS. BETTY COTTAM

Oil Family on a Verandah	14 in × 19 in

JOHN HARVEY COLLECTION, SANTA FE

Oil   The Road to Mitla (by Brett and Lawrence)

BIBLIOGRAPHY

I ABBREVIATIONS FOR SOURCES OF PUBLISHED LETTERS

Boulton   James T. Boulton, ed. *Lawrence in Love: Letters to Louie Burrows*. University of Nottingham, 1968.

Brewster   Earl and Achsah Brewster. *D. H. Lawrence: Reminiscences and Correspondence*. Secker 1934.

Carswell   Catherine Carswell. *The Savage Pilgrimage*. Chatto and Windus, 1932.

Centaur   *The Centaur Letters*. Humanities Research Centre, Austin, 1970.

Corke   Helen Corke. *In Our Infancy*. Cambridge University Press, 1975.

Cushman   Keith Cushman. 'D. H. Lawrence and Nancy Henry.' *DHLR* 6, i, 1973.

Damon   S. Foster Damon. *Amy Lowell: A Chronicle*. New York, 1935.

Delaney   Paul Delaney. 'D. H. Lawrence: Twelve Letters.' *DHLR* 2, 1969.

Douglas   Norman Douglas. *Looking Back*. Chatto and Windus, 1933.

Finney   Brian Finney. 'A Newly Discovered Text of D. H. Lawrence's "The Lovely Lady".' *Yale Univ. Library Gazette* 49, Jan. 1975.

Fraser   Grace Lovat Fraser. *In the Days of My Youth*. Cassell, 1970.

Gallup   Donald Gallup. 'D. H. Lawrence's Letters to Catherine Carswell.' *Yale Univ. Library Gazette* 49, Jan. 1975.

Heilbrun   Carolyn Heilbrun. *The Garnett Family*. New York, 1961.

Hobman   J. B. Hobman, ed. *David Eder: Memoirs of a Modern Pioneer*. Gollancz, 1945.

Huxley   Aldous Huxley, ed. *The Letters of D. H. Lawrence*. Heinemann, 1932.

Irvine   Peter Irvine and Anne Kiley. 'D. H. Lawrence: Letters to Gordon and Beatrice Campbell.' *DHLR* 6, spring 1973.

Irvine 2   Peter Irvine and Anne Kiley. 'D. H. Lawrence and Frieda Lawrence: Letters to Dorothy Brett.' *DHLR* 9, spring 1976.

Jooost   Nicholas Joost and Alvin Sullivan. *D. H. Lawrence and The Dial*. Carbondale, 1970.

Lacy   Gerald Lacy, ed. *The Escaped Cock*. Los Angeles 1973.

Lawrence   Frieda Lawrence. *Not I, But the Wind . . .* Santa Fe, 1934.

Lawrence-Ada   Ada Lawrence and Stuart Gelder. *Young Lorenzo*. Florence, 1932.

Luhan   Mabel Dodge Luhan. *Lorenzo in Taos*. New York, 1932.

Mackenzie   Compton Mackenzie. *My Life and Times: Octave Five*. Chatto and Windus, 1966.

Mohr   'Briefe an Max Mohr'. *Die Neue Rundschau* 44, April 1933.

Moore   Harry T. Moore, ed. *The Collected Leters of D. H. Lawrence*. Heinemann and Viking 1962.

Nehls   Edward Nehls, ed. *D. H. Lawrence: A Composite Biography*. 3 vols. Madison, 1957–9.

Priest   Harry T. Moore. *The Priest of Love* Heinemann 1974.

Ross Charles Ross. 'The Composition of *Women in Love*'. *DHLR* 8, Summer 1975.

Russell Harry T. Moore, ed. *D. H. Lawrence's Letters to Bertrand Russell*. New York, 1948.

Sagar Keith Sagar. 'Lawrence and the Wilkinsons.' *Review of English Literature* 3, Oct. 1962.

Sagar 2 Keith Sagar. 'Three Separate Ways: Unpublished D. H. Lawrence Letters to Francis Brett Young.' *Review of English Literature* 6, July 1965.

Schorer Mark Schorer. 'I Will Send Address.' *London Magazine* 3, Feb. 1956.

Secker Martin Secker, ed. *Letters from D. H. Lawrence to Martin Secker*. Bridgefoot, 1970.

Seltzer Gerald Lacy, ed. *D. H. Lawrence: Letters to Thomas and Adele Seltzer*. Los Angeles, 1976.

Zytaruk George Zytaruk, ed. *The Quest for Rananim: D. H. Lawrence's Letters to S. S. Koteliansky*. Montreal, 1970.

2 ABBREVIATIONS FOR OTHER BOOKS AND ARTICLES CITED

A B C and E refer to those sections in Roberts.

Aldington Richard Aldington. *Portrait of a Genius But . . .* Heinemann, 1950.

Arnold Armin Arnold. *The Symbolic Meaning*. Centaur Press, 1962.

Boulton 2 James T. Boulton, ed. *Movements in European History*. Oxford, 1971.

Boulton 3 James T. Boulton. 'D. H. Lawrence's "Odour of Chrysanthemums".' An Early Version. *Renaissance and Modern Studies* 13, 1969.

Branda Eldon S. Branda. 'Textual Changes in *Women in Love*.' *Texas Studies in Literature and Language,* VI, 306–21.

Brett Hon. Dorothy Brett. *Lawrence and Brett*. Santa Fe, 1974.

Bumpus *David Herbert Lawrence: An Exhibition*. April-May 1933 at John and Edward Bumpus Ltd. London, 1933.

CP Vivian de Sola Pinto and Warren Roberts, eds. *The Complete Poems of D. H. Lawrence*. Heinemann and Viking, 1971.

CPlays *The Complete Plays of D. H. Lawrence*. London, 1965.

Cecchetti Giovanni Cecchetti. 'Verga and D. H. Lawrence's Translations.' *Comparative Literature* IX, 1959, 333–44.

Corke 2 Helen Corke. *D. H. Lawrence's Princess*. Thames Ditton, 1951.

Croydon Helen Corke. *D. H. Lawrence: The Croydon Years*. University of Texas, 1965.

Cushman 2 Keith Cushman. *D. H. Lawrence at Work: The Emergence of the Russian Officer Stories*. University of Virginia, 1978.

DHLR *D. H. Lawrence Review*. University of Arkansas.

Davis Herbert Davis. '*Women in Love*: A Corrected Typescript.' *University of Toronto Quarterly* 27, Oct. 1957, 34–53.

Delavenay Emile Delavenay. *D. H. Lawrence: L'Homme et La Genèse de son Oeuvre*. Paris 1969.

Delavenay 2   Emile Delavenay. *D. H. Lawrence: The Man and his Work.* London, 1972.

ET   Jessie Chambers. *D. H. Lawrence: A Personal Record.* Cape, 1935.

Farmer   David Farmer. 'D. H. Lawrence's "The Turning Back": The Text and its Genesis in Correspondence.' *DHLR* summer 1972.

Ferrier   Carole Ferrier. *The Earlier Poetry of D. H. Lawrence: A Variorum Text.* Doctoral dissertation at the University of Auckland, 1971.

Ferrier 2   Carole Ferrier, 'D. H. Lawrence's Pre-1920 Poetry: A Descriptive Bibliography of Manuscripts, Typescripts and Proofs.' *DHLR* 6, fall 1973.

Finney 2   Brian Finney. 'D. H. Lawrence's Progress to Maturity: *The Prussian Officer.' Studies in Bibliography*, 1975.

Finney 3   Brian Finney. 'The Hitherto Unknown Publication of Some D. H. Lawrence Short Stories.' *Notes and Queries*, Feb. 1972.

Ford   George Ford. *Double Measure: A Study of the Novels and Stories of D. H. Lawrence.* New York, 1965.

Ford 2   George Ford. 'Prologue to *Women in Love.' Texas Quarterly* 6, 1963, 98–111.

Ford 3   Geroge Ford. 'The Wedding Chapter of D. H. Lawrence's *Women in Love.' Texas Studies in Language and Literature* 6, 1964, 134–47.

Frieda   E. W. Tedlock, ed. *Frieda Lawrence: The Memoirs and Correspondence.* Heinemann, 1961.

Kalnins   Mara Kalnins. 'D. H. Lawrence's "Odour of Chrysanthemums": The Three Endings.' *Studies in Short Fiction*, fall 1976.

Kinkead-Weekes   Mark Kinkead-Weekes. 'The Marble and the Statue' in Mack and Gregor, eds. *Imagined Worlds.* Methuen, 1968.

Levy   Mervyn Levy, ed. *The Paintings of D. H. Lawrence.* Cory, Adams and Mackay, 1964.

Littlewood   J. C. F. Littlewood. 'D. H. Lawrence's Early Tales.' *Cambridge Quarterly* 1, 1966, 115–19.

McDonald   Edward D. MacDonald. *A Bibliography of the Writings of D. H. Lawrence.* Philadelphia, 1925.

McDonald 2   Edward D. McDonald. *D. H. Lawrence: A Bibliographical Supplement.* Philadelphia 1931.

Miscellany   Harry T. Moore, ed. *A. D. H. Lawrence Miscellany.* Carbondale, 1959.

Phoenix   Edward D. McDonald, ed. *Phoenix: The Posthumous Papers of D. H. Lawrence.* London, 1936.

Phoenix 2   Warren Roberts and Harry T. Moore, eds. *Phoenix II: Uncollected, Unpublished and Other Prose Works by D. H. Lawrence.* London, 1968.

Poste   Harry T. Moore. *Poste Restante: A Lawrence Travel Calendar.* California, 1956.

Powell   Lawrence Clarke Powell. *The Manuscripts of D. H. Lawrence.* Los Angeles, 1937.

Roberts   Warren Roberts. *A Bibliography of D. H. Lawrence.* Rupert Hart-Davis,

1963.
SP   Keith Sagar, ed. *D. H. Lawrence: Selected Poems*. Penguin, 1972.
Sagar 3   Keith Sagar, ' "The Best I Have Known": D. H. Lawrence's "A Modern Lover" and "The Sades of Spring"'. *Studies in Short Fiction,* winter 1967.
Sagar 4   Keith Sagar,'The Genesis of "Bavarian Gentians"'. *DHLR* 8, i, 1975.
Sharpe   Michael C. Sharpe, 'The Genesis of D. H. Lawrence's *The Trespasser.' Essays in Criticism*, Jan. 1961.
Skinner   Mollie Skinner. *The Fifth Sparrow*. Sydney, 1972.
Smailes   T. A. Smailes. 'Seven Hitherto Unpublished Lawrence Poems.' *DHLR* 3, i.
Spender   Stephen Spender, ed. *D. H. Lawrence: Novelist, Poet, Prophet*. Weidenfeld and Nicolson, 1973.
Tedlock   E. W. Tedlock. *The Frieda Lawrence Collection of D. H. Lawrence Manuscripts: A Descriptive Bibliography*. Albuquerque, 1948.
Waterfield   Lina Waterfield. *Castle in Italy: An Autobiography*. New York, 1961.
Young Bert   *Young Bert: An Exhibition of the Early Years of D. H. Lawrence,* Nottingham, 1972.
Zytaruk 2   George Zytaruk *D. H. Lawrence's Response to Russian Literature*. The Hague: Mouton, 1971.

3   WORKS OF D. H. LAWRENCE PUBLISHED SINCE ROBERTS

A   Books
The Paintings of D. H. Lawrence, ed. Mervyn Levy. Cory, Adams and Mackay, 1964.
The Complete Poems of D. H. Lawrence, ed. Vivian de Sola Pinto and Warren Roberts, Heinemann and Viking, 1964. Revised ed. 1971.
The Complete Plays of D. H. Lawrence. Heinemann and Viking, 1965. Contains the first publication of 'The Daughter-in-Law'.
Phoenix II, ed. Warren Roberts and Harry T. Moore. Heinemann and Viking, 1968. Contains the first publication of 'Lessford's Rabbits', 'A Lesson on a Tortoise', 'Germans and English', 'Return to Bestwood', and the Preface to *Black Swans.*
Movements in European History, ed. James T. Boulton. Clarendon Press, 1971. Contains a previously unpublished Epilogue.
The Mortal Coil and Other Stories, ed. Keith Sagar. Penguin, 1971. Contains a later version of 'The Fly in the Ointment' than that printed in *Lawrence Ada* and *Phoenix II.*
The Princess and Other Stories, ed. Keith Sagar. Penguin, 1971. Contains the first publication of 'The Wilful Woman', the first chapter of Lawrence's projected novel based on the life of Mabel Luhan; also the later ('unexpurgated') version of *Sun,* not reprinted since the Black Sun Press edition of 1928 [A35b].
D. H. Lawrence: Selected Poems, ed. Keith Sagar. Penguin, 1972. Contains the first book publication of the prose-poem 'Fire', first published in *Smailes,* but incorrectly, as verse.
The First Lady Chatterley. Heinemann, 1972. First English Edition.
John Thomas and Lady Jane. Heinemann, 1972. First publication in English.

B Contributions to books

Word for Word, by Wallace Hildick. Faber and Faber, 1965. Contains passages from early drafts of *The White Peacock,* 'Odour of Chrysanthemums' and *The Rainbow.*

The Priest of Love, by Harry T. Moore. Heinemann and Farrar, Strauss and Giroux, 1974. Contains a previously unpublished epilogue to *Fantasia of the Unconscious.*

C Contributions to Periodicals

'The Man Who Was Through with the World,' ed. John R. Elliot. *Essays in Criticism,* July 1959. Collected in *The Princess and Other Stories.*

'Prologue to *Women in Love,*' ed. George Ford. *Texas Quarterly,* spring 1963. Collected in *Phoenix II.*

'The Wedding Chapter of D. H. Lawrence's *Women in Love,*' ed. George Ford. *Texas Studies in Language and Literature* 6, 1964 (134–47).

Anonymous reviews of *The Oxford Book of German Verse* and *The Minnesingers,* ed. Armin Arnold. *PMLA* March 1964. Reprinted from *The English Review* of Jan. 1912. Collected in *Phoenix II.*

'D. H. Lawrence's "Odour of Chrysanthemums": An Early Version,' ed. James T. Boulton. *Renaissance and Modern Studies* 13, 1969.

Anonymous review of *Contemporary German Poetry* (reprinted from *The English Review,* Nov. 1911) and 'With the Guns' (reprinted from *The Manchester Guardian,* 18 Aug. 1914), ed. Carl Baron. *Encounter,* Aug. 1969.

'Seven Hitherto Unpublished Lawrence Poems,' ed. T. A. Smailes. *DHLR* 3, i.

'An Unpublished Version of D. H. Lawrence's Introduction to *Pansies,*' ed. David Farmer. *Review of English Studies* 21, May 1970.

'D. H. Lawrence's "The Turning Back": The Text and its Genesis in the Correspondence,' ed. David Farmer. *DHLR* summer 1972.

'Two Missing Pages from "The Ladybird",' ed. Brian Finney. *Review of English Studies* 24, May 1973.

'A Newly Discovered Text of D. H. Lawrence's "The Lovely Lady",' ed. Brian Finney. *Yale Univ. Library Gazette* 49, Jan. 1975.

Passages from 'Ecce Homo', ed. Alvin Sullivan. *DHLR,* summer 1976. An early version of 'Eloi, Eloi, Lama Sabachthani?'.

'Throstles in the Cherry Tree,' ed. Emily Potter Brooks. *DHLR,* summer 1976. An intermediate version of 'Cherry Robbers'.

INDEX

273

Index

Index

Index

284

Resurrection (poem), 75, E346
Resurrection (essay), 66, 140, 142, E346.1
Resurrection (painting), vii, 159, 161–2, 175, 267
Resurrection of the Flesh, E346.5
Return, E213, E320.1
Return Journey, The, 44. See *Twilight in Italy*
Return to Bestwood, 154, 271, E31, E144
Revelation of St John the Divine, Introduction to, 190
Review of the Scots Guards, The, E317
Revolutionary, The, 105, 113
Rex, 93, 101–2, E349.5
Riches, 179
Rise in the World, A, E302
Risen Lord, The, 186, E27, E350
River Roses, E318, E319.7
Road to Mitla, The, 141, 267
Rocking Horse Winner, The, 149, E351
Rondeau of a Conscientious Objector, E317, E351.3
Rose is not a Cabbage, A, E266
Rose, Look Out Upon Me, E49
Roses, E302
Roses on the Breakfast Table, E318, E319.7
Ruination, E320.1, E320.2, E352.3
Running Barefoot, E320.1, E320.4

Saga of Siegmund, The. See *The Trespasser*
Saïd the Fisherman, Review of, 146
St John, 105, E352.5
St Luke, 105, E352.53
St Mark, 105, E352.55
St Matthew, 105, E47
St Mawr, 137–9, 143, E352.6
Saint, The, E49
Salt Licks, 179
Salt of the Earth, 179
Samson and Delilah, 74, 117, E352.7
San Gaudenzio, 38, 64–5. See *Twilight in Italy*
Sardinian Films, 110. See *Sea and Sardinia*
Saturday Morning, 141, E227.7. See *Mornings in Mexico*
Scargill Street, 32–4
Scent of Irises, E320.1, E352.9
School, E317, E320.1
School on the Outskirts, E269.5, E320.2
School on the Waste Lands, The, E320.2
Schoolmaster, The, 27, E213, E320.1
Scripture, E320.1
Scrutiny of the Work of John Galsworthy, A, 157–9, 165, 173, E181.3
Sea, The, 25, E320.4
Sea and Sardinia, 109–10, E355
Sea Bathers, 184
Seaweed, E302, E319.6
Second Best, 18, 22, 52, E356.5
Second Contemporary Verse Anthology, Review of, 130
Second Harmony, E320.1
Second Supper, Introduction to, E356.7. See *The Story of Dr Manente*
See Mexico After, 142, E357
Self-Contempt, 17, E145.5
Self-Pity, E302
Sentimental Correspondence, E320.2
Separated, E320.1, E320.4
Service of All the Dead, 38, 66
Sex Appeal, 178, E591.1
Sex Locked Out, 178
Sex Versus Loveliness, 178, E359.1
Shades, E359.3
Shades of Spring, The, 18, 24, 38–9, 42, 53, 55, E359.4
Shadow in the Rose Garden, The, 8, 42, 52–3, 55, E359.5
Shadow of Death, The, E320.1, E320.2, E320.4
She Goat, 119
She Looks Back, 28
She Was a Good Little Wife, 27, E319.2

Index

Index

GENERAL

291

Index

Jaffe, Else, 33, 151, 184, 187
Jennings, Blanche, 8–9, 11, 17, E67, E342, E389.6, E436
Jester, Mr, 144–6
Johnson, Willard ('Spud'), 134–7, 147, 171, E13
Jones, Hilda Mary, 11
Joseph, Michael, 153
Juta, Jan, 112

Karavas, Saki, 267
Kennerley, Mitchell, 43–4
Knopf, Alfred A., 146, 170
Knopf, Blanche, 144, 146
Koteliansky, S. S., 54–6, 60, 72, 81, 84, 88, 95–8, 111–12, 130, 134, 160, 166, 180, 190
Kouyoumdjian, Dikran, 68
Krenkow, Ada, 18
Krenkow, Fritz, 17
Krout, J. A., 147, E297

Lahr, Charles, 182, 186, E154.7, E266
Lancret, 112
Land and Water, 94, 103
Lane, John, 107
Lasca, Il, 177–8, 185–7, E356.7, E379.9, E380, E380.1
Laughing Horse, The, 134, 138, 147
Lawrence, Ada, 14, 18
Lawrence, Emily, 177–8
Lawrence, Frieda, 45, 57, 96–7, 101, 104–5, 122–4, 128–9, 135, 137–8, 140, 143, 147, 151, 155–6, 164, 168, 172, 175, 180–1, 187, 190, 267, E3.6, E9.5, E23.1, E87.1, E116, E272, E340.5, E371.5, E401.6, E440
Lawrence, Lydia, 14, 16–18
Leader, B. W., 2
Leslie, Shane, 146
Lockhart, John G., 34
London and Provincial Press Agency, 12
London Mercury, 164, 166
Lorenzetti, 107, 109

Lowell, Amy, 80, E269.5, E314.3
Luhan, Mabel, 122, 124–5, 134, 136–9, 180, 271, E432.7

Macartney, Laura, 20
McDonald, Edward, 78, 93, 139, 170
Mackenzie, Compton, 82, 104–5, 151
McLeod, A. W., 24, 33, 45
Magnelli, 158
Magnus, Maurice, 119–20, 138
Manchester Guardian, 54
Mann, Thomas, 36, 38–9
Mansfield, Katherine, 35–6, 57, 65, 70–2, 92, 130
Marsh, Edward, 45–6, 66, 100, E133.5, E152.5
Masaccio, 117
Mason, Anges, 34, E430
Mason, G. H., 2, 21
Mathews, Elkin, 182
Maugham, W. Somerset, 174, E377.5
Maunsell, 81
Medici Society, 112–13
Melville, Herman, 71–2, 88, 124, E382
  Moby Dick, 71
Meredith, George, 5
Methuen, 51, 58–60, 67
Metropolitan, E437
Meynell, Viola, 58–60, 62
Minchin, Cecily Lambert, 96
Mohr, Max, 187–8
Monk, Violet, 96
Monro, Harold, E314.2
Monroe, Harriet, 38, 55, 66, 76, 125, 132, E47, E113.2
Morrell, Lady Ottoline, 57, 59–62, 75, 85, E365.5
Morrison, Nellie, 170
Moult, Thomas, 96, E269.6
Mountsier, Robert, 109–10, 113, 115, 117, 120, 122, E47, E314.5
Mudie's Circulating Library, 101, 106
Murry, John Middleton, 36, 65, 70–1, 92–3, 95, 98, 131, 133, 135, 147,

292

Index

Survey Graphic, 180
Swan, J. M., 2, 20
Swinburne, Algernon, 5

Taylor, Rachel Annand, 14, 16
Teniers, 93
Terborch, 112
Thaulow, Fritz, 11
Thayer, Scofield, 161
Theatre Arts Monthly, 138
Thomspon, Clarence, 137
Thurlby, Mabel, 2
Time and Tide, 21, E86
Times, The, 83
Times Educational Supplement, The, 90
Tomlinson, H. M., 155, E145
Tramp, The, 12
Trotter, Philip, 176

Uccello, 93–4
Unwin, Stanley, 103

Van der Goes, 112
Van Gogh, 59
Van Vechten, Carl, 157, E271
Vanity Fair, 131–2, 141, 152, 174,
    178–81, 183, 189, E274, E337,
    E422.7
Verga, Giovanni, 115–16, 119–22, 124,
    127, 130, 161–2, 164–5, E416
    Cavalleria Rusticana, 115, 124,
        164, 165, E62
    I Malavoglia, 115

Mastro-don Gesualdo, 115,
    119–21, 130, E230.9
Novelle Rusticane, 115, 121–2,
    127, E204
Vogue, 152, 174, E377.5

Wallace, Miss, 103
Warren, Dorothy, 175
Waterfield, Lina, 46
Watson, Jean, 174, E31.3
Weber, Alfred, 29, 187
Weekley, Barbara, 149, 181
Weekley, Ernest, 33
Weekley, Frieda, 24, 26. See Law-
    rence, Frieda
Wells, H. G., 182, 153
    The World of William Clissold, 153
West, J. Walter, 2
Wheelock, Miss, 107, 109
White, Walter, 157
Whitman, Walt, 86, 88, E382
Whittleys, 104
Wilkinson, Arthur Gair, 152–3
Wilkinson, Lilian Gair, 152–3
Wilkinson, Walter, 161, E307
Williams-Ellis, Clough, 174, E377.5
Wilson Charles, E41, E319.4
Wingate, J. Lawton, 2
Woolf, Leonard, 112, 124, E143.3
World, The, 97

Yale Review, 81, 82–3
Young, Francis Brett, 99

294